Frances Osborne worked a[s ....], then a journalist before becoming a full-time writer. She lives in London and Cheshire with her husband and two young children.

This is her first book.

www.booksattransworld.co.uk

LILLA'S FEAST

A True Story of Love, War and a Passion for Food

Frances Osborne

BLACK SWAN

LILLA'S FEAST
A BLACK SWAN BOOK : 9780552771887

Originally published in Great Britain by Doubleday,
a division of Transworld Publishers

PRINTING HISTORY
Doubleday edition published 2004
Black Swan edition published 2005

5 7 9 10 8 6 4

Set in 10.5/12pt Melior by
Falcon Oast Graphic Art Ltd.

Black Swan Books are published by Transworld Publishers,
61–63 Uxbridge Road, London W5 5SA,
www.rbooks.co.uk

Addresses for companies within
The Random House Group Limited can be found at:
www.randomhouse.co.uk/offices.htm

The Random House Group Limited Reg. No. 954009

A CIP catalogue record for this book
is available from the British Library

The Random House Group Limited supports The Forest Stewardship
Council® (FSC®), the leading international forest-certification organisation.
Our books carrying the FSC label are printed on FSC®-certified paper.
FSC is the only forest-certification scheme supported by the leading
environmental organisations, including Greenpeace. Our
paper procurement policy can be found at
www.randomhouse.co.uk/environment

MIX
Paper from
responsible sources
FSC® C016897

Printed and bound in Great Britain by Clays Ltd, St Ives plc

For Luke and Liberty,
two of Lilla's many great-great-grandchildren

CONTENTS

A NOTE ON CHINESE NAMES

In 1976, English-language newspapers changed from the old, Wade-Giles system of romanizing Chinese names to the modern Pinyin. As Lilla's story is set in the past, nearly all of it prior to 1976, I have used the Wade-Giles system. The Chinese names in this book are all, therefore, written differently today. This may give the impression that the places Lilla went to no longer exist. And, as you will discover, they don't – at least not as she knew them.

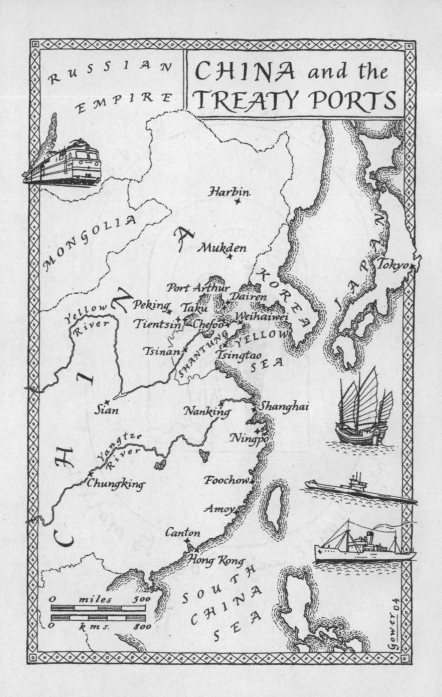

CHINA and the TREATY PORTS

RUSSIAN EMPIRE

MONGOLIA

Harbin

Mukden

Port Arthur

Peking   Taku   Dairen

Tientsin Chefoo Weihaiwei

Tsinan   SHANTUNG YELLOW

Tsingtao SEA

KOREA

JAPAN

Tokyo

Yellow River

CHINA

Sian

Nanking   Shanghai

Yangtze River

Ningpo

Chungking

Foochow

Amoy

Canton

Hong Kong

SOUTH CHINA SEA

0   miles   500

0   kms.   800

Gower 04

The Bride of to day

The House wife of tomorrow

PROLOGUE

IN THE IMPERIAL WAR MUSEUM in London there is a cookery book. It's there because it was written in a Japanese internment camp in China during the Second World War. When the book was given to the museum back in the 1970s, prime-time television was still packed with dramas about Japanese prison camps and the war, and the museum put it on display in the front hall. Thirty years later, it has slipped further back in the building, into one of the galleries about battles we're growing too young to remember.

There its old-fashioned Courier-type pages lie open, each chapter a rusting paper-clipped bundle of different coloured leaves. Most sheets are scraps of what was once white paper, but which has now yellowed with age. Some are torn from old account books. Some have 'American Red Cross' stamped on the back in red. There is even the odd sheet of Basildon Blue. And many of the pages are typed on blank ricepaper receipts so thin that you can see right through them and marvel at how they survived the click and return of an old metal-bashing typewriter, let alone the war in which the recipes were written.

11

It's when you actually read the book that the real surprise comes. For it's not what you would expect from a wartime recipe book, all rations and digging for victory – or subsistence on rotting vegetables and donkey meat in a Japanese internment camp. It's quite the opposite. It's a book that's written as if the war wasn't there at all. As if everyone was back in their warm, safe homes with their families and friends, the larder full and the table heaving with fresh, just-cooked food. It gives advice on how to make good things last longer, how to live and eat to the full. The pages are jam-packed with recipes with old-fashioned names: cream puffs and popovers, butterscotch and blancmange, galantine of beef and anchovy toast, jugged hare and mulligatawny soup. There are dinner-party menus, children's menus, cocktails, ice creams, sweets. It's a book for making the best of times in the worst of times, a book which makes you believe that if you could fill your mind with a cream cake or anything delicious then you could transform the bitterest experience into something sweet and shut out the things that you needed to forget.

And that's what my great-grandmother, who wrote this book, believed.

My great-grandmother's name was Lilla. She'd been christened Lilian, but her stutter stopped her reaching the third syllable. So Lilla it was. I remember her vividly. She didn't just survive the camp, she lived for another forty years – until she was almost one hundred and one, and I was almost fourteen. Even at the end of her life she was extraordinarily elegant, her long hair gently twisted up at the back of her head, her enviable legs always neatly crossed, and she only ever wore fitted black lace and diamonds that sparkled like those still-burning bright blue eyes. When we children scuttled through the door, this slim, birdlike creature would lean forward from where she perched on the edge of a sofa and whisper that it was 'w-w-wonderful' to see us as she could never understand what the grown-ups had to say. In ten seconds flat we had fallen under her spell. Jumping over the two bossy generations in between, our great-granny was our ally.

Lilla made the end of her life appear effortless. She trotted a mile to the shops and back each day. She had more descendants than she could count. Her bedroom was a through-the-looking-glass museum of furniture, pictures – even costumes – from every corner of the world in which she had lived: China, where she had been born; India, where she had been a wife; even England, where she'd ended up when she had nowhere left to go. She behaved as if she had sailed through life, and nothing could have been better.

She rarely mentioned the camp.

Still, there were a few snippets that didn't add up. A few phrases that slipped out in those grey hours after the funerals of each of her two children. There were her three 'husbands' waiting in heaven, and her worry as to which one she should live with 'up there', if any of them. There was an allusion to a 'real father', who she said had shot himself when she was very young. There was her obsession with having something to leave her children and grandchildren. And there was the unheard-of child that, in a whispered confession, she said she had made herself miscarry.

At the time, these were mysteries that simply added to Lilla's exotic charm. It was only years later when I started to unravel them that I began to realize that they were, in Lilla's way, cries for help. Calls to understand that, beneath its polished surface, Lilla's life had been far from effortless. Clues not just to the pain of internment, which at least she had shared with others, but to another story, one that she had endured alone. A trail of dozens of surviving friends and relations – there's a tendency to longevity in our family – led me to the British Library. There I soon found myself staring at a long, thin box thickly packed with faded letters that had flown between Lilla, her first husband (my great-grandfather), his parents and his siblings, almost exactly one hundred years ago. As I pieced together the story that unfolded in them, I began to cry. Salty tears ran down my cheeks and dropped on to the thin paper of the letters, almost washing the words away. I wiped my face with a handful of tissues, smearing mascara around my eyes until I looked like I'd been in a fight. One of the librarians came over and asked if I was all right. Emotional outbursts must be rare in those dimly lit reading rooms on the Euston Road.

It took me two years to return. When I walked back into the Oriental Reading Room, changed, a mother now, and hoping to be able to judge the story in a more objective light, the librarians recognized me instantly. And, almost before I could ask, they had gone to retrieve that old ballot box whose contents had made me cry.

The letters I read made me understand how Lilla had found the will to write those recipes. If it hadn't been for what she had been through long before the camp, I'm not sure she would have had the determination, the imagination, to shut out the bad things by writing down not just the odd recipe but a complete cookery encyclopaedia that runs chapter by chapter from a course of cooking to soups, to fish, to game and on to hints on homemaking, and get right to the end.

My father was always the one who was going to write Lilla's – his grandmother's – story. I remember him standing on the first-floor landing of our house in London on the cold January morning after her funeral. He was examining a photograph of Lilla's terrifying-looking first husband, his grandfather, that he had just hung on the wall. What a book it would make, he said. 'It would be a sizzler. My God, she had a life.' But my father has written several books since then, and none of them has been about Lilla. Eventually he handed me a pile of old photograph albums and a briefcase heavy with Lilla's papers and documents, and the mantle passed to me.

I went back to the Imperial War Museum for the first time since I was a child and read the recipe book under the reading-room dome. I went to the British Library to see if I could find out a little more about who did what when and unearthed that ballot box of letters, there because one of my great-great-uncles had become Foreign Secretary to the government of India and a poet. And as I started to turn over long-forgotten stones, more letters and newspaper clippings emerged from the bottom of dusty attic boxes, from the backs of once-flower-scented drawers. And more photographs appeared. Some from the vaults of university libraries. Others from the albums kept by Lilla's identical twin sister Ada, spirited over to me from New Zealand. And a few from the collections of each person I went to see.

Then there are the family stories. I tracked down a web of long-lost relations by plucking names from newspaper reports of weddings written a century ago and persuading directory enquiries to do national searches. I've discovered dozens of cousins I never realized I had. I flew from London to Vancouver for the weekend to stay with one of Lilla's nephews, and met a lady who had known Lilla in a Japanese prison camp. I found others scattered around the coast of England, in Suffolk, Cornwall and Kent. All of them have their stories to tell about Lilla. The things they overheard their parents discussing as children, and the secrets she confided to them during her long years in England at the end of her life. There are non-family stories, too. Thousands of documents record the minutiae of Lilla's home, the treaty ports of China – extraordinary enclaves of Western

15

life that used to be dotted up and down its shores.

The way in which each record has been kept tells me almost as much as its contents. Like the sepia portraits of British families and children, dressed as for a London street a century ago but taken, as the fraying cardboard around them reveals, in Shanghai. And it is not just *how* memories have been preserved but *why* that has been revealing, too. There are those British Library letters, self-consciously gathered by Lilla's in-laws, the Howells, a family thoroughly sure of both its intellectual ability and its literary skills, as 'they will very likely be interesting reading a hundred years hence if the world moves on as fast as it has done'. Several key letters and files seem to have escaped the fire or waste-paper basket only because they make some reference to money, and were kept by people who had lost a lot of it, and hoped that one day some might come back. And there are the letters and notes that have not survived – destroyed because the reader wanted to keep the correspondence tantalizingly private, or because the writer assumed that nobody would be interested. As one of my many great-great-aunts writes of her diary, 'as I am not very likely to become famous and have a biographer, I have burnt it'. Oh, how I wish she had not.

Even the stories I have been told face to face vary in nature according to the teller, and what they have found interesting enough for their memories to retain. Detailed accounts of great journeys, moments of battle, business deals and mouth-watering meals from my male relations. The intricacies of who said what to whom when, loves, heartbreaks, homes, clothes, possessions and eating habits from the women. Some old and lonely by the time I found them, their minds still fixed on a glorious past.

However, it is far from new to declare that all 'facts' are inextricable from the person and medium used to record them. As Queen Victoria wrote, 'I had long learnt that history was not an account of what actually happened, but what people thought had happened.' And every day, in courtrooms all over the world, a row of witnesses will stand up and give widely differing accounts of an identical incident. Some may be lying, but the majority will believe what they are saying. And where in all this does 'the truth' lie? With the judge and jury, who will rely on what they think they see and hear, and their view of human nature, to form opinions that will be held up for posterity as fact.

I haven't attributed every single fact given to me to the particular source that provided it. To do so would make the text unreadable. In many cases I have been given so many accounts of a single episode – each providing a different camera angle on Lilla's life – that the only intelligible way of reproducing them has been to edit them into a single movie. However, where it adds to the understanding of the story, and is not self-evident, I explain how details came to light.

But by far the hardest question surrounds the gaps in the story. Where, perhaps playing the role of a lone jury-man, I have had to deduce how it must have felt to Lilla to be in a certain place, at a certain time. I read her recipe book again and again, my mind tasting the food she loved to cook. I went to China and marvelled at the beauty of the bay in Chefoo, where she was born. My sister and I ate cakes in the grand hotels of Shanghai, as Lilla and her sister once did. I put on her shoes and walked through her life with her. Where Lilla smiled, I smiled, where she cried, I cried, and where she made decisions that today seem strange, I began to understand what she had done. After all, I knew Lilla. The blood of her stories runs in my veins. Standing there with her, in other times, in other worlds, I closed my eyes and could almost see and hear what must have happened to her. Could imagine what she might have thought and felt.

Lilla's story is not large-scale history. She was not a grand or famous person orchestrating world events. She was in many ways very ordinary, a typical woman of her time. And this is a story of what large-scale history does to the small-scale people caught up in its events. There were a lot of events. Two world wars, a couple of civil wars, and a complete change in the choices open to women in the Western world. When Lilla was born, she was brought up to be a wife and nothing else. But she ended up working and starting her own business. And I hope that my children, who never had a chance to meet Lilla and to whom this book is dedicated, will take its most enduring lesson to heart. That is, however bad things may be, somewhere inside all of us is the strength of spirit to overcome them. Never give up hope.

London, January 2004

~ PART I ~
Love

SHRIMP PORK

Vermicelli	pork,
onions	shelled shrimps
garlic	mixed vegetables
margarine	salt

To serve say five people.

¼ lb vermicelli (boiled until soft), 3 large onions, ½ lb pork cut into dice when fried in the margarine until tender. Chop the onions & fry until golden brown, shell the shrimps about 4 ozs, prepare the vegetables then cut into small pieces. If garlic is liked chop a very small piece. Boil the vegetables.

When all is ready, add onions, drained vermicelli, pinch of salt, chopped pork, vegetables (about 2½ lb), shelled shrimps. Put into a saucepan and heat until very hot.

1

THE SWEET SMELL OF SPICE

Chefoo, North China, the second last day of March 1882

ADA WAS BORN FIRST, taking Lilla's share of good luck with her. Or so everyone said. I'm not sure whether this was a Chinese myth to do with twins or just some family comparison of their two lives – for who can resist comparing the lives of twins? But when Lilla struggled into the world thirty minutes after her sister, she wailed, fists clenched, as if she already knew that she was going to have to fight to make up for being born without her fair share of fortune.

As far as the amah who looked after the two of them was concerned, Ada was Number One Daughter and Lilla Number Two. When the amah picked up Ada to be fed first, Lilla learned to scream so that she was not forgotten. On the cold, dark mornings of those freezing North China winters that numbed the babies' fingers and noses, Ada was the first to be swaddled in layers of warm clothes and Lilla had to shout to show that she was cold too. The moment that a thick, slippery silk ribbon was carefully woven into Ada's plaits, Lilla pushed through her stutter to demand one for herself. And if Ada's ribbon was pink, Lilla made sure that she had a pink one as well. 'Right from the start,' I was told, 'they had the most terrible fights – their shoes had to be put on each foot at the same time.'

To look at, Lilla and Ada were identical. Rummaging through the archives of the School of Oriental and African Studies at London University, I found a photograph of the pair of them, taken by a visitor to Chefoo when they were about eight years old. In it, they have exactly the same pale, heart-shaped faces with high cheekbones and delicately pointed chins and noses. And the same long, dark brown – almost black – hair and bright blue eyes.

But only one of them is smiling. And I cannot tell which.

It was when the twins began to move around and talk – almost as soon as they did so developing a twinly private language – that a difference emerged between them. The moment Lilla opened her mouth, her stutter betrayed her, while Ada spoke in smooth, clear tones. And when the pair of them started to totter around their red-brick, two-storey, end-of-terrace home in the Chinese port of Chefoo (correctly pronounced Shee-fu, but anglicized to Chee-foo) – a house designed to give its inhabitants the illusion of living in a safely British town – it was always Ada who went first. Lilla, a few paces behind, struggled to catch up with her elder sister as, black-booted and white-frilled, they clattered down the steep stone steps that led from the grand European villas and mock-castles on Chefoo's Consulate Hill to its port. There they peered out over a harbour full of junks and beyond them to a volcanic reef of green-pointed islands like the spines on the back of a storybook dragon sitting down in the water. They watched as a coastal steamer from Shanghai slid through the water, and a regatta of tall, swaying sailing ships and puffing, coal-driven barges from India, from

Russia, from Japan, some even straight across the Pacific from San Francisco, nudged their way into moorings. They saw hundreds of barefooted coolies staggering up and down gangplanks loading silks and peanuts to go to every corner of the world – and unloading packages of narcotic brown powder from the hills of India, their conical straw hats shielding their dark-ringed eyes from the sun and hiding their sidelong glances in the direction of the sweet-smelling smoke seeping out from the doors of the opium dens.

And when Lilla and Ada played at being grown-up, they strolled down the gentle slope on the far side of Consulate Hill that slid into the higgledy-piggledy beach-front. They promenaded, tiny parasols in hand, alongside the rattle of rickshaws and the pong of mule-carts that wafted into the sea air. They wandered past the white-washed Western holiday hotels, past the clink of glasses on the suburban-style Chefoo Club terrace, and past the square, squat tower of the austere St Andrew's Church with its triangular hat of a spire.

Wherever they were, Lilla was always abreast of Ada, as if she needed to make sure that she was never left behind again.

Lilla's parents had ended up in China by chance. They met aboard a salty steamer puffing the long haul from London to Australia in early 1876. The ship was bulging with excited families on their way to start a new life, eager young men hoping to strike gold and make their fortunes, and Lilla's mother, Alice Simons, who didn't want to be there at all. Alice, who dreamed of being an opera singer, 'was a bit of a handful', writes one of her granddaughters, and had been caught as 'she appeared to be about to elope with her music master'. Her family had therefore packed her off as governess to a family emigrating to Australia.

Alice could think of nothing that she would rather do less. The thought of becoming a bespectacled, grey-clad, hair-scraped-back, schoolroom-bound miss, even for a week, filled her with horror. Both her parents had died by the time she was five years old and Alice and her orphaned siblings had been split up. Alice's sister Lucy had been sent to live with her mother's puritanically religious family in York. Her brother Tom had been dispatched to boarding school. Alice, the lucky one, was sent to her Jewish grandmother, her father's mother, Mrs Simons, near London.

Although Mrs Simons lived under a veneer of anglicization, calling her granddaughter Alice instead of her first name of Elizabeth, she was still – so the story goes – passionate about music and food in a thoroughly unBritish way. Alice grew up in a household where the smell of cooking was always in the air, one meal barely finishing before the stirring, baking and roasting began for the next. Mrs Simons was well off. She had several servants and 'spoiled my mother', wrote Lilla a century later, with countless lace dresses and 'a good boarding-school at Ealing', then just west of London, where she learned how to live the life of a grand lady.

Nonetheless, back at home, Alice and her grandmother would have been endlessly in and out of the kitchen. I can imagine them standing in their stiff Victorian dresses, using worn wooden spoons to try to scoop up squares of lamb bubbling in a stew, like small children attempting to catch leaves as they dance to the ground in autumn gusts. Dipping their fingers into the powdery new spices from the far corners of the world, whose tastes must have made Alice dream of the smoky, heaving bazaars that she had seen pictures of in books. And the table in the dining room next door laid, for just the two of them, as if for a feast: rows of silver knives and forks, crystal glasses, thick starched napkins, finger bowls, imitation Sèvres and flowers bound together in precious-looking posies.

In the evening, Alice played the piano and sang. It was all she wanted to do, and Mrs Simons hired her the best and most fashionable music master that either of them had heard of, to come to the house. He was, wrote Lilla, 'a famous teacher'. I can see Alice leaning over the piano, being showered with praise as her bosom rose and fell with each note. Standing there singing, being told that she was the most beautiful, talented creature alive, she must have felt as though she was opening the doors of heaven – her music master no doubt impressing upon her that he held the key. And Mrs Simons watched her beloved granddaughter blossom and bloom, naively paying for ever-longer lessons.

It's not clear at what stage the planned elopement was discovered. However far it had gone, it was certainly far enough, and the puritanical posse that made up Alice's maternal uncles and aunts insisted that she was sent abroad. Somebody had heard of a couple who were moving out to Australia and needed a young lady to go with them to teach their daughters. They were leaving almost immediately. A governess it was.

Not that, without eloping, Alice had much of a choice as to how she spent her life. For a supposedly proper middle-class girl like her living in England in the 1870s, the only socially acceptable forms of employment were teaching other middle-class children or marrying a middle-class man. The type of man who, Alice must have feared, wouldn't let her spend all her evenings singing. Yet, by the time she was en route to Australia, marriage was her only way out of a schoolroom fate.

On board ship, somewhere in the east Atlantic or perhaps the Mediterranean, as the sun began to take enough bite out of the sea air for the passengers to idle rather than stride around the decks, and attempt a conversation above the engine noise, she met Charles Jennings.

One of the eager young men off to make his fortune on the other side of the world, Charles Jennings was working his way out to Australia by acting as the ship's purser. It was said that he had land in Ireland but, frankly, I reckon that this was a lie to cover up that he hadn't a bean. Apart from the fact that he loved boats, and dogs, precious little else is known about him, not even what he looked like – although from looking at his sons he was probably fairly tall and thick-set. Anyhow, somewhere between the sea and the soot pouring out of the steamer's chimney, he fell madly in love with Alice.

By the time the ship docked in Australia a couple of months later, Alice and Charles were engaged. They married soon after arriving and then, as Charles had 'an opportunity' in China, they boarded a boat for Shanghai. Alice had escaped the schoolroom.

Shanghai in the 1870s had the feel of a humid Wild West. It was a city that you sailed into and either sank or swam. You could make a fortune in a day and then lose it overnight – if you didn't die of disease or trip and fall into one of the numerous stinking creeks on the way home. Each morning, the horse-drawn carriages of the newly rich trundled past doorways filled with what looked like piles of rags but which, all too often, were beggars who had either frozen or starved to death in the night. And even if you managed to bank a few dollars and dimes, there was always a risk that the natives outside the town's gates would swoop in and raze the place to the ground. Instead of regular raids, those inside Shanghai's city walls lived with an ever-growing rumble of discontent from millions of Chinese. The Chinese might be slow to react – time in China passes with its dynasties and not its days – but when they did their protests would be bloody and brutal.

As far as the Chinese were concerned, their foreign invaders hadn't just stolen their land, they had poisoned the population and humiliated the whole country.

Round-eyed Europeans had started trading in China almost two hundred years before Charles and Alice arrived. China was not a country that had ever wanted much contact with the outside world. But in 1685 the emperor K'ang-hsi, unable to resist the opportunity of filling China's coffers with outsiders' money, had opened the southern port of Canton to foreign trade.

Business took off. The British were already downing vast quantities of tea and the new Chinese tea was thought to be much better than its Indian cousin. Within a few years, the silver bullion to pay for it was leaving Britain for China in tons. The hitch for the British economy was that the trade was almost all one way. Desperate to rectify the worrying – and increasing – balance of payments deficit, the British government turned to the only two commodities that the Chinese appeared to be interested in. Both were produced in British-controlled India. One was soft, at times pretty, and harmless to the Chinese. It was cotton.

The other was opium.

Opium smoking – like many historical regrets – seems to have evolved from a series of unfortunate co-incidences. In this case the unfortunate coincidences were, in the following order, a seventeenth-century Chinese craze for smoking North American tobacco in pipes; the decision of the Chinese emperor to ban tobacco-smoking; the ingenuity of the Chinese in taking the Dutch sailors' habit of mixing Indian opium with their tobacco in the belief that it prevented malaria, and turning it to smoking pure opium in their pipes instead;

and the sudden influx of opium into China so that the British could balance their economy. 'And thus,' writes Martin Booth in his history of opium, 'was born one of the most evil cultural exchanges in history – opium from the Middle East met the native American Indian pipe.'

In a deeply ironic reversal of China's initial trading success, the Chinese regarded Indian opium as far better than their home-grown affair. And 'as the availability of opium rose so did the demand for it', writes Booth. Eventually, in 1799, China declared opium imports illegal. In response, Britain made the gesture of ceasing to ship opium from India to China on the government-controlled East India Company's ships. Instead the East India Company took its cases of opium down to the Indian port of Calcutta, where it auctioned them off to British and American shippers who then smuggled the opium into China themselves.

The continuing opium trade was so profitable that a new style of ship that could sail against the wind – the clipper – was developed just so that opium could be sailed to China throughout the seasons. And, perhaps because taxes on Indian opium were earning the British government just under £1 million a year – a fortune back then – it decided to compound its hypocrisy by increasing poppy cultivation in India. By the 1830s, about 1 per cent of the Chinese population was believed to be addicted to opium. In China that made four million people. And by 1836 enough opium 'to cater for more than twelve million addicts' was being shipped in.

Inevitably, tension between the Chinese authorities and the mainly British opium traders mounted. In 1840 the First Opium War broke out between Britain and China. There were no legendary battles in this war, just a succession of military skirmishes that seemed to drag on. By the time a victorious Britain wound up the war in

August 1842, more British soldiers had died from malaria and dysentery than in the fighting itself.

As a prize for its victory, Britain's peace treaty, the Treaty of Nanking, demanded the opening up to foreign trade of five 'treaty ports' – Foochow, Canton, Amoy, Ningpo and Shanghai. Shanghai became the unofficial capital of these new open ports. Britain also took the island of Hong Kong in its entirety, to turn into a full-blown British colony. Shortly afterwards, the other trading nations began to pile into China too. A couple of years later, in 1844, the Americans negotiated a further treaty with China, which also allowed them to construct Protestant missionary churches, hospitals and cemeteries. The French followed suit.

For the next fourteen years, an unsteady peace reigned over the China trade as the number of opium addicts and pirates roaming the South China Sea grew. Opium clippers were hot targets for pirates as they would be loaded with valuable opium on their way out to China or silver bullion on their way back. But any ship was worth a hit. Most of the pirates were Chinese, but some were British and American. Many registered their ships in Hong Kong and sailed under the British flag. In October 1856 the Chinese impounded a ship with an expired Hong Kong registration upon suspicion of piracy, and this gave the British the excuse they needed to launch the Second Opium War – for several years they had been unsuccessfully negotiating for further trade concessions, and a successful war would allow them to take what they wanted in another peace treaty. This time, when one of their missionaries was murdered in 1857, the French joined them.

The Second Opium War lurched on until 1860, when the Chinese government finally agreed to raise a tax on opium imports – effectively legalizing the trade. It also granted foreigners unfettered access to the great Yangtze river that curves its way through inland China, and gave in to the establishment of more treaty ports.

Many of these new treaty ports were lonely spots dotted along the vast belly of China's coastline and up its wide, muddy rivers. The sites chosen were often pre-existing Chinese ports and villages where first the British, then the Americans, the French, the Italians, the Germans, the Russians and the Japanese literally staked out their own territory in which they could live – so the agreement was – happily immune to Chinese law. This principle was known as extraterritoriality. As far as the Chinese were concerned, it added insult to injury, effectively turning little patches of China into foreign soil.

As the foreigners arrived, they built. And, as if to deceive themselves into believing that they were as safe as they were at home, they built in the style of their own national architecture. By the time Alice and Charles arrived, Shanghai was already becoming a patchwork of English stately homes, French chateaux, East Coast townhouses, Alpine chalets, Mediterranean villas and palatial office buildings that wouldn't have looked out of place on Madison Avenue. Yet in between these imposing buildings ran dirt streets packed with faces from every corner of China: elevated cheekbones from the unforgiving Mongolian desert and bitter, windswept Manchuria, sun-shielded eyes from the Himalayan hilltop kingdoms that scraped the sky and wide, open gazes from the water-logged paddy fields of Canton. Down by the waterfront, the smells of steaming rice and charring meat mingled with traces of opium smoke. And in the residential streets set back from Shanghai's muddy Huangpu river, warbling tonal calls to buy animal parts for medicines, for food, for luck, echoed against the high garden walls. The 'treaty-porters' may have convinced themselves that they were as safe as the houses in which they lived but they were out-numbered by a patient enemy, a thousand, ten thousand, to one – an enemy waiting for an opportunity to restore its pride.

The only gesture of order in China's treaty ports – apart from the Chinese police, whom the Westerners ignored – was the Imperial Maritime Customs Service. Chinese Customs, as it was known, ran the harbours full of square-sailed wooden junks and tall-chimneyed steamers and collected customs duty for the imperial Chinese government in Peking. It employed both foreigners and Chinese but was really run by the British. Its senior posts were filled with clever Mandarin speakers from the best universities. The reason Alice and Charles had sailed to Shanghai was that the Inspector General of Chinese Customs – the man who effectively ran China's treaty ports – was a man called Robert Hart. Charles's 'opportunity' was that he knew him.

Charles and Alice arrived in Shanghai to discover that Hart worked in Peking, hundreds of miles to the north. Alice was by now very pregnant and certainly not fit to travel further. Nor did Charles want to leave her alone in Shanghai. So he wrote to Hart. Chinese Customs ran a swift postal service between the treaty ports, and within a couple of weeks he had a reply.

Hart wrote back offering Charles a job as harbour master in Chefoo, one of the smaller treaty ports on the northern coast of China. 'The climate is very healthy,' wrote Hart, and suitable for a family. In the late summer of 1877, shortly after Alice had given birth to a boy, Vivvy, Lilla's parents took the coastal steamer north.

The journey took two days, one to reach the bottom of the Shantung peninsula and another to skirt around its rocky perimeter to Chefoo. The trip was far from pleasant. The Yellow Sea through which they were sailing was notoriously infested with pirates, whose raids left few survivors. To protect the passengers, all except the essential crew were locked below decks in stuffy, swaying cabins, where glints of sunlight occasionally made their way through the chained and padlocked grilles.

When they arrived, Chefoo must have seemed even more attractive than Charles and Alice had been led to believe. The port was surrounded on land by steep hills rising up sharply behind the town and at sea by that reef of dragon-spine volcanic islands curving through the water. In winter it was the most northerly harbour not to freeze over, and in summer the sea breezes kept the air cool and fresh. As Charles and Alice stepped off the steamer, the salty air would have hit the back of their throats, clearing away the stench of a boiling summer in Shanghai. Chefoo was, said a contemporary travel guide, 'undoubtedly the most salubrious' treaty port in China. Given that the foreigners in the rest of the country spent much of the year fighting a host of tropical diseases, this was high praise indeed. Each summer, Westerners flocked there from the sweltering cities of Shanghai and Tientsin, earning Chefoo the nickname 'the Brighton of China'.

But unlike Brighton, England, or even Brighton Beach, New York, Chefoo had barely two hundred Western residents. It was perched precariously on the eastern edge of China on a rocky peninsula that, in an atlas, looks like a dog's head barking at the country's unfriendly neighbours, Korea and Japan. Inland, beyond the hills, lay thousands of miles of muddy and rutted plains planted with peanuts, beans and mulberry trees crawling with silkworms. And in sharp contrast to the port's temperate seaside climate, this country inland from Chefoo was subject to near-Siberian winters, biblical floods and searing droughts. The year before Charles and Alice arrived, two million Chinese had died of famine in the Shantung province alone.

As in Shanghai, most of the foreigners in Chefoo made every effort to shield themselves from the gritty reality of Chinese life beyond the cradling green hills that rose up behind the town. Sixteen grand consulates were built on the high promontory – rapidly renamed Consulate Hill – that overlooked the town and divided the pleasures of the main beach, known as First Beach, from the business of the port. Bavarian chalets jostled with French villas along the seashore, together with Western shops and services. In 1877, there was a British butcher splitting the bloody carcasses of skinny Chinese cattle into anglicized ribs of beef and cuts that looked like Sunday joints. There was a German bakery exhaling damp baking dough and crisp, sweet chocolate pastries. And there were three storekeepers, three doctors, five holiday hotels and an architect.

Perhaps lulled into a false sense of security by the reef and the hills behind, the one thing that the foreigners in Chefoo didn't feel the need to do was to mark out any fixed territory. Instead of a segregated British compound as in most of Britain's colonies, or clearly defined foreign concessions as in the larger treaty ports, there was simply a vague area of international settlement where foreign houses of every nationality were freely interspersed with Chinese homes and buildings. Here the smell of fat German sausage, steak and kidney pudding and garlic and runny French cheese drifted out to meet the persistent wet vapour of Chinese cabbage and noodles.

As the years passed, Western buildings sprang up in every corner of the seaside valley. The informality of the town's layout, thought the residents, simply added to the easy-going holiday atmosphere of the place. The Chefooites must have felt so safe and secure in their pretty haven that they almost forgot they weren't in their own country at all. The Westerners began to give their roofs a Chinese tilt so that the ridges curved back upwards at the edges like a pagoda. They filled their houses with smooth, lacquered oriental furniture and cedarwood-scented painted screens. They began to cook food the Chinese way, lunching on the noodles of northern China, adding sweet and sour sauce to their evening meals. They wandered into the narrow alleys of the old Chinese quarter and gazed at the flutter and screech of hundreds of animals in cages and cautiously sniffed at the curious Chinese medicines on sale. The temple pagoda that stood at the top of the hill on the western edge of the town, towering far above the mansions on Consulate Hill, became a pleasant spot for a picnic. From it the Westerners could survey their little world tucked into the bay. And the caravans of chewing camels and mule trains that stank of dung and desert and had crossed Asia before making their way to the coast from the inland city of Sian – the far eastern end of the old Silk Road – were regarded as charming curiosities for the children to look at. Not a stark reminder that, despite its carefully manufactured home-grown atmosphere, Chefoo was in a very foreign country, on the far side of the world. A place where the native Chinese still carried out their own, as opposed to Westernized, forms of justice – casually beheading their equally casually convicted criminals behind the rocks at the far end of Second Beach, just outside the town. Leaving the sand there permanently stained a deep dark red.

For all the town's pleasure-oriented activities, riding, racing, boating, picnicking and so on, tourism was not the main business of Chefoo. That, as in all of China's treaty ports, was trade. Trade, the making of far greater sums of money than could be earned back home, was the reason why most of these Westerners were risking their lives in these distant soap bubbles of unreality. In 1877, Chefoo's exports came from the town's agricultural hinterland of the Shantung province. This produced vast quantities of peanuts, beans, straw braid 'consumed in the fabrication of fancy baskets and other articles of utility for the use of the fair sex', according to the Chinese Customs trade report for that year, and the region's glistening, double-threaded Shantung silk. Chefoo's main imports, however, were much the same as those of the other treaty ports: practical cotton and wool and the dreadful, inevitable opium. But by 1877 opium imports were on the wane. After steadily losing ground to improved domestic poppy cultivation and opium production in China, they had halved in just three years. Nonetheless they still made up 'nearly one third of the entire revenue for the year'.

Most of the six trading firms operating in Chefoo when Charles and Alice arrived bought and sold whatever they could turn a profit on as well as acting as agents for the bevy of insurance companies that underwrote shipping in China. There were about thirty full-time traders in Chefoo, and it took another twenty – and that was just the Westerners – in Chinese Customs to back them up. At the top of the Customs hierarchy stood four British Mandarin speakers known as 'Indoor Staff'. Below them came the less genteel 'Outdoor Staff', who were concerned more with the physical business of moving boats in and out of the port. As the harbour master and head of the Outdoor Staff, Charles Jennings had to walk a political and social tightrope between the two camps.

Chefoo was home to one other big foreign industry in China: religion. To the Chinese, the missionaries were at least as big a part of the foreign occupation as the traders. There were missionaries throughout China. Unlike the business communities, which tended to stay inside the treaty ports, the missionaries travelled as far inland as they could. They lived with the Chinese, in their huts and villages. To many of the millions of Chinese who didn't live near a treaty port, 'foreign devil' simply meant missionary. Missionaries were the only foreigners that they had heard of or seen.

Within the treaty ports, the missionary communities tended to keep to themselves. In a way, the preachers and the traders were trying to do the same thing – make the most of the new mass market that China offered. They had both been given access to inland China by the same agreement – the 1860 Convention of Peking – that had brought the Second Opium War to a close. Neither, however, saw it like that. The preachers disapproved of the opium trade. And the businessmen thought that the missionaries simply stirred up trouble. As a rule, the rift ran deep. Although, in 1908, domestic political pressure would bring Britain to agree with China that the opium trade should be brought to a halt, the missionaries and businessmen in China would continue to live quite separate, parallel lives.

The missionary community in Chefoo, on the other hand, was a little different. Almost as soon as the treaty port had been opened, two missionaries had decided to set up a boarding school in Chefoo, to which missionaries isolated in inland China could send their children. The school campus sprawled along several hundred yards of the beachfront, at the far end of First Beach from Consulate Hill and the town centre. In order to start the school off, the missionaries agreed to accept children from the business community, immediately breaking down the boundary between the two groups. Just as the foreign nationalities in Chefoo were jumbled up with each other and with the Chinese, so the missionaries began to mix in too. There were football and cricket matches between the school and the town – usually under the banner of the Chefoo Club, hub of the trading community's social life. The trading firms lent boats for school trips to the outlying islands. There were joint picnics to the temple pagoda. And so it went on.

* * *

Charles and Alice reached Chefoo just as the summer season of 1877 was drawing to a close. They moved into the harbour master's new red-brick house on the edge of Consulate Hill, where first another boy, Reggie, and then Lilla and Ada were born. They bought pet dogs. Alice decorated the small house, painting friezes of flowers on the edges of table-tops, on the backs of chairs and around the walls in each room – as she did every house she lived in. She and Charles made a few good friends in the small community that worked in Chefoo throughout the year. When they came round for dinner, Alice, who was never a person to do anything by halves, would have shown her Chinese cook how to produce great banquets of overflowing dishes. Some steaming with the same spices whose densely coloured powders would have stained her fingers and tongue as a child. Others exuding the comfortingly familiar aromas of gravies, steak and kidney puddings and roasts, sweeping her guests through the icy night air back to their nurseries, their mothers' laps, and rolling green hills several thousand miles away.

Even at family meals, as far as Charles's harbour master's salary allowed, Alice would have brought out soups and starters, teaching her children to ease crab-meat from its shell, flip the bones out of a fish, wolf watery noodles without spilling a drop, eat hot, spicy foods without letting their eyes water. Lilla's earliest memories must have been a riot of different tastes and textures: mousses so light that you could scarcely feel them on your spoon, barely steamed vegetables that crunched between her milk teeth, vermicelli that slithered down her throat like the snakes she and Ada ran from in the grass, and great hunks of dense German rye bread that sank to the bottom of her stomach, weighing her down like the stones with which she filled her bucket on the beach.

Most evenings Alice sang and, Lilla later said, she became 'well known in China' for her voice. Charles must have listened, mesmerized and bursting with pride, to every note. And, despite the possible convenience of their marriage, Lilla was told that her parents fell deeply in love and lived a more or less idyllic, though relatively modest, family life.

And so it should have continued: the boys growing up and joining Chinese Customs or a local trading firm; Lilla and Ada marrying and staying close to home; Charles and Alice greying hand in hand as they watched the sun set each evening behind the town's high hills, the last glints of sunlight separating into a rainbow of different colours on the sea.

But, on the bitter, icy morning of 20 December 1884, when Lilla and Ada were just three months short of their third birthday, Charles Jennings apparently scribbled a note to a friend of his in Chefoo called Andrew Eckford, asking him to look after his family. He then picked up his harbour master's pistol, loaded it and went outside. His boots crackled through the frost as he walked across the rough-grass lawn to the shed at the bottom of the garden. He stepped inside, shut the door and blew his brains out.

The sound of the pistol shot ricocheted around the garden walls. Alice came running, to find the family's house-servant shivering outside the padlocked shed. Charles had told him to lock him in and not to open the door 'until you are certain that I am dead'.

Alice ordered him to unlock the door. Charles lay on the ground, his pistol a few inches from his motionless fingers.

Lilla was later told that one of the pet dogs had turned rabid and bitten him. There was no cure. Faced with the prospect of a creeping, agonizing, even dangerous death – during which he might well have gone mad and attacked his family – her father had chosen to take his own life. And thus Lilla's happy family idyll was brought to an abrupt end.

Alice was devastated to lose Charles, she told her children. That she was stranded in China with hardly a penny didn't matter. In fact, that was the easiest part of the situation to solve. The combination of a shortage of women and the sense of community spirit in British outposts around the world had led to an unwritten tradition that one of the bachelors in town would marry the wife of any man who died out there. And Andrew Eckford proposed to Alice. Andrew was a partner in one of Chefoo's largest trading firms and therefore one of the wealthiest men in the port. He was as Chefoo establishment as a man could be. His firm even ran the local mail service. Andrew asked Alice to marry him and offered to take on all her four children. Strangely, Alice turned him down and took her children 'home' – as Victorian expatriates called England. Andrew escorted them all to Shanghai and bought the family tickets on the next steamer out. It would take two months to reach England. He installed them on board and waved goodbye.

The return to England was not a success. Mrs Simons had died, her savings exhausted by all those music lessons and boarding-school fees. The few relations who were still around simply didn't have enough spare cash for Alice and her four children by an unknown and now dead husband. Alice found herself struggling to put food on the table.

Andrew Eckford turned up on Alice's doorstep in January 1886. The custom in the treaty ports, and in colonial life in general, was for expatriates to return home on leave every few years – often for a year at a time as travelling each way could easily take a couple of months. A businessman would leave his firm in his partner's hands. And Andrew had handed over the reins of his firm, Cornabé Eckford, to Cornabé and taken some leave in order to return to England and pursue Alice.

It was a year since he had seen her off in Shanghai. He proposed again. This time she accepted. They married in England and Andrew prepared to return to China. Vivvy and Reggie, aged nine and seven, were sent to boarding school in England, along with thousands of other little boys whose parents worked in the far reaches of the British Empire. Lilla and Ada were still just too young for this and, in any case, being girls, their education simply didn't matter as much. They went back to China with their mother.

As stepfathers go, Andrew Eckford was a good one. He threw himself wholeheartedly into his new family and treated Lilla and Ada, the boys too, more or less as his own. More or less because, in just one respect – one that would turn out to be important for Lilla – he held back. However, then, none of them was old enough to notice or care. Lilla, Ada, Vivvy, Reggie, all called him Father. And within a terrifyingly short space of time it was as if their real father had never existed. After her misery over losing Charles, Alice seems to have made a decision to start again with Andrew. There were no pictures or mementoes of Charles Jennings, not even hidden away in some drawer – he simply ceased to exist. She even informally switched her children's surname to Eckford, extinguishing the evidence of her former, poorer life. The children forgot Jennings, almost forgot that they had ever had another father. He disappeared into the furthest recesses of their memories, surviving only in the traces of his features on their faces.

Alice continued to run her new family in the same way

as before. She sang to her children, and made every effort to convince them of the pleasure of mealtimes – encouraging them to stand on stools in the kitchen, cut raw biscuit dough into animal shapes, lick their fingers for that sweet sugary tingle on their tongues, and vie for the last teaspoonful of butter, eggs and sugar scraped from the mixing bowl. This time around, however, Alice's budget was without constraint. Each morning, when Andrew wandered into his study, a fresh bunch of flowers would be waiting on the desk. Every month or two, Alice – an avid shopper – would sail south to Shanghai and return followed by great cases of elegant Chinese and English reproduction furniture, delicate, whispered ink drawings by the Chinese artists that everyone was talking about at the time, and voluminous silk dresses with corsets that crushed her ribs as they wasped her waist and thrust her chest forward. And each time Andrew, or even just the children, sat down at the dining-room table, they were confronted with a panorama of mouth-watering smells, steaming northern Chinese dishes so hot that you could burn your hands as you spooned out a helping, dishes from western China deceptively cool to the touch but whose spices threatened to lift the roof off your mouth, and the best cuts of meat from the British butcher followed by weighty puddings of suet and flour laced with sherry and jam.

There were other ways in which Alice's life was better. And as I write this it forces me to reconsider the story I have already told – the story as Lilla knew it. Alice didn't just love her life with Andrew Eckford, she loved him, too. In fact, I am assured by all who knew her that Andrew Eckford was the love of her life. Andrew Eckford, not Charles Jennings, not even the unnamed music master. And maybe, just maybe, that was why Alice didn't marry Andrew in China just after her husband had died. Because they already loved each other. And heaven forbid that anyone should know.

I wonder whether Lilla's father was really bitten by a rabid dog. Whether he ever wrote that note to Andrew Eckford.

Or whether he killed himself because he knew his wife was in love with another man.

If Lilla ever suspected this, she didn't mention it. All she recalled was how her new life as an Eckford was, in all material ways, considerably better than she had been told her life was before. She and Ada spent the next few years living in the grandest house in Chefoo, attending the mission school at the end of First Beach, making grand shopping excursions to Shanghai with their mother and chattering away to each other in a language indecipherable to anyone else. Every summer the town filled with more and more new families as the treaty ports flourished. There were parties, picnics, boat trips and races – their new daddy owned one of China's most famous racehorses, Recruit. They had every toy that they could want, and two of each – one for each twin. They wore the prettiest of dresses made out of the lightest of silks and the smoothest of cottons, with no limit as to the number of petticoats, bows and ribbons. And, as Alice quickly gave Andrew two children of his own, they even had a new baby sister each – Edith and Dorothy – to play with.

There was one other thing that Lilla didn't mention. It was so terrifyingly normal back then that it would never have crossed her mind to bring it up later. That Andrew – dear, sweet, kind Andrew, whose firm shipped a little bit of everything in and out of China – was, more likely than not, making money out of opium too. Money that was buying Lilla and Ada all those toys and dresses and ribbons, and turning them into a pair of little princesses. Enabling them to have one of everything each – even an amah each, so Lilla stopped having to wait her turn. So much so that, at some point during this golden childhood, the idea that Ada had stolen Lilla's share of good fortune was almost forgotten.

2

HEAVENLY TWINS

THE RECIPE BOOK is unbound. Its flyaway leaves are cradled between a pair of black leather-topped covers decorated on the front with a sketch of a young couple holding hands and wearing uniform. If you run your fingers over its lines you can feel that they have been embossed deep into the board beneath. Above this sketch the title reads *A House Wife's Dictionary and Suggestions*. The drawing is by Lilla's eldest brother, Vivvy, a gentle giant in whose large hands a pen could create an entire world on paper, and whom one cousin remembers giving her art lessons back in the London suburb of Blackheath in the early 1950s. 'Poor as a church mouse by then,' she gushed, 'but still the handsomest man in the world.'

It was Vivvy who gave Lilla the idea of writing the book when they were both in Chefoo, waiting for the full blast of war to hit them, with little to do and too much time to think. So it's hardly surprising that he offered to fill it with illustrations. Beautiful, tiny pen-and-ink drawings of pots and pans and cakes and puddings and barefoot men pulling wheelbarrows and wearing pointed hats are scattered throughout its pages.

Whatever else you might say about Vivvy, he could certainly draw.

Lilla's book starts with a course on how to cook. 'Cooking stands today amongst the most important arts,' she writes. 'A few suggestions in boiling, simmering and roasting will be found useful.' Useful, that's what she wanted the book to be. Then comes a basic guide on how to turn every foodstuff from raw to cooked. At first the suggestions are general. How to roast meat, what you do with fish. And then there are a few gems such as: 'If fish is boiled too long and breaks, it is best to add white sauce and chopped up hard boiled eggs mixed with it, and serve it as Fish Fricassée,' and 'See that the fruit is dry before it is added to the cake. Steamed puddings are lighter than boiled ones.' There are rules for cooking vegetables, time limits for each one, and for poultry and game, tips about the right fat for frying, and how to cook casseroles. Then a table of measures 'and their equivalents'. The chapter ends with 'Suggestions for a list of kitchen utensils required' and almost-forgotten words like double boiler, pastry board, enamel saucepan, tin plates, salamander and jelly moulds (you needed two of these). And some items that sound surprisingly modern: a coffee percolator, a mincing machine.

There's an introduction too: 'This book has been compiled to help the House wife to select her menus. There are many little items in everyday life that a House wife would like to know, not only in her kitchen, but in sickness, and household hints. *House Wife's Dictionary and Suggestions* will give enough information to help and advise the House wife.' Help and advise. That's what Lilla wanted to do. Help and advise the housewife, whom Lilla puts right up on a pedestal – the star of the social and domestic show.

At the bottom of the introduction is a drawing of

wedding guests leaving a church. Below that is a quote from *Alice's Adventures in Wonderland*. Even as she started to write it with the war closing in around her, Lilla knew her recipe book would be a fantasy. The quote reads, 'A book without pictures, is not interesting says "Alice."' And the frontispiece shows a bride and groom leaving the church. Around it are written the words: 'The Bride of today The Housewife of tomorrow.' The groom is in uniform, looks like he has a moustache and has exceptionally broad shoulders, but he stands little taller than the bride. The couple look just like Lilla and her first husband, my great-grandfather Ernie Howell, in the old wedding photograph hanging in my parents' house. I wonder whether Lilla asked Vivvy to draw it that way or whether that's just how it came out.

Chefoo, North China, summer 1901

The summer of 1901, Chefoo was heaving with soldiers on leave from their stations in China. Uniforms from almost every Western country, every service, every brigade, jostled side by side. Red twill, white cotton, blue wool and plain green serge waltzed around each other on the packed beach promenade. Glints of gold braid, shiny silver epaulettes and well-burnished leather caught the sunlight as their wearers edged slowly along the seafront,

weaving in and out of the crowds. China was under foreign occupation following an infamous episode, immortalized both in print and on celluloid and known as the Boxer Uprising.

There are a host of theories about the mystical and mysterious origins of the Boxers. They are generally believed to have sprung from a religious group based in the Shantung province. The group held that its followers would become invulnerable in battle, and its members were called Boxers as they preached through boxing demonstrations in town marketplaces. The Boxers drew their support both from peasants who, after a serious flood in 1898 followed by two years of searing drought, feared a regional famine, and from China's widespread anti-Westernism.

The initial targets for Boxer anger were Chinese Christians, who vied with the Boxers for recruits in Shantung's towns. The Boxers blamed them for the floods and the drought, and started to attack both Chinese Christians and the foreign missionaries who had converted them, killing a few Chinese in the process. This alarmed the foreigners in China enough for them to ask the imperial court to suppress the Boxers. The Boxers' response was to develop a series of popular jingles posted on street corners. According to Jonathan Spence in *The Search for Modern China*, one translated as 'Their men are all immoral; Their women truly vile. For the [Foreign] Devils it's mother-son sex That serves as the breeding style.'

By the beginning of June 1900, Boxers were roaming the streets of Peking and Tientsin wearing red leggings, white bracelets and turbans in red, black or yellow. Anyone in possession of foreign objects such as clocks, matches or kerosene lamps was subjected to a witch-hunt-style trial by holding burning paper. If the holder was innocent, the ashes rose. If they fell, he was guilty.

Boxers roaming the streets of Tientsin, 1900.

And even though the Boxers had a women's brigade, known as the Red Lanterns Shining, women were regarded as unclean and had to stay indoors after nightfall.

The most curious Boxer target, however, was the railway system. Railways were not just 'an obvious manifestation of foreign intrusion', writes Frances Wood in her superb account of treaty-port life, *No Dogs and Not Many Chinese*, but – in as clear a sign as any that nations need to stop and think before imposing their own cultural values upon others – the railways also directly interfered with Chinese traditions. The rail tracks altered the Feng Shui of the land, thus bringing bad luck to all the areas in which they were laid. Passing trains potentially shook the tombs of ancestors, preventing their spirits from resting in peace. It was even alleged that the foreigners buried a dead Chinese under each railway sleeper – perhaps a metaphor for the jobs lost on the roads and canals. And in the second week of June 1900, the Boxers dug up as much of the Peking–Tientsin Railway as they could.

One week later Western troops stationed at Tientsin seized several forts that controlled access to the city, forcing the imperial court to back either the Boxers or the treaty-porters. Fearing a popular rebellion if it sided with the West, the court took up the Boxer cause – in a dramatically unsuccessful attempt at self-preservation – and a full-scale war broke out. The Boxers took the endorsement as encouragement to do their worst and they swept inland, murdering any Chinese Christians, missionaries and their families that they could find. In one town, the Chinese governor made the grand and apparently brave gesture of offering all the local missionaries protection. And then, when they arrived, he slaughtered every man, woman and child.

* * *

For the foreigners, the most celebrated area of action was in Peking itself. There, everyone retreated into the American, British, Russian, German and Japanese legations – diplomatic compounds – which nestled side by side in the city, and barricaded themselves in with sandbags, timber and whatever furniture they could find. Between 20 June and 14 August, an infamous fifty-five days, they were under siege, resorting to eating their ponies and horses, which had been performing in the May races shortly beforehand.

However, as the Boxers had cut the Peking–Tientsin telegraph along with the railway, the news flow at the time was limited and some confusion arose. On 5 July the *New York Times* splashed, 'All foreigners in Peking dead', then, eleven days later, printed the lurid details of the alleged massacre: 'Foreigners all slain after a last heroic stand – shot their women first'. But when the rescue force, an early UN-like combination of twenty thousand Japanese, Russian, American, British and French troops, arrived in August (to be followed later by a German contingent), they found just seventy of the several hundred foreigners dead and the rest alive.

Foreign retribution was severe. 'Russian and German troops in particular embarked on a campaign of rape and terror. Hearing that valuables were sometimes hidden in coffins along with dead family members awaiting an auspicious date for burial, they broke open any coffins they could find and even dug through the cemetery, flinging bodies away to be eaten by stray dogs.' The rest of the foreign soldiers set about sacking the palatial red-walled maze of the Forbidden City and beheading every Boxer they could find, grimly posing with their victims for photographs like big-game hunters who had tracked down their prey.

And the effect on the Chinese imperial court of first siding with the Boxers and then losing to the foreigners yet again would turn out to be disastrous. Various financial and political penalties were imposed upon it by the occupying powers. But the most demeaning outcome was perhaps the breaking of the majestic isolation in which the imperial court had kept itself, as the empress dowager now found herself holding receptions – tea parties, I imagine – for the wives of foreign diplomats. And, in the longer term, the Boxers and their anti-foreignism defeated, the young Chinese started to examine their country's own fallible imperial institutions in their search for a solution to China's problems, so marking the first step on the road to a tumultuous and bloody upheaval.

Chefoo, despite being an obvious Boxer target with both the Chefoo school for the children of missionaries and the bases of several missions in the town, seems to have been spared the worst. The clearest account is in a history of the school, which suggests that the town was only threatened for a week, and although the children 'slept with a pillow-case containing a complete change of clothes ready by their beds', they never needed it. Nonetheless, it must have been terrifying for those there. One former China resident writes that her missionary parents first ran to Chefoo from their station inland and from there fled China altogether, 'travelling steerage' to Japan, her mother sitting up all night 'to keep the rats off her babies' – including the author, who was just a few months old at the time.

Although the foreign forces took Peking in August 1900, the military campaign throughout the rest of the country dragged on, leaving several thousand troops stationed in the treaty ports. The treaty-port residents took it upon themselves to entertain them. There were tea parties in the afternoon, regimental balls in the evening, and

The Heavenly Twins: Ada and Lilla, Chefoo, 1901.

First Beach from Consulate Hill, Chefoo, 1900.

hunting at dawn the next morning in the countryside around the treaty ports. And when the cities turned into saunas the following summer, the soldiers decamped to seaside resorts like Chefoo whenever they were given leave. There the entertainment went on. There were thinly sliced and peppered cucumber sandwiches at picnics in the hills, early morning canters kicking up the sand along the beaches, energetic boat trips out to the islands that circled the bay, with well-muscled arms wielding oars instead of swords, race meetings at the track on the far side of the old town, with bets and adrenalin running high, and dancing whenever there was the slightest excuse. And with all too few young women around, Lilla and Ada's days were bursting at the seams with invitations.

It was a high time for the twins. They were nineteen years old and just back from finishing school in Germany. Those impish grins had blossomed into flirtatious flickers. Their heart-shaped faces had softened. Their thick, dark hair was piled up on their heads as the fashion dictated. But those two pairs of blue eyes still sparkled as if their owners were just twelve years old.

Lilla and Ada were pretty and knew it. They knew how to hold themselves in a corset, move their arms gracefully in the lightly frilled high-collared shirts of the moment, step not stride in slimmed-down skirts and perch their boaters at just the right angle. And they knew how to flirt. 'They were extraordinarily interested in pleasing men,' I'm told.

Their mother, Alice, showed them her other ways of making a man happy too. How to make a room look inviting, pulling back the furniture to open it up yet not placing the chairs so far apart that a secretive whisper couldn't travel from one to another. How to bring a garden indoors without creating a greenhouse. How to display the latest tastes in fashion, art and music so that your husband feels he is ahead of his peers. How to keep a house fresh, the air so gently scented that you long to breathe in yet more of it, without it growing too hot or too cold inside. How to turn your kitchen into an ever-simmering workshop of succulent roasts and irresistible sweet bakes and soft spices to tease the tongue – because, however many servants you might have cooking for you, they would only be as good as you yourself could teach them to be. These, Alice taught her daughters, were the tools for marriage, the skills for the only life that lay ahead of them. These were the unseen keys, I can almost hear her murmuring, to unlocking a husband's heart. Spoil him rotten, she would have whispered, cater to his every need and he will not be able to help himself but show you love in return. And as Lilla and Ada watched Andrew dote on their mother, his eyes following her every time she swept in or out of the room with a rustle of silk petticoats, they could only have agreed.

Lilla also had charm. Her stammer gave her the air of an innocent about to surrender. And to keep up with Ada, she tried to please. Ada simply swanned around. Then that was Ada, everyone says, she never had to try. Unlike Lilla, whose need to work at whatever she turned her mind to meant that, even in her nineties, she would still have a young man eating out of the palm of her hand within minutes. At nineteen, however, the pair of them were dynamite, an ever-shifting double image tantalizing admirers, who found it hard to tell which one they were addressing. They had endless breathless energy with which to picnic, ride, play tennis, chatter and dance until dawn. Their feet barely touched the ground. And the soldiers who came to Chefoo, Lilla said, called them 'The H-h-heavenly Twins' – a nickname stolen from a contemporary popular novel about a pair of wicked but irresistibly engaging children. One of Ada's grandsons sent me a cartoon from New Zealand. It was drawn in China, that summer of 1901. It shows several officers weeping because they weren't given leave to go to the races in Chefoo and see the leaping pair of parasolled figures in pink and blue, marked 'THE HEAVENLY TWINS'.

Then, just as Lilla thought they were having such a good time that she never wanted it to stop, Ada fell in love. And it wasn't just a passing infatuation. Ada was head over heels in the going-to-get-married unstoppable sort of love with a naval officer called Toby Elderton. Toby was tall, handsome and a bit of a hero in Chefoo. He had been in charge of the ships that had ferried the rescue troops at breakneck speed to Peking, and he had already won one of the top British military medals, the Distinguished Service Order, twice over. He dazzled Ada with his self-assurance and charm. He was already thirty-six years old, so sweeping a nineteen-year-old girl off her feet must have been a walk in the park.

Part of Lilla would have been thrilled for Ada. Marriage was what they had been brought up to do. A husband was their career. And Ada was doing just that – and basking in the romantic glow that had seeped out from the pages of the novels they had read.

Ada was mesmerized and could barely take her eyes off Toby. She dressed for him, wanted only to spend time with him. She stopped speaking to Lilla quite so much in their private language – and started speaking to Toby about things she wouldn't repeat to her sister.

The rest of Lilla must have been quite desperately jealous.

Jealous not just of Ada, who, for the first time since their birth, had something Lilla didn't have and couldn't simply demand to have as well. But, as having an identical twin is like already having a husband, a wife, a lover, she was deeply jealous of Toby, too. His arrival made Lilla ache in a place that she couldn't quite pinpoint. Ada's glazed, flush-cheeked look haunting her and her nights plagued by disturbing images of Ada disappearing up an endless church aisle, her rippling train slithering through Lilla's outstretched fingers each time she tried to grasp it.

The visceral, umbilical cord that had, until then, still joined the two of them was beginning to tear.

Ada wasn't just going to marry Toby. She was going to leave China with him too.

One year after the Boxer Uprising, the foreign occupation of China was coming to an end. Power was going to be handed back to the reinstated Chinese government, and the invading armies would disperse. Toby was a member of the British-run Indian Navy. He had come to China from his base in India. When he went back, he would take Ada with him.

Ada would write. But it would still take six weeks, at the very least, to send a letter and receive a reply. And Lilla would be left behind in Chefoo, the unmarried twin. The spinster sister. The one who wasn't whisked off to India. The one letting the side down.

As an identical twin, Lilla would have found it very hard to imagine living without Ada. When she was with Ada, she felt complete, safe. Alone, it was as though some part of her was missing, tucked away in the purse that Ada had carried off with her.

Lilla had plenty of admirers that summer.

If she wanted, she could go to India, too.

Lilla met Ernie Howell through Toby. Ernie was a stockily handsome, fiery, reddish-haired man with solid-muscle shoulders almost as broad as he was tall — which was not very. His blue eyes blazed and even from his

ORR & BARTON,   PHOTOGRAPHERS,
BANGALORE.

Ernie Howell.

photographs you can see he exuded a very physical energy that matched Lilla's own.

Ernie and Toby were good friends. Ernie was, at thirty-two, a few years younger than Toby but still a dozen years older than Lilla. He and Toby had worked together on the Boxer Campaign. Ernie, a supply and transport captain in the British-run Indian Army, had liaised with Toby, a captain in the supply and transport division of the Indian Navy. They'd even sacked the Forbidden City together, Ernie walking off with the great prize of one of the extravagantly embroidered thick silk cloths that had covered a mandarin's chair in the council chamber. (It still hangs in the English bedroom of one of my cousins today.) And, crucially, once the military occupation of China came to an end that autumn, Ernie, like Toby, would be going back to India. To the great naval port of Calcutta, where Toby was expecting to be sent too.

Ernie probably didn't stand a chance. That summer Lilla must have perfected her way of taking a man's hand gently in hers and looking at him expectantly, as though the next thing he uttered would be the most wondrous words she had ever heard. And then, in an endearing stammer, whispering back.

Within days Lilla's wide-eyed enthusiasm and whispered promises reeled Ernie in. Ernie had been looking for a wife. 'An unmarried man is a ship without ballast,' he'd written home barely a few months before. And Lilla, it clearly seemed to him, was just the ballast he needed. Upon his arrival in Chefoo, Ernie must have been rapidly entranced by the charms of the Eckford women. Skirts rustled around him like paper-thin brown leaves parted by a gentle breeze. Smiles and twinkling eyes surfaced in front of him as the Eckfords' engulfing armchairs and abundant wine threatened to lull him to sleep. Before he realized that he was thirsty, a drink was by his hand. Before he had a chance to feel hungry, plates

of cakes, biscuits, sandwiches, floated around the room.
He sat through feast after feast at their shining dining-
room table. He watched Lilla playing the piano after
dinner and must have hummed along as Alice sang. He
would have noticed how every room was arranged so
that it both caught the eye and welcomed a visitor in,
with a sense of style lacking in his own family of intel-
lectuals and civil servants scattered around the globe.
Wherever he went in the Eckford house, he would have
been surrounded by tantalizing smells – flowers, scented
woods, baking cakes. Seen how every dark corner had
been brought to life with hand-painted friezes of flowers.
He must have quickly realized that Andrew Eckford was
the biggest taipan in Chefoo. And Lilla had such a pretty
little face. A way of looking at him that would have made
him want to grab her.

Ernie was an impetuous man, easily enthused by new
passions. He had been a wild and out-of-control child,
I've always been told, frequently clambering on to the
roof of whichever Indian home his parents were living in
at the time and refusing to come down. At the age of ten,
he had been so enchanted by his first sea voyage that he
had immediately decided that his future lay with the
navy and insisted on going to a naval school the following year. When, at fifteen, he had failed to pass the navy's
entrance exam, he had rushed to sign up to the merchant
navy as a sea cadet. It was only then that he discovered
he suffered from appalling seasickness and had to resign,
joining the Indian Army instead.

Here in Chefoo Ernie was quickly dazzled by Lilla. She
is 'a charming young woman', he wrote. 'She really loves
me for myself.' 'She is only 19,' he continued, and 'very
pretty. She is very musical and plays the violin beautifully . . . She is good as gold – no nonsense about her and
quite unspoilt by contact with modern society. We shall
be as happy as the day is long.'

Lilla and Ernie's wedding. Standing, left to right: Toby Elderton, Ada, Reggie, Ernie, Vivvy's wife Mabel and Vivvy. Seated: Andrew Eckford, Lilla and Alice. In front: Edith and Dorothy.

Rushing like a dog out of the starting trap, he proposed. Lilla accepted.

It's hard to say whose the mistake was. Was Ernie, already in his thirties, old enough to know better than to follow some impulsive affection or believe that he could transplant this domestic bliss to a tougher life in India? Or should the nineteen-year-old Lilla have been more discerning in her choice? Should she have waited, as Ada was doing, for a lengthy courtship to run its course, allowed a while for any difficulties to bubble to the surface, before they were both plunged in at the deep end, miles away from home?

But life, especially when it comes to love or lust or whatever you want to call the forces propelling Lilla and Ernie towards each other, doesn't always happen as it should. They didn't have time to wait. Ernie was likely to have to leave China any day — even before Toby.

Lilla and Ernie were married in St Andrew's Church, Chefoo, on 16 October 1901. For all the swiftness of the wedding's organization, it was a full-blown affair. Alice Eckford was determined to show her daughter off at her best. Lilla wore a dress of 'rich white satin, the skirt and bodice trimmed with chiffon', said the *North China Daily* in an article headed 'Hymen at Chefoo'. A long train trailed behind, made out of such obviously expensive silk that no decoration was needed. The bridal bouquet consisted simply of 'white chrysanthemums, tuberoses, and maiden-hair fern'. The church was filled to over-flowing with white flowers and palms. The bridesmaids, who were Lilla's sisters — Edith, Dorothy and the as yet unmarried Ada — carried 'white flowers in dainty baskets and wore gold cash bracelets, a gift of the bridegroom'. Alice herself may have gone a little over the top. Her blue-grey silk dress was trimmed with black lace and solid beads of jet. Her headdress was a concoction of black and gold net 'trimmed with autumn foliage'. Andrew Eckford – no mention in the *North China Daily* of 'stepfather', no mention of Charles Jennings at all – gave Lilla away. Toby Elderton was best man.

The reception was held at the Cornabé Eckford offices, known by the firm's Chinese 'hong', or trading name, of Hokee. Lilla and Ernie's two hundred and fifty-odd wedding presents were spread out on display. Tall silver coffee pots and squat silver teapots. Heavily engraved silver punchbowls and telegraph-pole candlesticks. Silver toast racks, mustard pots, salt cellars and ice buckets. And photograph frames of such delicate silver lace that they look as though they might crumble between your finger and thumb.

But by the time the wedding party went outside to be photographed, some of the day's gloss must have been starting to wear thin. The picture I have shows a cross-legged Edith and Dorothy sulking in the front row. Alice sits behind with a terrifyingly stern expression on her face. Ernie, standing, stares impatiently to the side as if he can barely wait to be away. And Lilla looks quite miserable. Almost as if she is about to dissolve into tears.

Something must have gone wrong.

But the *North China Daily* only tells us that, shortly afterwards, 'amid hearty cheers and showers of rice and shoes', Ernie whisked Lilla off to the smaller seaside resort of Tungshin, a couple of miles down the coast.

Two days later, they set sail for Calcutta.

3

A NOT QUITE PRUDENT MARRIAGE

Calcutta, India, November 1901

CALCUTTA WAS the political and trading capital of British-run India and many, many times the size of Chefoo. Grand municipal buildings and smooth-carved statues of generals towered over narrow streets packed with rickshaws and open carts overflowing with fruit, bags of rice and chickens, live and dead. Vast steamers sailing to and from every corner of the world jostled for space with the city's debris in its dark-watered, dark-smelling harbour on the Hooghly river. Even on land Calcutta was crowded. Houses were jam-packed together as in the oldest quarters of medieval cities. Property was so expensive that even many of the British living there could barely afford it.

As their ship eased into Calcutta's harbour, Lilla would have been burning with excitement. Arriving in a new city is always exciting and this was the beginning of her marriage, the greatest adventure of her life. In any case, whatever happened next had to be better than the past three weeks at sea. Ernie's seasickness meant that he had spent the entire journey green and grumpy. Now that they were reaching dry land, Lilla must have assumed that her husband's ill humour was over and that a protracted honeymoon was about to begin.

Lilla seems to have more or less decided to be besotted with Ernie, just as she had seen Ada was with Toby. But once she had made this decision, her feelings for Ernie appear to have taken on a life of their own. Part of this was probably sexual. Ernie's photographs show him to have been handsome, strikingly handsome, really quite a hunk, with those powerful shoulders and that square-cut jaw. And part, I'm sure, was because it gave her a role to play and she longed to weave around him the magic that her mother had shown her and create a cosy nest for them to snuggle into. Homemaking, after all, was what her new career as a wife was about. It was a role that Lilla had spent her nineteen years trying to learn how to carry out to perfection. But now she was married, she couldn't even have a go at it: she and Ernie didn't have enough money to rent a house in Calcutta.

That one respect in which Andrew Eckford had held back from treating his stepchildren fully as his own now reared its head. All his capital in Cornabé Eckford was destined for the two children he had had with Alice, his blood descendants, Edith and Dorothy. Not Lilla. Far from being an heiress with the right to a share in a prosperous China trading firm as Ernie must have originally assumed, Lilla was only a stepdaughter. Ernie would have been told this by Andrew Eckford when he went to him to ask for Lilla's hand in marriage. But at this late stage it would have been embarrassing for Ernie – cruel of him, even – to pull out of his courtship of Lilla. In any case by then he must have been desperate to marry and bed her. So Ernie had steamed ahead with his proposal. Nonetheless, Lilla's lack of money was enough of an issue for Ernie to feel that he needed to justify it to his family: 'She is not wealthy. I don't believe in rich wives for poor men. I should hate to have to ask my wife for money.' I think that, as he wrote this, he genuinely, perhaps again impetuously, believed that Lilla's lack of money wouldn't be a problem.

I wish he had been right.

But I fear that the reason everyone looks so miserable in that wedding photograph was that the ugly questions of finance and unmet expectations were already causing trouble.

Rather than rent a modest house outside the city and commute in each day, Ernie decided it was better to live centrally. He took a room for them in a boarding house run by a woman called Mrs Bridges at Number 14, Chowringhee – a thoroughfare in the centre of the city. In the daytime he went to his office. In the evenings he would have often gone to his club, or the officers' mess – places where, when he was still a bachelor, he had been able to spend all his evenings, drinking without restraint. But now he was married, Ernie was discovering that somehow his army captain's wages didn't stretch as far as they had before. And the knowledge that, while he was with his friends, his wife was sitting at home with nothing to do must have produced a distinctly irritating feeling of guilt.

Living in lodgings was quite different from how Lilla had expected her married life to be. Where was the house, the apartment even, that she would make a pleasure to look at inside and out? That she would fill with soft furniture, and chairs not so deep that it was hard to stand up. Where she would scatter pretty sketches, tactile sculptures, objects that caught the eye. Serve three steaming courses for every meal and four for guests. Afterwards, play the piano gently, unless the company called for a song.

In a bedsit in Calcutta, living like this was just a dream. And I am sure Lilla tried to dream it, thinking through how she'd arrange a sitting room – the chairs at just such an angle, the side-tables carefully strewn with plants and books. At least the fresh flowers she could do for real, balancing great bunches of bright, exotic, nameless blooms on the tiny table in the corner of their room until Ernie complained that they were in his way. And there would have been a piano in the parlour downstairs. Slightly clunky but playable. If Ernie came back at a reasonable hour, she could play for him until he stood up and said he'd had enough. But cooking, leaning over a steaming pan, sprinkling crinkly fragments of dried herbs, dipping a spoon slowly into a thick sauce, tasting sweet and sharp, smooth and crunchy, she had to imagine. I can see her standing there in a tiny rented bedroom trying to picture herself between a stove piled high with pots and pans and a kitchen table groaning with crisp, earthy vegetables and the sharpest of knives. Her hands moving as she dreams of peeling apples with insides like half-frozen snow, of slicing onions whose rubbery skin catches her knife before letting it crackle through the layers, of the gentle fizz of a simmering stew, its heat prickling her face as she breathes in its vapour to see whether it is done. And then the images flicker and vanish, leaving her staring out of a small window at a brown-grey sky, the stench of the gutter making her cough.

Lilla's days stretched emptily ahead of her. Some people might have been happy to idle away the hours reading the newspapers or strolling in Calcutta's botanical gardens, but Lilla loathed to waste time. She felt that she always needed to be improving something, creating something from scratch, something useful or something that would last. Up until the final years of her life, when she came to believe that heaven was her next stop, Lilla wasn't terribly religious. Agnostic at best. But if anything was a sin in her book, it was idleness.

Yet without a home to decorate and a kitchen to run, and missing the twinly competitiveness that used to drive her through the day, Lilla was at a loss as to how to fill her time. Even wandering along the shopping streets must have been frustrating. The flip side of Ernie's great passions for life was a tendency to blow his top at the slightest provocation and often in the direction of Lilla. Each time she bought anything at all he would have erupted, saying that they couldn't afford it. Lilla found herself side-stepping an ever-increasing list of activities that provoked him, staring longingly through the windows at all sorts of delights – cushions, lampshades, silks and dresses – that back in China she would have bought without hesitating. Lilla hadn't even been four years old when Alice married Andrew. She cannot have remembered money ever being an issue before.

Nor did she have any real friends to visit. The wives of some of Ernie's colleagues came by but Lilla had so little in common with the older, more India-entrenched, army wives that the conversation soon ran dry. For all Calcutta's superficial similarities to Shanghai – the incessant shouting, the spicy smells, the scuttling pace at which everybody rushed around – Lilla would have been beginning to realize that British India was a very different place from China. Even though, of all the cities in India, Calcutta was the most cosmopolitan, the most business-oriented, it was still governed by layers of terribly British officialdom in a way that China simply wasn't.

For a start, there were the armed forces, the Indian Army and Indian Navy, in which Ernie and Toby served. At first it appeared strange that they were Indian in name when they were so British in nature – the 3,000 most senior officers were British. But it rapidly became clear that, unlike China, where the foreigners lived perched on the edge of the continent in treaty ports while the rest of the country was left to carry on more or less as usual, in India it was quite the reverse. The British Raj had attempted to permeate every pore of Indian life, every village.

Like the treaty ports, the Raj had its own civil service. Yet again, whereas Chinese Customs concerned itself only with China's muddy harbours and convoluted trading terms, the Indian Civil Service – known as the ICS – aspired to regulate nearly every aspect of what the British saw as Indian life. Chinese Customs ignored, in so far as it could, Chinese life outside the treaty ports, and in any case it reported to the Chinese government in Peking. The ICS, on the other hand, piloted education systems and ran courts of law throughout the entire country. It reported to Whitehall, in London. It was so busy monitoring, regulating and reporting that governing the region – supposedly providing a mere support system for the business of bringing money home – had become a primary industry in itself. And this reverence for bureaucracy spilled over into everyday life. The British in India were a conformist caste. Things were done by the book, in the right way. British was best.

Lilla was British in name, but she'd been born in China. And, barring a couple of years of so-called education in England and on the Continent, she'd grown up there. True, the British had been predominant, had even stuck together to a certain degree, formed an Anglo-Chinese culture of their own. Anglo-China, however, was not introspective, quite the opposite. It was surrounded by a melting pot of Western nationalities. Most of them had their own stakes in the place. Many of them took part in the fairly lax self-government. And all of them openly pinched the best from each other's cultures. Whether it was the latest trimmings from French fashion, heart-opening notes of Italian music, foaming pitchers of malty German beer, the treacly sponge of Austrian cakes or mind-numbing Russian vodka, it all blended into a single treaty-port way of doing things – the newer the better. When treaty-porters deferred to a greater power, they did not look to London, they looked to Shanghai. And who you were or where you stood in the general run of treaty-port life depended simply on how well you were doing in business.

In comparison, British social life in India was a labyrinthine affair, a complex equation of rank, military or civil, family background and income. The British in India defended their respectability – an attribute at risk merely by being in India and not England – with a ferocious set of prejudices. Principal among these was a general feeling of superiority over, even a suspicion of, those from less prestigious parts of the British Empire. This meant everywhere except India. When it came to China, they drew a deep breath. China was certainly interesting, adventurous even, but best kept at arm's length. It wasn't even a question of being less smoky gentleman's club and more smoggy East End barrow boy – it wasn't even officially part of the empire. China, and Lilla with it, was off the scale. And Lilla's foreign status was aggravated by Ernie's decision to call her not Lilla, but the more oriental-sounding Lily.

Waiting for Ada to join her in the noisy, dusty, clammy city where every corner revealed an unfamiliar street and her clothes stuck to her skin as the dirt fought its way into her eyes and nostrils, Lilla must have felt all the loneliness of a stranger surrounded by thousands of people. The rest of her family were back in Chefoo, all together, preparing for Ada's December wedding. It must have been terribly hard for Lilla even to think about it. Not once in her nineteen years had she ever been so far from Ada for so long, and now she was even missing her wedding. She couldn't go. It would take three weeks at least to return to Chefoo; if she left now – almost as soon as she'd arrived in Calcutta – she'd only just make it. Besides, Ernie would make a fuss about the expense and it would hardly look right to abandon her husband just one month into their marriage. So be it. Ada would be coming to Calcutta with Toby soon. Two months apart were worth it if it meant more time together afterwards.

Lilla must have desperately tried to find something to distract her during the wait for Ada. And perhaps for a lack of anything concrete to busy herself with, I think she decided to focus herself entirely on Ernie – and his qualities expanded to fill her empty hours.

Ernie knew the city in which Lilla felt so lost like the back of his hand. And the rest must have followed – his heavy build making her feel protected when she stood close to him, his thick moustache tickling her upper lip reassuringly whenever he kissed her. Shortly, Ernie must have become her world, unable to do wrong and knowing exactly what was right and what was ill-advised. And when he lost his temper with Lilla, it was only, I fear she thought, because he wanted to discourage her from imprudent behaviour. The more frequent Ernie's outbursts of temper, the more Lilla found herself looking up to him, trying to anticipate what might please him and avoid what would not. And as Ernie was the one who was busy, the one with things to do, she was the one who had to seek his attention. The more she had to seek, the more her dependence on him must have evolved into something stronger. If she made her way through the streets against a tide of crowds and carts to meet him for lunch, Ernie, who would rather have been surrounded by his fellow officers in the mess, would only have told her that they couldn't afford the extravagance of eating out – leaving her reduced to waiting for him to return at night.

It wasn't as if Lilla wasn't keen on the idea of sex. Quite the contrary. Sex, or rather the vague promise of it, was an integral part of Lilla's charm. However, before her wedding night, she would have known little of its reality. When it came, it may have been a shock.

In his thirties, Ernie would have been sexually experienced. However, barring the luck of an affair with an already married woman – and Ernie was far too Britishly proper to do such a thing – this experience would have been limited to business propositions, a series of purely functional episodes, most of them in the Indian Army's regulated brothels. Eager by nature, he must have approached Lilla with a combination of unbridled enthusiasm and well-honed functionality, as Lilla struggled to work out what she should do. It can't have been the great romantic experience she had hoped for.

Nor can it have been what Ernie had hoped for either. If their private life had taken off, if Lilla had known how to twist Ernie round her little finger in bed rather than simply flirt with him as though she did, the nightly passion would have made up for everything else that was bothering him. For the cooling reality of everyday life. For the burden of having to look after somebody who didn't appear to fit into his Indian world. And, most importantly of all, for the unexpected shortage of money that was curbing his old freedom to do just as he pleased.

Instead, quite early on, Ernie began to retreat from Lilla, his regression marked by the increasingly violent outbursts of temper that Lilla still talked about at the end of her life. And instead of standing her ground in the face of her husband's flashes of anger, she made the terrible, naive, teenage mistake of – as one of her husband's sisters would put it – 'giving way to Ernie too much – she simply purrs around him like a kitten'. And the more she purred, the more capricious Ernie grew. The more capricious he grew, the less happy he became with being, as he put it, 'saddled' with a wife. And the more he blamed Lilla for his general feeling of discontent.

Lilla clung to the belief that if she looked after Ernie enough he would love her in the end. And she fussed around him like an army of handmaids.

This was not what her mother had taught her. Spoil your husband, Alice would have said, don't crowd him. But Alice was a long way away. And Lilla was too alone, a twin too unused to being alone, to realize what she was doing wrong. In pursuing Ernie, she succeeded only in driving him further away. The further he withdrew, the greater the air of desperation that must have surrounded Lilla's efforts. And the more desperate Lilla's efforts, the greater the distance that Ernie must have wanted to put between them. And as she pursued, Lilla was un-wittingly turning a potentially solvable financial problem into something that would threaten to destroy her marriage. Potentially solvable because had Lilla then quietly asked Andrew for help – quietly because Ernie, out of embarrassment, would have forbidden it if con-sulted – things might have run just a little more smoothly at that oh-so-important stage right after the wedding. But she didn't.

Eventually, Lilla's spirits began to waver. Ernie's remoteness may have made her keener than ever on her husband, but there was only so long that she could go on ignoring his rejection of her. When it began to batter its way in through her eyes, her ears – the way he moved his arm if she touched his skin – she must have started to ask herself whether she would ever succeed in making him love her.

Alone in Calcutta, Lilla had nobody to turn to. Even if she had, it would have been hard to admit her marriage was going wrong so soon. The only person she might have been able to open up to was Ada. Ada, whose absence had left Lilla unsteady. Ada, who had Toby doting on her every step. Ada, to whom Lilla could now only write – and then wait six weeks for a reply.

In families spread out around the world at this time, parents, brothers, sisters, even children, usually wrote to one another once a week. With separations often lasting for years at a stretch, letters formed the only relationship they could have. Sadly, I have very few of these from Lilla's own family. Three to be precise, all written to the same cousin, Lulu Covil, the daughter of Alice Eckford's sister Lucy, who had been brought up by their deeply religious uncle and aunt in York. And they are not even letters, just postcard scrawls, kept either for their techni-colour scenes of Chefoo and imperial life or, more likely, because they fell into a pile of papers that someone for-got to throw away. Unlike the Howells, who made a conscious decision to collect their letters as a record of colonial life, it wouldn't ever have occurred to the Eckfords to do so.

But Lilla and Ada wrote to each other far more often than once a week. Almost every single day that they were apart, they scribbled notes to each other. They both suffered from 'written verbal diarrhoea'. At the end of her life, Lilla scribbled endless postcards and letters to friends and relations, sending her Christmas cards out as early as November with her news attached. And she her-self admitted in one of the few notes of hers that made it into the Howell collection, 'How I *love* letter-writing!!!'

On the days that the twins didn't write to each other, it was because they had argued. Or because some more dreadful thing had happened. And there were plenty of those days to come. But still, they must have written thousands and thousands of letters to each other over the course of their long lives.

And not a single one survives. I am assured by every-one that, practical and houseproud, the last thing either

Ada and Toby.

Lilla or Ada would have done was keep a letter from her twin once she had read it. It would have gone straight on to the fire to bring a flicker more heat into the room.

At first, I found this deeply frustrating. But even if any letters had survived, I'm not sure that we would have understood them. As Lilla and Ada spoke to each other in a private language, they probably wrote in one too, to exclude everyone else.

Ironically, in that long red ballot box of Howell missives in the British Library there appeared to be more letters than I could possibly want. Dozens and dozens fired off by Ernie's parents and siblings, all bulging with the information and conversations that make up most of the next five chapters of this book, and many more details that I didn't need. Details of polo matches and promotions, details of day trips and digging in their Indian gardens, and endless details of the toing and froing that made up their daily lives in the three or four years during which their letters were collected.

The best letters are, perhaps unsurprisingly, the ones that were never meant to be kept – particularly one between Ernie's sisters that begins with clear instructions to burn it after reading. Instructions that were, thankfully, never followed. But I wonder for how many other, now vanished letters in this saga such instructions were obeyed. For of course anything that really mattered, anything that a recipient wanted to keep secret – the types of conversation that nowadays you would have face to face or over the telephone, as email has a terrifying habit of recording itself for posterity – would have been destroyed to prevent anyone else reading it.

Yet even the Howells' great collection has all too few letters from Lilla in it, particularly during the first year and a half of her marriage. In a way, this seems to accentuate the unfairness of what was about to happen to her. It is as though she wasn't even given a chance to speak up in her own defence.

In any case, back then in Calcutta, Lilla couldn't have put her fears in a letter to Ada without feeling a failure. Nor would she have wanted to tell Ada how unhappy she was when her twin was still too far away to do anything about it. It would only have made Ada unhappy too. Every letter Lilla wrote at this time must have somehow been holding back a cry for help. But by now Lilla was expecting Ada and Toby to reach India soon and, even if they didn't stay in Calcutta long, they would certainly pass through. So, terribly alone, with no hint of any guidance or wise words to rely on, she must have decided to wait until she could see her twin.

But plans change. And little did Lilla realize quite how long she would have to wait.

4

BURN THIS

India, Christmas 1901

A T CHRISTMAS, Ernie and Lilla made the two-day journey north from Calcutta to the East Indian hill station of Shillong. Here two of Ernie's sisters lived with their Indian Civil Service and Indian Army husbands, surrounded by the hypnotic rolling green of endless tea plantations and intoxicating rain that fell around their houses like the bars of a great cage. Barbie Somerset and, confusingly, another Ada, Ada Henniker – the name was in fashion at the time – were an intimidating pair. Barbie had read modern languages at Girton College, Cambridge, at a time when very few women went to university at all. Ada – who had disconcertingly attractive different-coloured eyes – hadn't been to university but she was still several years older than Lilla, and had the poise and confidence of a fully paid-up member of the Raj. Ernie's father had been a minor star in the Indian Civil Service. He had promoted a number of education reforms across the country and had ended his career in some grandeur as acting Resident – an ambassador of the British government in India – in the independent Muslim princedom of Hyderabad.

To Lilla, Barbie and Ada – the first members of Ernie's family that she had met – would have seemed friendly but daunting. In China only the cleverest people in Chinese Customs had been to Oxford or Cambridge. In the trading community, the men usually came straight back out to the treaty ports from boarding school in England – where, like Lilla's brothers Vivvy and Reggie, they would have been sent by their parents living in China – to launch themselves into business. Lilla had probably never met a woman who had been to university, and she must have rather admired Barbie for having done something that sounded so daring. Even Ada, so at ease with her husband and so familiar with India, must have seemed to Lilla to live on another plane. And Lilla must have rapidly found herself looking up to her sisters-in-law, wishing she could be more like them. Barbie and Ada always had something to say that was funny, or clever, or simply the right thing. They chattered about the ins and outs and whos and wherefores of Indian life with a familiarity that Lilla couldn't have imagined ever reaching. There were about twenty thousand British people in India and Ernie and his family seemed to have grown up with most of them.

As the news of strangers echoed around Lilla like some obscure tribal tongue, she must have watched Ernie nod at his sisters' every word and begun to wonder if that was what she was up against if she wanted to win her husband round. Would she have to swap her stutter for Barbie and Ada's cool, clear-cut tones reverberating off every hard surface in the dining room? Pull her shoulders back and her chest up further to gain the inches she needed to match the lanky Howell girls' height? But when she pictured herself coming out with witty interventions in their conversations, and precise answers to the barrage of questions being fired around the table, the image would have seemed as wrong as the reflection of her face in the polished silver spoons on the table – upside down, distorted into an unrecognizable mask. It wasn't her, couldn't ever be her, a smooth-talking intellectual making passing references to the latest scientific discovery or novel political thought. She, Lilla, and Ernie's sisters were inescapably, funda-mentally, even divisively different.

It wasn't just the years in India or the university education that separated them. Or even the fact that Lilla must have felt she had a pennant reading 'From an out-post in China' pinned to her hair. No, it was their whole approach to living. To Lilla, soft, silky fabrics that your fingers slid over, tantalizing perfumes that made you open your eyes and search for the source, food that conjured up an appetite even when you thought you had none, laughter, incessant music, were all priorities. The Howells, Barbie, Ada and Ernie – although Lilla knew, had seen in Chefoo, that he enjoyed the things she loved too – held a far more practical view of life. They seemed, my father assures me from his own experiences staying with them in England years later, to be impervious to their surroundings, their houses as chaotic and un-comfortable as armies of Indian servants allowed. They ate, Lilla must have felt as she picked at barely passable food, merely to survive. Or in order to gather and discuss politics, science, religion – topics that barely surfaced in Chefoo in the way they did here, with everyone expected to have a view on subjects that Lilla knew little about. In the letters that flew between Ernie's siblings at this time they talked about the great surge in scientific discoveries that were going to turn the whole world on its head, and the same topics would have dominated their conver-sations at breakfast, lunch and dinner. They were obsessed with education. Early education. Higher edu-cation. Education for women as well as men. Ernie's sisters had been part of one of the first generations of

British women for whom there were schools that offered an academic training, and the whole concept of educating women was still widely regarded as suspect by the overwhelmingly male establishment. The Howells, however, held the belief that women should – if only by studying and travelling before marriage – avoid being stuck at home with children all their lives. But, as Lilla would have seen, their homes were not a place where anyone would want to linger.

I don't think it occurred to Lilla that the difference between the Eckford and Howell styles of living was why Ernie called her extravagant. That, as much as he may have enjoyed creature comforts when they were on offer, he clearly wasn't prepared to fork out for them if it meant any cost to himself. That he'd rather live as his sisters did instead.

Nineteen years old and fresh from a silk-cushioned life in China, Lilla would have been horrified.

Most of the Howells' theories about life would have been new to Lilla. They must have sounded exciting, revolutionary almost. In any case, terrifyingly progressive. But it wasn't her world. She would have quite liked the idea that a daughter of hers would go to university but Lilla herself had been sent to finishing school, not Cambridge. And, while she was fascinated by everything new and had every intention of being as independent as possible, she still yearned to potter around a house and kitchen.

The one topic of conversation that Lilla could join in on was Ada's new son, Jack. But even this would have made Lilla a little uneasy. Jack had been born in October and Ada had been through a rough time. She had swelled up like a balloon during pregnancy and, in order to heal after the birth, she had had her knees tied together for several weeks. Then she had been given doctor's orders never to have another child. Lilla, who would just have been beginning to suspect that she might be pregnant herself, must have winced at every word.

In place of having the right thing to say, Lilla continued to fuss around Ernie. Making sure he was comfortable whenever he joked that his sisters appeared not to care. Sending his clothes to the laundry before they were dirty. Bringing him cakes and drinks and sweets in endless succession. And, to what must have been her intense pleasure, embedded in an armchair at his sister's house, he no longer pushed her away but settled into her flurry of activity.

Barbie and Ada watched as Lilla struggled to please their brother. They found their new sister-in-law 'really quite pretty', as they told their mother in London, but 'so very young, almost a baby'. Neither of them had married until well into their mid-twenties, and after 'seeing something of the world'. The way in which Lilla gave in to their brother's whims worried them. With a combination of sisterly prescience and a few more years' experience of life than Lilla, they both sensed trouble ahead.

Almost as soon as Lilla and Ernie returned to Calcutta, Ernie fell ill. In the days before penicillin, even a mild infection could rapidly become life-threatening. Ernie's health deteriorated quickly. Within a couple of weeks he had grown drawn and thin. The army medics took one look and ordered him back to England on sick leave. The conditions in India were renowned for being in-hospitable to good health. He was not to return for twelve months.

Ernie, with all the good grace of a bad invalid, would have been furious. He had been hoping for promotion to the rank of major, which would bring him not only some prestige but also a much-needed increase in pay, and this sick leave was going to set it back at least a year.

Lilla and Ernie, Calcutta, January 1902.

Unwilling to attribute the course of events to pure bad luck, his temper must have flared, scalding Lilla in its path as he, once again, started to push her away. So, just as Lilla received news that Ada and Toby had been ordered to remain in Chefoo for several more months, long enough to justify a visit home, a visit where she would be able to talk to Ada face to face, she found herself wrenched in the opposite direction as she and Ernie set sail for London.

The sea journey took almost a month. Ernie was sick and cabin-bound from the start. By the time the ship reached Southampton, Lilla was two and a half months pregnant and probably had waves of nausea rocking through her, too. To make matters worse, after encountering Ernie's sisters in India, she was terrified of meeting the rest of her husband's family in England.

London, February 1902

Ernie's parents, Arthur and Laura Howell, were wealthy enough to retire to England after a career in India. They had based themselves in London, where Ernie's intellectual father could spend his days playing whist at the Athenaeum – a club set up for 'individuals known for their scientific or literary attainments' and whose nineteenth-century members included Darwin and Dickens. Its eighteen-year waiting list meant that its green leather armchairs were full of elderly members being waited on hand and foot as they browsed their way through the library's legendary 70,000 books.

The Howells rented a house in Kensington Gardens Square, in the middle of the then relatively new area of Bayswater, which was fashionable with their colonial set. The house, Number 5, is now the centrepiece of a Best Western hotel that occupies the block. The front door,

*Mama and Papa: Laura Russell Howell and Arthur
Pearse Howell, Ernie's parents.*

were it still to open, would lead you straight into the bar. Yet the six-storey building still towers above the square's gardens. And the now-defunct doorstep still bears the original slippery black-and-white-patterned tiling that must have swirled under Lilla's eyes as she waited, giddy with exhaustion, while Ernie pulled the bell.

By the time Laura Howell, known to the family as 'Mama', reached the door she had already worked up a considerable degree of irritation with the new arrivals. Ernie had failed to telegraph ahead that he was on his way – 'I don't wonder Mama was annoyed at Ernie and Lily's sudden arrival,' wrote Barbie, 'it was stupid of E not to wire.' His turning up on the doorstep was therefore quite unexpected, meaning that absolutely no preparations had been made. Mama Howell was generally said to have been one of those who 'ruled India with an umbrella' and she did not take to 'casual visitors'. With a great flurry, the servants were diverted from whatever the task in hand and instructed to open up another dank bedroom and make it ready. Only then did she acknowledge the arrival of her son – whom she had not seen since his last visit home two years beforehand – and his 'Chinese' bride, Lily.

Mama and Papa Howell were already worrying that Ernie's marriage might have been 'not quite prudent'. They knew their son's tendency to rush headlong after the latest thing to take his fancy and feared that he had once more done just that. In the months before he met Lilla his letters home had been full of lonely assertions that the task of finding a wife 'is an awful lottery'. And, on one occasion, he had made the desperate suggestion – ignoring Indian Army regulations that forbad soldiers from marrying before thirty (until then they were supposed to be married to their regiment) – that 'all unmarried men over 25 years of age should be taxed'.

However, loneliness and the sexual frustration of bachelorhood were part and parcel of empire life. Even if you were married, you could easily find yourselves posted to 'a place where one never sees a soul week in week out and there is absolutely nothing to do but walk along the same bit of road evening after evening', and you would simply find yourselves feeling lonely together.

In his parents' view, Ernie should have calmly accepted the status quo and waited to meet somebody suitable to make 'an Indian life' with. Suitable meaning somebody whose parents they knew or, even better, whom they had introduced Ernie to themselves. Suitable also meaning having enough money. Actually having it. Not somebody you assume is wealthy but who turns out not to be because you have been 'not quite prudent'. Like Lilla. First they would have received a hurried wire announcing that Ernie was marrying a local business-man's teenage daughter in a holiday resort in China – making them fear that sexual attraction, although they would never have uttered the words, and not reason had driven his decision. The gushing letters that followed – explaining that Lilla was not rich but pretty – confirmed their suspicions. And, by the time Lilla and Ernie arrived in London, Mama Howell would have received – albeit only just – Barbie and Ada's letters detailing Christmas in Shillong. What she read about Lilla and how she fussed around a grumpy Ernie fuelled her fears. And, like all mothers, her sympathies lay firmly with her son. She believed that he had made a terrible mistake.

To Lilla, London must have appeared even less welcoming than Calcutta. Arriving in February, she would have found it as damp and dirty as Calcutta, but cold with it. Whenever she ventured out into the perpetual half-light – a result of the thick smog that hung around the streets – the fumes would have clung to her, woven their way into her clothes, penetrated every pore of her skin. As an Englishwoman from abroad, Lilla should have regarded London as the capital of her imperial universe. Instead she must have found it grey, bland, uniform, compared to Shanghai or even Calcutta. She would have missed the bustle of the foreign cities, their not-quite-right British or European-ness, their vivid colours, pungent, spicy smells and chaotic sing-song of human cries. Shanghai and Calcutta might have been intended to emulate London's finer qualities but, as far as Lilla was concerned, the copies were a great improvement on the original.

And, here in London, she still longed for a home, even just a kitchen of her own, but the beastly question of expense growled on. Rather than resort to the 'misery of squalid lodgings in the Hereford Road' as Barbie describes the temporary accommodation on offer to expatriates returning to London on leave, Ernie insisted on staying in the house in Kensington Gardens Square. Like the Howell sisters' houses in Shillong, it must have struck Lilla as horribly uncomfortable. But far worse than physical discomfort was the loss of privacy.

In Calcutta, she and Ernie might only have been living in a boarding house, but nobody – apart from an inevitably slightly curious Mrs Bridges, no doubt offering Lilla endless cups of tea – had intruded into their lives. But in London, if Lilla tried to cheer up her in-laws' house by bringing back flowers, tearing off the excess green leaves, cutting the stems to just such a height and angle, and arranging them in elegant, simple displays, she would have been told that she was far too extravagant. Her mother-in-law must have seemed to be always right behind her, looking over her shoulder, telling Ernie what to do, taking him off shopping with her, checking that he was comfortable, asking him what he'd like to eat, making Lilla feel redundant as a wife. Or, even worse, that Ernie would rather be married to his mother.

Although Number 5, Kensington Gardens Square, had a kitchen within Lilla's reach, it would certainly not have been at her disposal. Its boundaries were prowled by a cook doubtless selected for her ability to satisfy the Howells' taste for parsimony. Lilla yearned to make some mouthwatering, gooey cake whose sweet smell would float up from the basement, reminding Ernie of how happy they could be. She yearned to find the courage to make a dash for it and tiptoe downstairs to the ill-lit basement room, search the grey cupboards for flour, sugar, eggs, chocolate powder or lemon, anything with which to cook something sweet. And dreaded being caught midway by the Howells' cook, or even Mama.

At dinner each evening, Lilla struggled with overdone vegetables and drying meat, surrounded by the Howells' endless colleagues from India and a bevy of maiden aunts recounting stories about the old days and life in the Raj – the revelation that Lilla was from China producing at best an 'Ah, I see' and a mention of pigtails and bamboo. When it was just the family at home, the conversation wandered to the achievements of the Howell relations, the progress of the army officers and academics in their ranks, and the occasional enquiry as to whether there were any scientists in Lilla's family.

Whenever Lilla was forced to respond to these seemingly unanswerable questions, her stutter welled up, trapping her few words in the roof of her mouth – anything she said only disappointing Ernie. Every word she uttered broadcast what she didn't know, what she hadn't seen, what she found difficult to understand. And, now that her husband was with his parents, the stark contrast her conversation provided with theirs must have made her attentions seem more irritating than ever to Ernie. His disapproval would have radiated across the table, as chilling as the damp London air, as he drew away from her, shuffling his chair closer to whichever parent he was sitting next to, as if changing sides.

Tears of frustration threatened to bubble out of Lilla's eyes as she longed to cook Ernie the curries that he complained of missing. Brighten up the gloomy house – tidy up the piles of periodicals for a start. Buy a couple of comfortable chairs and rearrange the furniture so that you could have a jolly natter around the fire instead of sitting alone with a book in a corner of the room. Longed to repaint the peeling grey kitchen and throw more light into its basement room. Rewrite the weekly shopping list, ordering juicier cuts of meat and less-battered vegetables from a better greengrocer down the road.

Yet as in Calcutta, being a wife, looking after her husband in the way that she had been brought up to do, remained a fantasy. The only space Lilla and Ernie had to themselves was the bedroom. She would fluff up the thin pillows, drape a Chinese shawl over the worn velvet chair and wait for Ernie's footstep on the stairs after he had finished his cigar with Papa. Here was the sole place where she could still act as a wife, even though she was growing increasingly large. As the weeks passed, her waist expanded, her stomach bulged, and her breasts grew heavy and too tender to touch. As much as she thought Ernie handsome, even found his withdrawal from her a magnet that made her want to be with him more, nature would have made his desire wane. The pretty little thing that he had swept up out of her easy, voluptuous household in China was becoming an awkward and unhappy matron whose presence hung round his neck like an ill-fitting collar.

Lilla must have read her husband's thoughts in the furrow of his eyebrows, the strained curve of his shoulders and the peremptoriness of his touch. Watched him slip away from her like a ghost, his warm flesh dissolving to leave a cold, hard stranger in her bed. Lain awake, struggling to find a comfortable position, yearning for a single gulp of Chefoo air that would clear her head, the salty smell of the sea, a bowl of wet noodles, anything that would take her home – and yearning more than anything to see her twin, Ada. And, closeted with Ernie's family in London's sodden twilight, the confusion that Lilla had felt in India began to turn into despair. 'They called me the little white loaf,' she whispered years later, the tears still hanging at the back of her eyes.

And then a wire arrived from Shillong, bringing sad news that added to the household's uneasiness.

Ada Henniker's son Jack had died. As the letter that later arrived from Barbie explained, he had had a 'high fever and convulsions for nine whole days then nothing for 24 hours but his strength was gone & he couldn't rally – poor scrap, he had made such a plucky fight . . . How horribly final death is – one felt almost relieved and thankful to think at last he was in no pain and had no more to go through.'

Ada was distraught. What made the matter even worse was that she felt guilty for not having wanted a baby so soon after getting married. All of the Howell sisters, Lilla and her twin too, wanted few children. Having a large family was regarded as physically tough, each process of pregnancy, childbirth and nursing taking its toll on a woman's body, ageing her prematurely and possibly shortening her lifespan. There were contraceptives. Rubber condoms and diaphragms had been mass-produced since the invention of the rubber vulcanization process in the mid-nineteenth century. Even spermicides were available. Yet in the early twentieth century respectable doctors would still have had nothing to do with such things, and fewer than one in six married English couples were using them – those that were tended to be from the better-off, better-educated families.

Even then, contraceptives seem only to have been used once you already had children, as a means of stopping yourself from having more. It might have been socially acceptable to let nature take its course and then decide not to have any more children, but using contraceptives to prevent you having any children in the first place perhaps implied a scandalous interest in sex for pleasure only. Ironically, it was a pleasure that the heaviness of the condoms and diaphragms probably removed altogether, leaving people unwilling to use them for this reason too. In any case, the norm, even for the astonishingly well-educated Howell sisters, seems to have been to cross your fingers and hope for the best.

Ada Henniker had therefore been furious to find herself pregnant within weeks of her wedding and had spent most of her pregnancy wishing her bump would go away. After Jack was born she had spent several weeks regarding her new baby as a 'horrid little wretch', before conceding that he was 'not nearly as ugly as most'. Now she felt that his death was her punishment.

Mama and Papa Howell were sympathetic but philosophical. It was terribly sad, so distressing for both Ada and Barbie, all of them. Yet such things were part and parcel of Indian life. Frustrated by his inability to do anything to help his sister, however, Ernie's concern, like most of his passions in life, would have been dramatic. After all his poor sister Ada had been through during and after the baby's birth, nobody else's troubles were worth a thought. Not even his pregnant wife's.

Lilla was terribly upset, though her tears over Ada's baby would have been hiding other emotions. She still adored Ernie, but his attention was now entirely focused on events in Shillong. And, as Lilla remembered the umpteen times that she had resented her own expanding waistline, she must have begun to fear that Ada's 'punishment' would also be hers.

Barbie, Ernie's other Shillong-based sister, certainly feared this. Barbie too was 'booked', as the Howells called it, and her baby was due a month after Lilla's. Barbie had married three weeks after Ernie and Lilla and, until the death of little Jack, had been horrified to find herself pregnant so soon, too: 'I was hoping against hope,' she wrote back to her family in England. And as she sat in India, talking her sister Ada into believing that her son's death was not her fault, she found herself 'fighting the superstition' that her child would die too.

Out in Shillong, the grating sadness of baby Jack's death refused to go away. The month that it took for post to reach India by boat from England meant that, for 'weeks and weeks' afterwards, Barbie had to open her sister's mail to filter out letters responding to Jack's photographs that had been sent home a few weeks beforehand. 'The first ones arrived the morning he died,' she wrote. 'And yesterday a parcel from home came with pretty bits of embroidered material for his frocks – it nearly made me cry . . . I couldn't believe that a baby could leave such a blank . . . We were always picturing him at different ages – a little redheaded fellow rolling about.'

The lag in time between the child's death and the arrival of letters written while he was still alive made Barbie feel 'such a terribly long way from it all', just as 'if any star were to be extinguished it would go on shining for us for ages and ages'.

The one subject that Barbie didn't feel detached from was her family's dissatisfaction with Lilla. Ernie's married life had become such a topic of conversation in the letters that flew between his parents and siblings scattered across India that, even a month's post away, Barbie had ended up feeling quite involved. It may have been the fact that they were both pregnant, that they had married within weeks of each other, or perhaps Barbie was simply more generous than her siblings. Whatever the reason, Barbie took up the position of Lilla's firmest, indeed only, supporter among the Howells. Expressing this support, however, was difficult. It was one thing for the Howells based in England to send news of developments to isolated family members living abroad, but it was another entirely to send an opinion in writing back to 5, Kensington Gardens Square. In families scattered across the empire, letters could rarely afford to be personal. Instead they were public property, and a new letter would be read out aloud after dinner, left lying around or passed among family members and friends who wanted to catch up on news. So anything that Barbie wrote back to London ran the risk of being discovered by Lilla.

But the moans about Lilla rumbled on and Barbie could no longer remain silent. She wrote to her eldest sister, Laura Harmer. Laura was another Cambridge graduate, who had walked away with a glittering double First in natural science – not that, being a woman, she had been allowed to collect her degree. She had married another scientist and still lived in the university town, so she was close enough to events in London to be able to influence what was happening, yet far enough from Lilla to make writing safe. Laura was also, quite rightly, regarded by the rest of her family as terrifyingly bright. Among the Howells it was thought sad but inevitable that she had given up her scientific career when she married and had children. (Her husband was an eminent scientist called Sidney Harmer, later knighted for his discovery of tiny single-cell organisms called protozoa.) Laura herself found it hard: 'I find that domestic chores – when they take the form of curtains and turning out drawers – all day simply reduce one's brain to a pulp and make it impossible to think intelligently on any subject.' Laura, like most of her family, was clearly not designed for domestic chores. My father tells me how her husband

Sidney, 'a scientist second only to Alexander Fleming', was so perpetually half starved by the household's meagre meals that every lunchtime he disappeared into the bushes to eat cheese sandwiches with the gardeners.

Barbie wrote:

> And now as this is a 'strictly private' epistle and only
> written to be burned at once – promise – after you've
> read it, I will say what I have frequently thought but
> have never ventured to hint at to Mama as I know
> how her letters get bandied about through the family
> – why is everyone so hard on poor Lily – including
> Ernie! Poor Lily, she may not be a prodigy of wisdom,
> but she is such a baby still – I do think Mama and
> everyone seem hard on her. What do you think about
> her and Ernie? Are they a happy couple? I do hope
> so. But he writes of her so funnily one doesn't know
> what to think.

Laura's reply has been lost. However, the complaints about Lilla continued to reach Shillong. A month later, Barbie wrote to Laura again:

> It makes me awfully angry to hear the groans over
> poor Lily – I do call it so horribly unfair and it makes
> me very cross with Ernie, who was certainly no
> susceptible infant when he married her but a man
> with his eyes very wide open indeed – or ought to
> have been. Well, well of course you understand all
> this is not for publication in the family but I am sure
> you agree with me. No-one can be more awake to the
> horrors and folly – esp out here – of 'reckless and
> improvident marriages'.

It was about this time that Ernie must have told Lilla that, when he returned to India, he intended to leave her behind with his family. To those used to 'Indian life' this was not so unusual. The country's raging heat and outbreaks of disease often led husbands to leave their wives and young children in England for long periods at a time. Ernie, though, was talking about repeatedly going out alone for three years at a stretch and piling together his one-month's annual leave in order to squeeze in a quick trip home, then leaving her behind again and again. As it took a month to travel each way, that left just a month with Lilla in England – once every three years. At a time when divorce was unheard of, Ernie was suggesting a very thinly veiled long-term separation. And all because, as he must have made clear, keeping her and the baby with him in India would be, in his book, too expensive.

To be told by your husband, when you are nineteen years old, pregnant and far from home, that your company is not worth the cost of living together must be just about as emotionally devastating as it gets. It must also have been terrifying for Lilla. If Ernie left her and their baby alone with his family, what would become of her?

Lilla clearly realized that this was a problem she could no longer hide.

And when, on the other side of the world, Alice Eckford read a cry for help that must have brought tears of frustration to her eyes, she didn't hesitate to act. She packed up the house and, six weeks after sailing out of Shanghai, she arrived in England in a glittering caravan of silk and lace. With her came Andrew – who must have decided to take another year's leave, now that Vivvy and Reggie were old enough to help run the firm in his absence – and their two teenage daughters, Edith and Dorothy, trailing behind.

As if trying to make her family as appealing as possible to Ernie's, Alice rented a house in Bedford, a market town bursting with retired empire-builders, civil

servants and army officers – and within visiting distance
of both Papa and Mama in London and Laura in
Cambridge. Then she filled it to overflowing with fine
oriental furniture, spices and endless gratuitous cakes,
setting up an extravagant family camp that shouted out
that money was not an issue.

And she made it clear that she intended to stay.

5

POOR LITTLE LILY

Bedford, early summer 1902

I HAVE BEEN SCRABBLING through boxes and drawers, through albums and battered cardboard folders, looking for a photograph of the Eckfords' drawing room in Bedford. I am sure that I have seen one somewhere. An almost wide-angled lens view across a square room, taken from the corner opposite the door. But it is not in my files. Perhaps it is in one of the many dusty photograph albums lent by relations or which surfaced from the deep vaults of all those libraries and universities. Or, possibly, the photograph doesn't exist at all and the scene in my head has been conjured up by dozens of hints and clues. Photographs of other rooms arranged by Alice. Descriptions trespassing in letters on far more important topics. Or just a clear, clear picture that seems always to have been there.

It is a large, lightly decorated room. Instead of being draped with the dark velvets and brocades of a century ago – every curtain pelmet, stuffed cushion edge and sofa skirt weighed down with heavy fringes and tassels – the Eckfords' drawing room is light, fresh, modern. But then that was Alice's, and Lilla's, style. The sofas and big armchairs are upholstered in pale fabrics. There are three or four dark wooden armchairs with cream, almost white, seats and backs. Great ferns, or palms, reach into the room from its corners, their long, thin, pointed leaves dangling down like fingers aching to stroke the shining objects that glitter around the room. Or the cheek of a passer-by. And in between the sofas and armchairs are maybe a dozen dark, thickly lacquered side-tables. Standing against the calm palette of the walls are three-quarter-height painted Chinese cupboards with moon-like circles drawn round their strange brass locks. A couple of Japanese screens covered in figures telling epic tales of love and heartbreak, half concertinaed, frame the set. Their resined scent fills the room, seeping out from deep inside the wood, bringing years of memories with it.

In sharp contrast to the minimalism of the colour scheme, every surface is crammed to overflowing with photographs in thick silver frames, carved wooden figures and demi-gods. There are embroidered laces and linens – some so bright that they appear snatched from the seamstress's hands, others so faded and thin that they look as though they would fall apart if taken out of their frames. Curving porcelain vases and bowls too fragile – the china almost transparent – to pick up but whose ridges rise and fall under your fingertips, so that their painted surfaces seem to leap out at you. And hanging on the walls are more framed embroidery samplers, pen-and-ink drawings by Chinese artists and watercolour landscapes by Western hands, but again of Chinese scenes.

This was a room in which you could hear the breathy whisper of opulence. Even the thick, silk curtains – the material shipped over on great rolls from Shanghai – were as pale as the walls, their richness one that you felt as your arm brushed past a surface firm from the sheer weight of the fabric. This was a room in which Alice intended to make it quite clear to Ernie and his family that the Eckfords were not just colonial traders whose daughters could be picked up and dumped at will but a force to be reckoned with. Little did she realize just how impervious to her efforts her daughter's in-laws would be.

Socially, the Howells were as deeply conventional as they believed they were not. They may have mingled with scientists on the cutting edge of change. They may have foreseen the cataclysmic political changes of the twentieth century, pointing out in the letters that flew between them that 'things cannot continue as they are' and discussing the likely collapse of 'that wonderful house of cards which we call our Indian Empire' – even when that meant the end of the very traditions, the old order, that had nurtured them. They may have held strikingly liberal views on women's education – it was quite extraordinary that in the 1880s and 1890s, when few women were educated at all, the family had not just allowed but encouraged Laura and Barbie to go to Cambridge. And, of course, each of them felt that their experiences in India had given them a worldly-wise perspective from which to judge. Nonetheless, on social issues, they were the puritanical sort of small-'c' conservatives whose sympathies and aversions had long sustained the British class system. When it came to family pedigree, the longer the better. And on this point they chose conveniently to ignore the fact that until Papa's grandfather had ventured up to London and made a fortune shipping supplies out to the British Army in its various wars, the Howells had simply been the local butchers in Oswestry, a market town on the Welsh borders. Instead, they focused on the achievements of Papa's father, Sir Thomas Howell, who had been knighted for sorting out the shambolic logistics – or lack of them – that had left the British Army without enough boots during the first bitter winter of the Crimean War.

A couple of exceptionally procreative generations – Papa was one of thirteen and appears restrained in having only six children himself – had now subdivided the family money to a pittance. This left the short-of-cash Howells deeply suspicious of other people's fortunes, particularly those that were newly made – as the Eckfords' money was in China. It was an unspoken but fundamentally held belief among Lilla's in-laws that the pursuit of riches resulted in a neglect of more high-minded endeavours. 'They must be fairly well endowed with this world's goods,' wrote Papa Howell after meeting Andrew and Alice Eckford for the first time – implying that they lacked the non-material, intellectual assets that were worth more.

There was certainly an element of jealousy in the Howells' snobbery. Like Ernie, the rest of the men in the Howell family were perpetually moaning about a 'shortage of funds'. When translated into English pounds and prices, Indian Civil Service and Indian Army salaries were not generous. The mess bills, the uniforms, the cost of employing a valet, could easily make an army officer's career an expensive luxury rather than a gainful occupation. Ernie and his siblings, even their parents, were incessantly calculating how to live the lifestyle that they had been brought up to expect on the combination of salary and the tiny private income that each of them had. And while they whinged about the difference between extravagances and necessities, they were all aware that the Eckfords didn't have to make such distinctions.

This must have made it all the harder for Ernie to ask Andrew Eckford for help. When Andrew wrote out cheques to Lilla, Ernie must certainly have been grateful.

But admitting to a successful businessman like Andrew Eckford that he couldn't cope financially would have knocked a huge dent in his soldierly pride. The straightforward option – especially now that Lilla had her family in England – was to stick to his plan to go to India alone.

Money wasn't the only gulf between the two families. Lilla was already well acquainted with the sharp contrast between the Eckfords' love of luxury and the Howells' almost spartan lifestyle. For Alice, this would have come as a shock. She may have intended the display in the house in Bedford to bring the two families closer together, but instead it seemed to accentuate their differences.

The Eckfords' house in Bedford was everything that the house in Kensington Gardens Square was not. Number 5, Kensington Gardens Square, was an externally elegant white-stucco terraced house containing a smattering of functional furniture. Number 14, Lansdowne Road, Bedford, was, wrote Ernie's sister Laura after she had driven over from Cambridge to see them, 'not much to look at on the outside, but most comfortable inside'. To some extent, Laura was impressed. '[The house is] beautifully furnished. The drawing room is a perfect museum of Chinese and Japanese china, embroidery, carved work etc.'

But this attention to visual detail heralded – as Laura might have expected – a lack of the intellectual interests that the Howells cared so much about. The Eckfords' conversation, she nonetheless wrote, was 'not particularly cultivated'. Alice Eckford, in particular, she found 'suburban' and 'full of a fussy sort of kindness which is rather distracting'. 'She simply fazes me out,' continued Laura. 'She has discovered the secret of perpetual motion and has in addition an unending flow of small talk. I think there is nothing as tiring as having to talk for a whole day especially the make up kind of talk one has to keep up with a person with whom one has not really much in common.'

Poor Alice. She was trying so hard to make life easier for Lilla by being friendly and showing that her family was too rich to be ignored. Really, she would have done better if she had suggested that the Eckfords were impoverished artists with grand connections. If she had toned down the decoration, focused on her love of singing and chatted less, maybe the Howells would have warmed to her.

Lilla's baby was due at the end of August. By the beginning of July she would already have felt the size of a house and been torn between a longing to be rid of the huge weight she was carrying and a growing fear of the pain that lay ahead in what was euphemistically referred to by the Howells as her 'event'. The question arose as to where she should give birth and stay for her confinement afterwards. The convention then was that, after giving birth, a woman should 'lie in' – either stay in bed or take it very easy indeed – for six weeks.

Deeply relieved that some of her family was with her in England – even if it made her twin's absence all the more marked – Lilla assumed that she would go to her mother in Bedford for the birth and started organizing herself to do so. But when the Howells caught wind of this, they were aghast. Lilla was now a Howell, they pointed out, as the baby she was having would be, too. She should therefore be with her husband's family for her 'troubles'. Perhaps Ernie's family did not quite trust Lilla's 'suburban' mother to do things in the proper way, or held some suspicion that she might have picked up unorthodox childbearing practices in China. In any case, they professed amazement that Lilla could have been foolish enough to think that she should give birth

anywhere but in a Howell household. London was regarded as unhealthy for a newborn, particularly in the summer, so it was decided that Lilla would go to some cousins of Ernie's near Cromer, on the Norfolk coast.

Cromer may have been a fashionable seaside resort like Chefoo, but Norfolk is nothing like Shantung. Instead of a town sheltered by hills and beaches nestling between rocky coves, the Norfolk coastline is bare and flat. The only undulations along the East Anglian shore and inland are a few dunes whose sand has been whipped up into great piles by the wind, and the dips that mark the great watery channels which criss-cross the countryside, the marshlands known as the Norfolk Broads. Bar a few tufts of tough, shrubby grass, there is little to stop the great North Sea winds sweeping down from icy Scandinavia and levelling the landscape. Even in August, the hottest month of the year, Norfolk requires a thick fisherman's sweater. It is not a cosy place to give birth to a first child.

Not that Lilla can have cared. Ernie was still intending to go back to India without her. And although her mother was now there to encourage Lilla to hold back a little, not serve herself up to Ernie on a plate, telling her that he would come round once he held his child in his arms, Lilla must have been desperate to do anything to make herself seem less of a burden and easier to take with him. She agreed to go to Cromer.

Ernie didn't go with her. In late July, he dispatched Lilla to his relatives and took the sleeper to Scotland. There he joined his father, who had already taken up residence at the Royal and Ancient Golf Club in St Andrews. While Lilla was left among strangers in an unfamiliar place to grow larger, more exhausted and increasingly anxious about what lay ahead of her in childbirth, Ernie and Papa settled down for a month or so of father-and-son golf.

Alice followed her daughter from Bedford to Cromer, taking Andrew and their two girls, Edith and Dorothy, with them. She booked rooms for the family in one of the hotels and hovered as close as she could without interfering with the Howells' arrangements and upsetting matters more.

Again it was Barbie's lone voice, from miles away in India, that spoke up for Lilla. 'For this event of hers she seems to have been the last person to have been consulted, though one would have thought on this one occasion at least she was the first person to consider.'

Perhaps, if they had arrived in time, Barbie's words would have roused a flicker of conscience among her family back in England. But, of course, it was yet another month before they were read.

The baby was late. Luckily perhaps, for it was only towards the end of August that Ernie decided to return south. Papa was reluctant to see him go: 'I wish Ernie could have stayed longer with me.' Ernie reached Norfolk in the last days of the month. Papa planned to follow him shortly.

The first week of September passed. There was no sign of the baby. The second week dragged on with Lilla cumbersome, barely able to move, simply waiting on tenterhooks for the pain to begin. By the time September reached its third week, Alice decided to intervene. In her opinion – and she had borne six children herself – a bit of movement was what was needed. She took Lilla out for a carriage drive. The carriage was a fairly rudimentary pony and cart. Nonetheless, as my grandfather, Lilla's son, told me again and again, Alice set off at a rapid pace.

It's unclear whether it was a surprising corner or another vehicle that caused the crash, but shortly after leaving the house the horse bolted and the pony cart ended in the ditch. Lilla, shaken by the fall, felt her

stomach begin to contract. Alice's plan, in a roundabout way, had worked.

The baby, my grandfather, was a boy. Given the less than perfect state of Ernie and Lilla's relationship, this was probably a good thing. Ernie regarded baby girls as 'petticoats'. In any case, Lilla's in-laws were delighted. The baby was the first boy with the surname Howell to be born in his generation and, even better, the few wisps of hair on the top of his head were clearly the same reddish colour that Ernie and Papa Howell were so proud to bear. For once Lilla appeared to have done something right and, glowing with pride and keen to preserve this new state of affairs, she readily agreed to christen her son Arthur after Ernie's father.

Lilla's state of grace in having produced a son and heir was short-lived. Alice had seized the opportunity of being with Lilla for the birth and had whisked her straight back to Bedford. But the Howells must have wanted Ernie's son back. Just one week after the birth, when Lilla should still have been confined to bed, she made the day-long journey back from Bedford to Ernie's cousins in Norfolk. There, worn out from the trip and separated from her own family, things rapidly went downhill.

A couple of afternoons later, Lilla was alone with the baby when she began the usual struggle to persuade him to feed from her breast. Muddled by the soul-emptying exhaustion of childbirth and moving around the country, she was turning the tiny child every way round she could think of to find an angle at which he could latch on when the Howells' baby nurse came into the room. The nurse was horrified, as Lilla later said, to see her 'trying to feed the baby upside down'. She snatched Arthur from her and advised the family that Lilla was unfit to look after the child. From then on, the times at which Lilla could

J. Thomson. Bedford.

Lilla and Arthur, Bedford, 1902.

see her baby – under strict supervision – were limited.

Lilla was devastated. To take a newborn child from its mother is to tear her apart. Having given birth so recently, Lilla ached in every cell of her body to pull her son close to her, easing the physical pain and emotional turmoil that can make a new mother feel like she has been run over by a juggernaut. And she would have still felt so physically joined to her baby that whenever the nurse took Arthur from her and swept him out of her room it would have felt as though, like a medieval torturer, she had reached in and taken hold of Lilla's innards, dragging them behind her as she and the baby left the room. Each time Lilla watched Arthur's tiny, podgy hands and face disappear out of view, I'm sure she felt that part of her died.

And, a few days later, bad news came from India. Ernie's sister Barbie had also given birth to a healthy boy – Alan Fitzroy, known as Roy – just two days after Lilla. But she had since fallen dangerously ill with a post-natal infection. Such infections are a common complication of childbirth today, though they can usually be cured by a swift course of antibiotics. Back in 1902, the only way to recover was to ride the infection out. Or, in the worst cases, be operated upon – putting the mother at risk of yet more infection. The wire that the Howells received in England told them that Barbie's temperature had already been climbing steadily above 104 degrees for four days. Eight or nine days was the absolute maximum that a person could survive with a fever of this level.

Ernie left to join his parents in London the moment their wire reached him with the news.

For hours on end, Lilla was left alone in her room. Still exhausted from pregnancy and childbirth, still facing being abandoned by her husband and having been told by his family that she wasn't capable of looking after her own child, Lilla must have felt that she wasn't worth anything at all. And with her self-esteem shot to pieces and a tumultuous hormonal tide turning her mind and body inside out, it was almost inevitable that she began to sink into what Ernie was to call malingering but what any doctor today would instantly recognize as post-natal depression.

However long she spent in bed, Lilla still felt exhausted, drained of every ounce of her former energy. Too tired to concentrate on reading or any other distraction. Tracing and retracing the loneliness of the past year. Where had she gone wrong? Why couldn't she have her baby? And why wasn't Ernie with her? Why did she have to be so very far from Ada?

It took almost seven weeks for a letter to reach Ada in Chefoo from England. And seven weeks for the reply to come back. That made a long three months for Lilla to tell her twin something and receive a reply. It was too long a time to have a conversation about anything that really mattered. In any case, at this point Lilla would probably not have been able to write. Ada, who must have been desperately worried by her family's flying departure from Chefoo, had to rely on the occasional wire and her mother's more detailed but seven-week-delayed reassurances, or not, that Lilla was all right.

And as Lilla lay there, the questions, the self-doubts, kept on popping into her mind. Why couldn't she do anything right? Not even now that she had given her husband the son he'd wanted? The more that she tried to think things through, the more confused she became, her mind thickening and slowing down. Her body, overcome by the effort of it all, lying there listless, as though her limbs were lead weights pinning her down on the lumpy mattress. And the continuing ups and downs of Barbie's illness in India flinging her from tears to elation to tears again.

* * *

It would be another three months or so before Ernie's siblings made an overt decision to collect their letters. But they had for some time already resisted the urge to throw all their letters away. Especially the ones detailing the family drama that follows.

For five long days after Ernie left her to go to London, Lilla waited to hear, second-hand, of Barbie's fate. And then good news came through. Barbie had been operated on and her temperature had fallen from 104.8 degrees to a far safer 100. Ernie came back to Norfolk and saw a Lilla who hadn't had to have any operations, who hadn't been battling at death's door in a faraway country, being what he must have thought was self-indulgently tearful. So when, less than a week later, another message arrived from Shillong to say that Barbie was ill again and this time the situation was even worse than it had been before, Ernie packed his bags and headed off once more.

Lilla cried as he left. Not just for Barbie but because, even though Ernie wasn't supposed to be leaving her until he returned to India in January, still almost three months away, he seemed only too ready to go now. And because the more elusive he became, the more she loved him. And she didn't seem able to make him love her back.

Up in London, Ernie became totally absorbed in his sister's illness. So far the news from India had been brief, and confined to wires revealing only the extent of Barbie's fever, the fact that she had been successfully operated on, followed by 'Serious relapse, slightly better.' Any more details were still caught up in the relentlessly slow post. It took a good three weeks for a letter to reach London from Calcutta and Shillong was two or three days further away than that. For the next two weeks, the wires continued in the same vein. Barbie was still extremely unwell and showing no sign of improvement. Ernie stayed in London, waiting on every piece of news, with the added excuse that he needed to study for his promotional exams.

As Ernie's concern for Barbie grew, his notes to Lilla must have grown briefer and rarer. He hadn't yet left her for India – only gone as far as London. But back in Cromer, Lilla would have felt that she had as good as lost him already. Her own mother's visits can hardly have helped. The more Alice – who would have meant well, have only been trying to make her daughter better – told Lilla to pull herself together and stop her silly worrying, the more Lilla would have done precisely the contrary.

And then, in the middle of the second week in November, the news from India changed. Barbie's sister and husband had decided to move her to hospital in Calcutta. As Barbie was seriously ill they would have to travel slowly and the journey would take several days. But reaching proper medical care was her only hope of survival. The Howells, relieved that a clear decision had been made, drew in their breath to see what would happen next. Mama booked herself on the next boat out to Calcutta. Ernie was almost beside himself with worry. But his exams had finished. There would be no more news from India for a week or so. It was hard to justify staying in London. On 13 November, Papa wrote: '[Ernie has] gone back to Cromer to look after his sick wife. Poor old chap – he is by no means the light-hearted chap that he used to be.'

By now, Lilla's six-week confinement was more than up. But, far from having recovered, she was still languishing in bed, unable to rise, dress and appear downstairs. Alice decided that, again, it was time to step in. What her daughter needed was a change of scene. She whisked Lilla back to Bedford.

Even surrounded by her own family and allowed at last to look after her baby, Lilla remained a shadow of her former self. Before the birth, even when she had been upset by Ernie's behaviour, she had continued to try to please him. Now she had lost the will to do even that – although Ernie's approval was precisely the tonic she needed.

Ernie was not a patient man at the best of times. He can have made no effort to conceal his irritation with what he saw as Lilla's unwillingness to pull herself together. He had decided that Lilla was a burden even before she was ill and now he must have felt that, compared to Barbie, Lilla's tears and exhaustion were a fuss over nothing, addressing her as if she were a foot soldier in his regiment – come along now, time to buck up – the bullying officer streak creeping in.

Ernie's words passed over Lilla in a blur. In a world of her own, all she would have heard was the tone of his voice: thud, thud, thud, like a deep bass marching drum. All she would have seen were his stiff shoulders, his jaw clenched as if his teeth were perpetually on the verge of grinding against each other, his eyes darting around the room and back again to the door. I can see her lying there, her face pallid, her eyes vacant and her cheeks tear-stained, sinking further and further into her mattress.

Alice called in the grandest doctor she could find in the hope that he could explain why Lilla was wasting away. But post-natal depression wasn't a diagnosis a doctor was likely to make back then. After examining her, he suggested that Lilla had 'possible tuberculosis', the early twentieth-century catch-all for doctors who didn't know what was wrong. 'Doctors,' wrote Lilla's sister-in-law Ada Henniker, 'seem to me to have tuberculosis on the brain.'

But at the mention of tuberculosis – which would make Lilla a long-term invalid and yet more expensive to live with – Ernie became even more determined to leave her behind.

Shortly after this, a wire came from India saying that Barbie had reached Calcutta safely – 'Barbie better.' And then, hot on its heels, the letters detailing what exactly had happened to her started to arrive from Shillong. They had been written by Ernie's sister Ada to Mama. But Mama had already left for India. Papa opened them, forwarding them to Bedford, and Ernie appointed himself the family scribe, copying each one out several times, making a diary of the events described in them, and forwarding both to the rest of the family.

Lilla must have felt that, when she looked at her husband, she only ever saw the back of his head. And the sheer horror of the letters he was copying would have made her feel guilty for wanting even a scrap of his attention. As Ernie's obsession with Barbie's condition grew, Lilla may have begun also to fear that the same might happen to her. Perhaps she even hoped it, thinking that if she fell as ill as Barbie then Ernie would pay her the attention he was now paying to his sister.

Until the first letter arrived, Ernie and his family knew only that Barbie had been desperately ill. They had some idea that she had had a post-natal infection, but it was only now that they learned the gruesome details. And even today the following is not for the squeamish. Having a baby in an Indian outpost a hundred years ago, let alone falling ill afterwards, was a risky business. Yet another reason for wanting to have as few children as possible.

Perhaps held back by a Victorian sense of prudery, Barbie's doctors in Shillong did not decide to make 'a thorough examination of her' until she was unlikely to survive another twenty-four hours. The extracts that follow are from copies, in Ernie's handwriting, of letters from Ada Henniker to her mother.

Shillong, 20 October

[The doctors] found two large cavities full of pus one on either side of the vaginal passage. They washed these out and inserted a tube to carry off the pus in 2 hours her temp had fallen from 104.8 to 100 . . . Had they not found the seat of the fever she could not have lived another 24 hours as with 8 days of temp at 104 and over she was nearly worn out of course. Every day the cavities were left more accumulation was going on and the temp would have gone on rising. It was an awful time. I shall never forget it and even after the cavities were found the pain she suffered having them cleaned out was too awful and yet as her only chance of recovery depended on it it was obliged to be done in spite of her heart-rending cries. What she has suffered I should think very few human beings have ever been through as any one with a less strong constitution would have died long before. Of course her recovery after this long period of perpetual fever is fearfully slow and has been somewhat delayed (even now the cavities are healed) by the most fearful irritation of the bladder, which is now being cured and then when she is sewn up she really will be over her troubles, but she has had the most awful time anyone ever had, I think. However she is so much better now that I feel quite a different being.

Ernie had to wait nearly two weeks for the next instalment. And, compared to what was to come, Barbie's first operation would look like a quick trip to the dentist.

Shillong, 31 October

My darling Mama,
    I must try and tell you of some of the awful things that have happened since my last letter.
    Barbie fever every day – but what the cause was no one could tell – they thought it was from the bladder trouble. On Wednesday morning about 7 am Wyndham [Barbie's husband] rushed round to me on his way to the doctors to ask me to go at once as Barbie had fainted. I went at once and found her with Major Hehir and the two nurses putting mustard plasters to her legs and heart, while she was in a complete state of collapse, icy cold, and covered with cold perspiration. We never thought she could pull through it was too awful. However she did – by the evening was wonderful. We had in the meantime wired to Capt Dykes, the Gauhati man, who came up at once and was there that evening so they had a great consultation with result that they said they must perform an operation as she must have an abscess inside her. It was an awful thought of course she was so weak and I had a horrible haunting feeling it was a mistake. But against 3 doctors, what could I do? I argued against the operation but they said it is certain to be an abscess and if we wait longer it will have bored deeper and perforate the bowels. Wyndham and I were nearly mad with fears, but in the face of 3 doctors we gave in and today they performed the operation. Oh! Mama, the horror of it. Poor little Bar lying there & not knowing what was in store for her and asking me why I looked so sad. It nearly broke my heart – but of course I could not tell her – oh but the agony and suspense mingled with doubts and fears were so awful, I should have gone mad if I had not been set to work to carbolize towels

*and mix antiseptic lotions and then when they began
to work how Wyndham and I sat holding our breath
for nearly 2 hours. Every time she stopped groaning
my heart stood still as I said to myself 'they've killed
her' – I can't describe the agony of it all, as her
groans tore one's heart nearly out. At last the doctors
came out and said they had found no abscess at all
but had found she had got local peritonitis. I felt
absolutely crushed to think of all she had gone
through to find only that – I have done nothing but
blame myself all day for not having followed my own
instinct and persuaded Wyndham not to allow it. But
as I said before – in the face of three doctors, how
could anyone? Now she is lying all bandaged up and
when not under Morphia, in the most heart-rending
pain – all for nothing, all for nothing.*

2 November
*Since writing this we have had one awful day and 2
more than awful nights. Last night was the worst as
she began being sick about 10 pm and the pain this
caused her was almost unendurable and [when] she
thought she was going to be sick she got into a cold
perspiration or terror and clutched me on one side
and the nurse on the other, while her eyes started
from her head. I've never seen anything so ghastly.
This feeling came over her about every hour and a
half and lasted perhaps 10–20 minutes at a time. We
gave her ice and brandy, but all no good and by the
morning she was worn out and had more Morphia
which she is now sleeping off.*

Shillong, 10 November

My darling Mama,
*My brain is in a whirl. On Saturday the doctors
had a consultation about Barbie and said that she*

*would never get well here and that taking her to
Calcutta was the only chance and that of course was
a tremendous risk. However Wyndham and I decided
to risk it as it is very evident they have not the
slightest idea what is the matter with her and they
will probably only muddle her worse than they have
done. Oh it is too dreadful to see the poor little wreck
they have made of it. It is cruel cruel. Think how
splendidly strong she was and now she is nothing but
a little skeleton and aching all over. She cannot
lie on either side and her back has two sores
on it and causes her agony and she can't sleep
because she is so uncomfortable. It is simply piteous
to see the poor little soul's suffering. Oh! Mama I
believe they have killed her. I can't believe she can
survive the journey to Calcutta but it is her only
chance.*

By now Major Hehir was suggesting that Barbie might
have 'tuberculosis of the bowels' and was persisting in
'pouring some awful solution of mercury down her
throat'. A move to Calcutta was indeed her only chance.

From the moment Barbie arrived in the city, things
began to improve. She was taken to the Eden Hospital,
where, said Ada, 'they had a nice, airy room waiting for
her'. The doctors there diagnosed an abscess but said
that, as she appeared to be recovering, they would not
operate. The abscess burst, and Barbie, shrunken to six
stone, began to recover.

For the first time in three months she was able to hold
her son, who had been looked after by a nurse in
Shillong.

Not surprisingly, he would be the only child Barbie
would have.

Bedford, England, late November 1902

As Barbie recovered in Calcutta, Ernie's mind drifted back to his own family. To Lilla, it must have seemed like a double miracle. Barbie had been all but dead and Ernie all but lost to her and their tiny son, but now both had been brought back. Not only was dear Barbie getting well, but for the first time in months she could see the front and not the back of Ernie's head. He was talking to her. And, even if he hadn't yet turned his attention to her in the same way that he had fixed it on Barbie, at least he was focusing on their child.

The first item on Ernie's agenda was his son's christening and, on the last Sunday in November, Arthur was christened in Bedford. He was given two middle names: Howard, after his godfather, a cousin of Ernie's called Howard Hill, and, strangely as it was not Lilla's real name, Eckford. I remember Arthur teaching me his names when he stayed with us one Christmas in our cottage in Wales. 'Arthur Howard Eckford Howell. My initials spell aheh! That's almost a word,' he said. Eckford, he told me then, was his grandfather's surname. And as I remember this scene – Arthur, Grandpa, his hair still reddish rather than grey, in a faded olive-green cardigan and shirt and tie, always a shirt and tie, standing in front of the theatrical dark-pink sofa in our drawing room and bending down to match my eight-year-old height, his hands gripping his legs just above the knee to keep his balance – it dawns on me that maybe Arthur never knew about Jennings. Or did he just choose to ignore him? As Lilla or Ernie – and at this time any decision was probably Ernie's – chose to do. Maybe Ernie was trying to rewrite the history that had turned his rich sweetheart into a not-so-rich wife. Trying to encourage Andrew Eckford to overlook the difference between his own children and his stepchildren. Anyhow, what seems important now, a century later, is that christening his son Eckford may just have made Ernie a little better disposed towards Lilla, if only because he hoped Arthur might one day inherit some money.

The christening was a success. 'It went off very well,' wrote Papa Howell to his youngest son, Evelyn, who was, as Papa had been, in the Indian Civil Service, and stationed in Peshawar, on the North West Frontier. This was, and still is, an area infamous for the guerrilla warfare waged by its local tribes, the Pathans, who make the most of the rugged mountain terrain to resist any form of outside control.

Lilla, who was 'going on well but still a sad invalid', must have begun to feel a glow of approval penetrate the thick cloud around her head. Two and a half months after having her baby, the torrent of hormonal change and exhaustion that had been raging through Lilla's body would have been ebbing, the world around her beginning to appear less distorted. And as she began to focus again, the picture that emerged must have shocked her into action. Ernie was cooing over his son's pram and writing to his sisters that 'Arthur is so pretty that people stop his pram in the street and admire his pretty colouring.' But in just a month's time, in January, his year-long sick leave would be up. Her husband was going back to India, and he was still insisting on leaving her behind.

If Ernie left without her, or without even agreeing that she should follow him shortly, their marriage would be as good as over. Lilla would be stuck with her family in England. When the Eckfords returned to China she would either have to stay alone with the Howells or face the public humiliation of returning to Chefoo having clearly been abandoned by her husband. Divorce was still completely socially unacceptable. So she wouldn't even be free to find someone else. She would spend the rest of her life as a single mother of one.

*   *   *

Then, just as Ernie was about to pack his bags, he failed his medical. He would now remain in England until March.

That gave Lilla two more months to turn the situation around.

Somewhere deep inside her, a fighting spirit stirred.

6
MELTING BITTER LEMONS

The Eckfords' house in Bedford, December 1902

DETERMINATION FLOODED BACK INTO LILLA. It thawed her stiff limbs, her frozen face and jaw, leaving her free to speak her mind. What she needed to do was cast some of that old Eckford magic over Ernie. She needed to cook for him, arrange a house for him, pamper him. Show him that she was worth taking to India whatever the cost. And that it wouldn't cost much. Slowly – still prone to great bouts of tiredness – but up, functioning, moving again, she set to work, gently guiding her mother's English cook through making a curry and cooking rice until it was just so. Making rich liver pâtés, folding in lashings of Grand Marnier and cream. Baking pastries with crusts crisped to not-quite-burnt, their biscuity and hot-jam smell seeping out under the kitchen door, and which dissolved into a featherweight crumbling crunch at first bite.

This was the first time, the very first time, since their marriage that Lilla had been able to look after Ernie in this way. She probably hoped, almost expected, that as soon as she waved her wand he would turn back towards her, his eyes glinting with desire again.

But Ernie didn't flicker. He noted perhaps that Lilla was about and dressed, her hair up, earrings on, a hint of make-up. He would have helped himself to the plates of pastries that appeared in the drawing room at teatime, sat down to Lilla's curries at dinner and bantered a little with Andrew Eckford about the progress of politics and the sporting events with which I guess, as neither of them was working at the time, they were filling their days. But, from all he said later, his shoulders remained raised, his expression sullen, emanating a general dissatisfaction with affairs as he muttered about his return to India and his irritation that it was delayed. And whenever Alice, his mother-in-law, drew close to him, he must have drawn in his breath. When she spoke to him, I can see him freezing, his fingers clenched in an arc over the wide arms of his chair.

When Lilla noticed this, she would have felt a rush of both relief and fear. Relief that Ernie's irritability was not her fault alone. Fear that some hidden agenda had set her husband against her mother and that it would ultimately drive him away. Alice was not the easiest of characters. She was voluble, extravagant and strong. Even 'overbearing' probably plays her down. But the intensity of Ernie's dislike of her mother sent a shiver down Lilla's spine. Somewhere, somehow, at some stage, something had clearly gone very wrong between them. And if Lilla couldn't work out what it was, then she had to take Ernie away. So when Edith and Dorothy Eckford went down with measles in Bedford and Papa Howell invited Ernie and Lilla to remove their baby from the infected house and move into Kensington Gardens Square with him, she leaped at the chance.

London, January 1903

Papa Howell welcomed his son Ernie and young family

with open arms. Since Mama had gone to look after Barbie in India, he must have been rattling about the house alone, and was now pleased to have company. 'Ernie, Lily and the infant are with me at 5 KGS and it is very nice to have them. The baby is splendid and never cries – at least I never hear him which comes to the same thing.'

For Lilla, returning to the Howells' house in London no longer heavy and pregnant, her every move no longer watched by Mama, must have felt like arriving in a new and different place. Now that she wasn't lugging a leaden belly from floor to floor, the six storeys of the house were not an interminable ladder to climb but a mountain to conquer. She must have swept up the stairs, her long skirt rustling over each step, shaking the dust off old photograph frames, pushing the curtains right back to let in an extra chink of light. By the time she had reached the top and opened the doors and windows of the empty bedrooms, flapping the dust sheets in the air like great flags, she would have felt as though she was breathing cool, clear fresh air again, not the choking London smog.

Then, just as she had longed to do all those months beforehand, she rewrote the shopping list. And rather than follow the usual practice of handing it over to the servants in the house, who would arrange to have the food delivered, Lilla surprised both Ernie and his father by setting off to the shops herself, in what Papa describes in a letter to Ada Henniker as 'quite the German Haus Frau fashion'. The German hausfrau – who took legendary pride in running her own home rather than delegating everything to the servants – having a style completely alien to the Howells' way of living.

Number 5, Kensington Gardens Square, stood only a few hundred yards from a glittering department store, Whiteley's, one of the first in Britain. William Whiteley, known as the Universal Provider, had made his name

Whiteley's of Bayswater, Westbourne Grove, c.1900.

famous all over the world for being able to provide everything from 'a pin to an elephant'. Or, more precisely,
anything from a pin to a new hairstyle to food to coal to
a new home – Whiteley's included an estate agency,
home removals and a domestic staff employment bureau
– to doctors on call.

Today the Whiteley's building towers over Queensway
– a vast domed affair that looks more than a little like a
cross between an office block and St Paul's Cathedral –
and has become a chain-store-packed shopping mall with
a multiplex cinema, a parade of themed restaurant concessions and a children's activity centre. I take my
children, Lilla's great-great-grandchildren, there to play.
A hundred years ago, however, Whiteley's stores stood a
block further north, where Whiteley had bought up a row
of neighbouring shops along the Queen's Road – as
Queensway was known back then – and round the corner
on Westbourne Grove. The stores themselves were just
the beginning of Whiteley's property empire. He had also
bought up entire streets in the neighbourhood in which
to house his thousands of staff, and he even ran his own
farms outside London, from where fresh produce was
brought in twice a day.

In 1903, department stores were relatively new, and
regarded as risqué by a society still in the shadow of a
repressive nineteenth-century morality that was as
prudish as the real, raucous and half-hidden night life
around it was not. The abundance of tempting silks and
lace in department stores was thought to lure young
women into sin. Female customers might be tempted to
shoplift. And the shopgirls, thought to be extremely
attractive and flirtatious, might be encouraged to earn
extra money by performing sexual favours for the gentlemen customers they served. In fact, these beliefs reveal
more about the behaviour and desires of the male-
dominated society that held them than about what

actually happened. If anything, department stores were a venue to which sexually desperate men could go in order to rub themselves up against women in the crowd.

Of all the London stores, Whiteley's in particular was a racy place to visit. Ladies were believed to use its reading room to write letters to their lovers. At one stage, white slavers were rumoured to hover in the powder rooms, waiting to grab young women. Moreover, the general suspicion of dangerous sexuality in the store was given some life by William Whiteley's well-known liaisons with his staff.

Lilla was clearly unperturbed by these rumours. For her the store would have held comparatively innocent attractions. One of these was its prices. These were so much lower than the local tradesmen's that one Guy Fawkes' Night the area's angry shopkeepers burnt an effigy of William Whiteley himself – and they were said to be the perpetrators of the recurrent fires that beset his premises. And Whiteley's gave Lilla the opportunity to inspect the food she was buying, instead of simply receiving whatever the butcher decided to deliver.

I imagine Lilla slipping into the store through one of its awning-shaded entrances on Westbourne Grove and entering an Aladdin's cave of tantalizing foods. She would have smelled the fruit, searching for just that level of sweetness that would tell her it was ripe – and avoiding the more sickly, fermenting odour of pieces that had been on the shelves too long. Prodded the fish, to see whether the flesh was still firm and good. And eyed the colour of the meat to work out just how long ago the blood had stopped pumping around its donor's veins.

And then, flaunting convention even further, Lilla didn't ask for the food to be delivered to her house later but, as Papa's letters reveal, took it back home with her straight away, as if to ensure that she had exactly the meat, fish, fruit and vegetables that she had paid for and not whatever was left to send on later. She must have had an errand boy trotting behind her, his arms full of oozing brown-paper packages tied up with string. Until the Second World War, there used to be a golden rule that a lady should never be seen in public without a hat and gloves or carrying her own parcels. Breaking this would only have turned Ernie further against her.

As Lilla's deep-red joints of meat were slapped down on to the kitchen table, the mood in the Howells' house must have changed. Instead of the bland, damp institutional smells that had risen from the basement, reminding Papa and Ernie of their years of boarding school and mess dining, rich, mouth-watering vapours started to waft up the stairs. I think Lilla determined to cook her way to Papa's and Ernie's hearts. She must have heated the oven up to the soaring heights she describes in her recipe book – the kitchen maid shovelling in more and more coal – until she reckoned it hot enough to sear the outside of the joint, sealing the juices within. Then opened the oven door again, the hot air blasting out and scalding her face as she slid a cooling bowl of water in to bring the temperature down so that the meat would simmer gently. And when she thought a roast might bore the men, she would have had beef and ham, chicken and lamb, chopped and mixed and moulded into rolls and loaves and pies . . . praying that even the most fixed of husbands would find them hard to resist.

Papa was the first to fall under Lilla's spell. Usually fanatically abstemious as he feared developing his father's gout, he was hypnotized by the richness of the household's new food, no doubt piling so much into his long, lean frame that after dinner he had to sit quite still for a while, his head spinning. After a day or two, merely the smell of Lilla's cooking made him dizzy with

anticipation. But Lilla's real route to her father-in-law's
heart was via his purse strings.

Papa was obsessed with expense and the avoidance of
it. 'Each of you boys has cost me £2000/- at least [over
£100,000 today],' he would complain to his sons. One of
the reasons he whiled away his days in the Athenaeum
may well have been that he could lunch there for
sixpence – the equivalent of £1.35 now. A couple of
months earlier, Papa had commended Ernie's decision to
leave Lilla and his child behind and live alone in India
as a good financial move: 'Ernie will escape the heavy
expenses of the double establishment, so he really has
done very well for himself in the way of escaping the
usual consequences of a not quite prudent marriage.'
However, now that Lilla's careful shopping expeditions
had cut his household bills dramatically, the same 'not
quite prudent' daughter-in-law had suddenly become a
star. He invited Ernie and Lilla to stay on in the house for
as long as they liked. And, as he set off on his annual
winter ice-skating trip to St Moritz, like a true convert,
Papa began to preach his new gospel to anyone who
might listen.

'The house is in excellent hands,' he wrote to Evelyn,
'and I can now go away with an easy mind.' To his
daughter Ada, back in Shillong, he wrote that 'Dear Lily
... proved herself a quite first class purveyor.' Even
Mama, to what must have been her great surprise, found
herself on the receiving end of her husband's eulogies:
'[Ernie and Lily] get on perfectly with the servants so you
can be quite easy about the house.'

Mama was not as convinced as her husband of her
daughter-in-law's domestic prowess. 'I do hope Lily and
the baby did not bring up measles to London with them,'
she wrote back upon hearing the news. Happily for Lilla,
as Mama was in India her protests were stuck in the
interminable post.

But Ada – who back in the summer, when Ernie's elder brother Auberon Howell had become engaged to a wise and worthy-sounding woman known as 'Bob' Ramsden, had been quick to comment, 'I bet she's a great contrast to poor little Lily' – had now started to write of her quite fondly: 'It is dreadful to think how Barbie and Lily have suffered . . .' Seeing Barbie so ill seems to have softened Ada towards her young sister-in-law.

Barbie, however, needed no converting to Lilla's merits. She simply absorbed Papa's new approval of her sister-in-law and passed it on. She wrote to Laura in Cambridge, reporting Ernie's joyous descriptions of Arthur in his pram as if they showed a glimmer of hope that their brother's marriage might finally have taken a turn for the better.

Back in England, a few days after Papa's departure for St Moritz, Ernie began to soften too. After fifteen grating months of mock-marriage in lodgings and staying with in-laws, it seems to have taken Lilla just a few days of looking after him to begin to win him back. A few days of showing him that she could run a house, pamper her husband and produce meal after intoxicating meal without spending a fortune. A few days of no mothers-in-law to irritate either of them. No family to show them up. A house more or less to themselves at night. Now, almost four months after giving birth, Lilla's body would have begun to feel caressable again. And by now she had learned – or worked out for herself – what she should do.

Shortly after Papa's departure, in a great rush of new-found enthusiasm for his wife, Ernie agreed that Lilla should join him in India that autumn after the country's blistering summer heat had subsided.

When Ernie at last gave in, after almost a year of threatening to leave her behind, Lilla felt the tension flood from her body. I can see her sinking into a chair, wanting to exhale great sobs of relief. And remembering to choke them back – lest Ernie change his mind.

For the problem with Ernie's great passions was that, once they had subsided, change his mind was often what he did.

I wish Lilla had stopped him from charging back to Bedford. But she didn't. As soon as Ernie had decided that Lilla should join him in India, perhaps still riding the crest of a wave of born-again love, he wanted to head back to Bedford. His ebullience must have made him feel that nothing could touch him now. That living again with his mother-in-law would no longer make him feel like 'a bear with a sore head'. That he no longer needed to incur the small expense of paying for his family's food in London, when he could live with the Eckfords in Bedford for no cost at all.

And on 18 January 1903, Ernie and Lilla arrived back at Alice Eckford's house in Bedford.

And everything that had just started to go so right began to go so wrong.

Of course it was a mistake to go back there. Within days, the old animosity between Ernie and Alice Eckford had reared its head. And probably caught by the trough that always follows a wave, Ernie once again, as Laura put it, found Alice 'a pest' and 'could not endure living with her'. He immediately reverted to his earlier intention of leaving Lilla in England and using his three months' leave every three years to come home, spending just one month with her. 'I should kick against that arrangement if I were Lily,' wrote Laura to her and Ernie's younger brother, Evelyn, as she took her sister-in-law's side, too.

Lilla, now, would certainly have tried to kick. Tried everything she could to change his mind, to drag him away from her mother's house. One of Ernie's letters mentions a plan for him, Lilla and their baby to spend a month playing golf in St Andrews – freezing and damp in February but the other end of Britain from Alice. They didn't go. Ernie must have decided it was too expensive. He was not to be moved either from his money-saving plan to leave Lilla in England or from a house in which he could live for free during his last weeks in the country. Instead he grated around the house in Bedford, his unexplained resentment of Alice growing more open by the day. Inch by inch, the gap between her and her husband that Lilla had managed to snap shut so briefly, cracked its way open again. Lilla felt the strength she had found in London being ground away by the friction between her husband and her mother. I imagine her lying on her bed in the daytime. Hugging her knees to her chest. Curled up in a ball. And then some news began to filter back from India that must have made the blood in her veins run cold.

Mama Howell had been staying in Calcutta as Barbie slowly recovered in hospital. The Howell clan in India had descended upon her for Christmas. Ada Henniker was still with her and Barbie in Calcutta and their husbands had come down from Shillong. Ernie's elder brother, Auberon, and his wife Bob had come down from Kohima, another hill station, where he had been drafted into the civil administration from the Indian Army. Even Evelyn, the youngest Howell sibling, had travelled right across India from Peshawar. For most of them, it was the first time that they had seen each other, and their mother, in two or three years. But, as soon as Christmas was over, they had all dispersed back to their posts. And, alone in Calcutta – apart from Barbie, who was still in hospital – Mama had begun to make some social calls.

One of her first stops was with Toby Elderton and Lilla's twin sister Ada. After an extended stay in Chefoo,

the Eldertons had at last come to India. A day or two after
Christmas, they arrived in Calcutta. Toby had been
Ernie's best man, and politeness decreed that Mama
should see Lilla's sister. She met them for lunch.

It was a roaring success. 'They are a very jolly couple,'
wrote Mama. And Ada, despite looking 'exactly like
Lily', to the extent that Barbie's Indian ayah from
Shillong thought she was Lilla 'turned up again
with a new husband', quickly met her approval: 'she is
very pretty and well dressed'. Mama arranged to meet
them for dinner the following night.

And so it went on. Shortly, it seemed as if Mama's
enthusiasm for Lilla's twin and her husband knew no
bounds. Unlike Ernie, Toby faced few money worries in
Calcutta. For a start, as a naval captain, he held a far
higher rank than Ernie's army captaincy and therefore
received a better salary. He also had enough money of his
own not to have to blink at what he and Ada spent. So,
after staying in a 'grand hotel' and paying an extravagant
'18 rupees a day for one bedroom' – as Mama gushed in
her letters home – he and Ada rented a large house in a
fashionable suburb of Calcutta. She sketched a floor plan
of the magnificent 'The Grange, Alepore', and enclosed
it. Within a couple of weeks it was decided that Barbie
would move in with the Eldertons before going back to
England with Mama. And the week after that – just about
the time when Ernie and Lilla had returned to Bedford
and Ernie had reverted to his plan of going to India alone
– Mama's letters began to reach England.

The news of Ada's new-found popularity with the
Howells hit Lilla like a punch in the stomach, knocking
the last remnants of breath out of her. Ada, whom she
hadn't seen since her wedding day. Ada, without whom
her life had turned upside down. Ada seemed to be the
daughter-in-law that Ernie's family wanted. Not her.

The news continued to flow. There were dinners with the Eldertons, picnics with the Eldertons, hotel recommendations given by the Eldertons. Each new titbit that Ernie read out must have cut into Lilla more deeply. And then came the final blow: Mama arranged that, when Ernie returned to India, he would move into the Eldertons' house in Calcutta. 'Truly it is a comfort,' ended Mama, 'to think Ernie has got a decent home at last, poor child.'

It was a terrifyingly perfect solution. Ernie could both save money and be looked after if he lived with Toby and Ada. It made it senseless for Lilla to go to Calcutta too. But for Lilla, even worse than the prospect of a life alone was the prospect of a life alone while Ada had Ernie. Ada, who was identical to her in every way but . . . but what? But for whom things appeared to go so right. But whose every success seemed to mark another of Lilla's failures. But who always had something – something indefinable, something hard to put your finger on – that Lilla didn't. And who now, even though Lilla was doing all she could to keep him herself, was going to have her husband as well.

Lilla still loved Ernie very much. To love somebody who has said and done so many awful things to you sounds silly, certainly weak. But Lilla was very young, not even twenty-one. And the whole course of her life depended on winning him back before he left for India.

He was due to set sail in mid-March, just one month away.

She had either to work out what annoyed him so much about her mother and resolve it if she could, or persuade him to leave the Bedford house so that she could again weave the magic that had worked so well before.

He insisted they couldn't afford to do that.

But by now, all his brothers and sisters were on Lilla's side.

'When I think how fortunate Ada & Barbie & I have been in our marriages,' Laura wrote to Ernie's younger brother, Evelyn, 'I can't help feeling most awfully sorry for poor Lily. I'm afraid there's no denying the fact that Ernie is selfish, very much so, & that the trials of matrimony have caused a rapid evaporation of his affection . . . I am afraid that Lily stands a poor chance of much happiness in her married life, poor child – she is only 20!' And at this point, cool, calm, scientific Laura decided to intervene and talk to Ernie: 'I hope I shall not do more harm than good.'

'Rub it into Ernie well,' replied Evelyn. 'I have not much right to talk but the words "for richer, for poorer, for better & for worse, in sickness and in health" are not mere rhetoric but are a standard one should try & live up to however difficult it may be.'

Desperate to escape the house during the day, Ernie had started to bicycle over to see Laura in Cambridge, taking the train back to Bedford in the evening. Laura tried to talk him round but 'like most attempts of that kind it was a failure'. What she did manage, however, was to discover why Ernie had taken against Alice Eckford so strongly.

Ernie told Laura that he was convinced that Alice Eckford had 'caught' him out in China, ensnaring him into a mistaken marriage with Lilla. 'I am thankful,' wrote Laura, 'that Mama did no "catching" for any of us.' Back then, 'catching' was rife. One of the by-products of empire was a social ritual known as 'the Fishing Fleet'. British women who had failed to find a husband 'at home' went on a tour of India. Out there, the shortage of unmarried women and abundance of unmarried men was thought to raise their stakes in the mating game. The 'fish' were torn between the attractions of the Fleet and their awareness that the systemic imbalance between the sexes made them liable to be 'caught'.

Being 'caught' was feared like venereal disease. It was a risk inherent in expatriate bachelordom, and to be avoided at all costs. The pervading view was that the best wives were to be found in Europe. The women who had to travel east to find a husband were regarded as second best.

The Fleet's nets were tightly spun. In the early twentieth century, dating was unheard of. A British man in India who wanted an alternative to the institutional brothels had to find a married woman to have an affair with, or else marry himself. To a man who had not seen an available European female face for a couple of years, the Fleet were tempting bait. Rushed to the altar by, shall we say, considerations other than lifelong companionship, many a foolish man, it was whispered, awoke on his honeymoon to realize that he had made a mistake. Looking for somebody to blame for his error, he accused his wife, or her accompanying mother, of entrapping him.

Ernie felt that he was one of these men. Within days of talking to Laura, he wrote a letter to Evelyn. Evelyn's self-confessed 'not much right to talk' was the result of having broken off his own engagement in India. Luckily his ex-fiancée had decided not to sue him for breach of promise as she could have done – possibly winning damages of several hundred pounds (worth tens of thousands of pounds today). Ernie wrote:

> Well, I must congratulate you on what I cannot help describing as a most fortunate escape. You are indeed well out of that business . . . Matrimony is not all that it is painted. Mothers in law are pests and no peace and no pocket money is the usual cry of the Benedict.

It is very easy to get into but, like the lobster pots, a rare game to get out of. Matrimony under the most favourable circumstances, as pictured in the marriage service, is no doubt a most excellent institution, but alas such ideals are rarely met with nowadays. So as regards your future, take my tip and thank Heaven you have option of taking it. Don't marry for money but only where money is, as the waters of matrimony do not flow smoothly unless there are banks on both sides. The genus spinster in the east is a deception 'don't you 'ave none of 'em.' Go to Cairo or St Moritz at the right time of year and make the best of your chances. Girls swarm in England and you can have a selection from a vast crowd. If you want to marry and don't marry well at home, well you have only got yourself to blame. Once bitten twice shy and so I feel quite confident as to your future. There is no snare so dangerous as the matchmaking Mama with daughters to dispose of, accompanied by a host of blessings and a box of old clothes.

Shortly afterwards Ernie followed this up with:

Take Bacon's advice, I wish I had done so, and limit your expenditure to half your receipts and you will soon save enough to enable you to go home & take your place in the best society and with any sort of fortune you ought to land a nice fish with golden scales to keep you company for life. I married for love solely, which you very nearly did, and I was not wise in my generation – in fact I was a fool. There is no such fatal disease as the insane desire to support someone else's daughter.

Ernie's letters are appalling. His would-be gold-digging is certainly as calculating as the baiting of the Fishing Fleet.

Even if Alice Eckford did, as is probable, let Ernie assume that Lilla was richer than she was to encourage him to propose, what he wrote still makes him immensely dislikeable. However different the world was then, thinking and writing that you shouldn't have married someone you loved just because they didn't have enough money, that you should only marry 'a nice fish with golden scales', is horrid.

Especially when that is what he thought about dear, sweet, elegant Great-granny. Thinking about how desperate she must have felt back then still makes me want to cry. She was desperate for Ernie. But all Ernie was, was this.

On the last day of February, Lilla finally persuaded Ernie away from Bedford to stay with Laura. From there they went on to London, where they joined Papa, who had returned from St Moritz – and was therefore buying the food – to await Mama's arrival from India. Ernie was going to sail for India in a fortnight, just after Mama was due to return from Calcutta. And Lilla's in-laws might now have been on her side, but it was up to Lilla herself to turn her husband's plans around.

The manipulation of emotions is not a rational, button-pressing affair where single causes can be identified and held to account. Instead moods and opinions sway with circumstances, with a little bit of thinking this, and a little bit of seeing that. Now that Lilla had taken Ernie away from her mother – whose every word made Ernie think that he should never have married Lilla in the first place – she had to convince him that having her with him in India would make his life wonderful and wouldn't cost him a bean.

Maybe she impressed the finality of parting upon him. Maybe she opened his eyes to the fact that he would miss seeing his son grow up, and would be unlikely to have any more children. Maybe, in those last two weeks in London, Lilla simply recast her spell, drowning Ernie's resistance in rich gravies, thick spicy sauces and ladles and ladles of cream, luring him back to her side. I wonder when she worked out that her sensuous cooking for her husband was a way of making love? As would become clear, she certainly worked some other, more private tricks upon him, appealing to the instinct that rushed him to the altar and made him a father within a year of the wedding.

A fortnight later, Mama returned to find Ernie impervious to suggestions that he should live in India alone. At the last minute, he delayed his departure by almost a week. He took Lilla back to Bedford. On 18 March they had 'a tearful parting', at which even Ernie seems to have shed a few watery drops. He 'was very cut up at parting from Lily and the little son', wrote Barbie, who had just returned to England with Mama. It was agreed once again that Lilla and baby Arthur should follow Ernie in October, after 'the hot weather'. The Howells, whose sympathy for Lilla – Mama perhaps excepted – was now as fervent as their antipathy had been just a couple of months beforehand, were thrilled. Ernie, wrote Papa, 'went away in capital spirits'. From Port Said, Ernie even wrote to his mother asking her to look after Lilla while he was away: 'dear little soul, I am sure that she feels parting with me dreadfully'.

Lilla had caught Ernie's coat tails as he disappeared through the door, and pulled him back into a full embrace. She and Ernie would spend just six months apart, and then they would be together. For a few short days Lilla, although missing Ernie dreadfully – she 'does not yet realize,' wrote Papa, 'that such partings are almost a condition of Indian life' – must have felt that she was on top of events. And then, almost as soon as she appeared to have made everything all right, her world again turned on its head.

At times it seems that whatever Lilla did, however hard she tried, something would always trip her up before the finishing post. This time, it was the very act of winning her husband back that had caused her downfall.

A few days after Ernie's departure, Lilla was already feeling unwell – or, as Barbie put it, 'very seedy'. At first the Eckfords and Howells simply assumed that she was finding it hard to cope with Ernie's leaving. But within a couple of weeks Lilla had worked out what the matter was. She was pregnant.

The baby was due late November or early December. There was no way that Lilla would be travelling to India in October that year – or even before the temperature began to rise the following spring. That meant she would have to wait until India's cool weather the following year. Now, in spite of everything that she had done, Lilla still might not see Ernie for another year and a half. A year and a half must have seemed an impossibly long time to her then – would he, could he, still love her after all that time? And even more painful for Lilla was the fact that, for all that time, Ada would have him instead. It was as though Lilla was a child again, fighting to keep up with Ada, who was offered everything first. Ada, whom the Howells seemed to prefer. Whom Ernie might learn to prefer, too.

Lilla realized that if she wanted to hold on to the fragments of her life that she had just sewn back together, she had to go to India sooner than the autumn of the following year. And by now she had learned the hard way that the only person who could give her the life she wanted was herself.

She determined to take matters into her own hands.

7

IN THE LAP OF THE GODS

Bedford, summer 1903

SOMETIMES WE DO THINGS that we know are wrong. When it appears that every other avenue is closed to us. And when the consequences of doing nothing, of letting fate push us along the seemingly downhill path she has mapped out, look worse than any possible retribution for the transgression itself.

Back then, with Ernie heading towards her twin's clutches, with the prospect of not seeing him for such a long time that he might have forgotten that he loved her, again facing the possibility of becoming an abandoned wife stranded in grey England, the consequences of doing nothing were intolerable for Lilla.

She did try to persuade everyone to let her follow Ernie out to Calcutta as the weather was cooling in September and have the baby there. Ernie's family thought she was mad. She had been very ill with her last child and they didn't believe that she was fully recovered. 'I do not think she should travel until she is quite fit again,' wrote Laura. Even Alice, who usually batted so hard on her daughter's side, who was firmly of the belief that a wife should always be with her husband, thought Lilla was not well enough to go.

And then the tide turned just a little in Lilla's favour. Perhaps as a result of his well-connected father pulling some strings for his son, Ernie's posting was moved from Calcutta to Kashmir, India's mesmerizingly scenic mountain kingdom in the foothills of the Himalayas, and both a holiday destination for British expatriates and home to some of the best hunting, shooting and fishing in the British Empire. He was delighted. 'A prime billet for a man of my rank,' he wrote to Evelyn, in anticipation of the hours of recreation that lay ahead. 'I cannot tell you how pleased I am & so will poor little Lily be when she hears the news.' She must have been. Kashmir was a long way from the charms of her twin in Calcutta. And there was a fighting chance that she might be allowed out to India a little sooner.

The climate in mountainous Kashmir was the reverse of that in the rest of India. Whereas by April Calcutta had grown unbearably hot – a breeding ground for disease and entirely unsuitable for a young baby – in Kashmir a cool, gentle spring was just beginning. So, although there was no question of Lilla going out to meet Ernie in Calcutta the following March when her new baby would be only a few months old, there could be no objection to her going out to Kashmir then.

But March was still the best part of a year away. To the twenty-year-old Lilla, it seemed like an eternity. She may have professed to Barbie to be 'quite consoled' to 'having another infant' but it was far from the truth. In order to keep busy, she immersed herself in the practicalities of Ernie's move, trying to look after him from afar and writing to him 'all my spare time'. She suggested that he looked for a house outside Kashmir's notoriously flood-prone capital: 'It would be most unwise to live in

Srinagar this winter as the house could not possibly be dry.' She asked him to buy 'only camp furniture' until she arrived and could take charge of their new home, their first proper home. 'I am sure I will be able to make the house quite nice and pretty, without any expense.' Ernie's enthusiastic replies urging her not to 'be discouraged, sweetheart', by their prolonged separation made Lilla feel closer to him than she had ever been. 'Oh if I had my Ernie,' she wrote, 'how happy I should be.' She longed to feel him hug her again as he had done in those last few days in England, or even just touch her. But whenever his letters launched into a lengthy description of his new life in his new home, or his job organizing the visits of Lords Curzon and Kitchener, India's viceroy and commander-in-chief, to Kashmir that year, she felt him slipping out of reach.

For a while, Lilla persevered. But as she packed his 'winter garments' to send out to Kashmir – 'he did not take any thick things with him, thinking he was to remain in Calcutta' – I think something in her began to crack. Perhaps folding his heavy tweed coats while the July sunshine beat in through the windows made the distance between them seem irrecoverably large and she could hardly bear to close the trunk lid. As Ernie's possessions disappeared from her sight behind a row of heavy brass locks, it was as though she was packing their relationship away. Kashmir, the label on the trunk read. The other side of the world.

I can see Lilla standing there, the fuzzy sunshine coming through the window on to the back of her neck, looking at Ernie's locked trunk, her spirits sinking. The old sadness creeping up on her again. A dark shadow beginning to cloud her field of vision, shutting out the light.

It may have been an old wives' tale that she had picked up, or just parlour gossip. I don't think she cared. The thought of it made her feel quite sick. It was a horrible, horrible solution. But right then it seemed to be her only hope.

Lilla feigned tiredness and excused herself from the day's visiting planned by her mother. Then went up to her room as if to take a nap and waited for the house to empty. When the last squeak on the stair had died away, she stood up on her bed and, as she told her grand-daughter years later, began to jump. Up and down, bending her knees and heaving her five-months-pregnant frame into the air. Raising her arms and trying to reach for the ceiling. Bouncing on the springs as they creaked and caved and sprang back. The head of the bed rattling against the wall. The bedposts grinding against the floor. She jumped and bounced and bent and reached until she could heave no more. Then collapsed on to the bed in a ball of exhaustion, and wept.

Shortly afterwards, she miscarried the child.

India, autumn 1903

Lilla sailed from Liverpool for India at the end of September with the now year-old Arthur and a nanny, Mrs Desmond. Her boat trip back to England with Ernie had been miserable. But this time she was bubbling with excitement, professing to Ernie 'in raptures', as he later wrote, to find the ship comfortable, the service attentive and even the food good. Not only was she going to see Ernie, she was also going to see Ada, who, with Toby, had been transferred to Bombay, on the west coast of India. The very port that Lilla was heading for.

Like Calcutta, Bombay was a grand imperial city. Perhaps even grander than Calcutta, for, as Jan Morris wrote in her great guide to the British Empire, the *Pax Britannica* trilogy, Bombay was home to 'probably the most daunting group of buildings in the Empire'. I have

in front of me a postcard, one of the three I know of
written by Lilla's own family. It was sent by Ada from
Bombay. Dense corridor-infested buildings that seem to
shout administration from every Victorian Gothic arch
and medieval portal squat in a row as far as the eye can
see. In front of them is what, on the postcard, looks like
a racetrack but which must be Morris's 'brownish turf'
and 'riding-track called Rotten Row' – after the track in
London's Hyde Park. Beyond this lay the beaches.
Perhaps the location of these grand buildings had been
chosen so that the British and Indians burrowing through
mounds of paper in Bombay's infinite offices could
glance up and see the waves ruled by Britannia stretch-
ing out before them back towards London.

Behind this gleaming show of imperialism was hidden
the chaos of the Indian city. Rickshaws, feathered
squawkings and a rich variety of stenches spread into the
distance. This contrary combination of all-British
grandeur and impoverished street life must have
reminded Lilla of Calcutta. But her time there was now
far away. It was almost two years since she had left that
city and now she was going to meet an Ernie who loved
her. And, for the first time, they would have a proper
home of their own.

It was also two long years since Lilla had last seen Ada.
Ada, who had always been a step ahead of her. Ada had
grown yet further in stature, almost rising to meet the
imperial edifices that the two of them would have trotted
past in tongas (the horse-drawn two-wheeled carriages
used as taxis in India). Toby was an important man in
Bombay, and Ada, even though she was only twenty-one
years old, had become a grand lady. Lilla must have felt
almost childish, girlish, in comparison. Ada and Toby's
comfortable house and servants must have made a stark
contrast to her old lodgings in Calcutta. And as much as
she talked about the importance of Ernie's new position,

it was clear that she and Ernie were on a very different path in life to Ada and Toby.

Even so, I don't think Lilla envied Ada one bit. Despite Ada's trappings of success, in reality her life had been far from perfect. Over the past two years, Lilla might have been almost abandoned by her husband, but she had succeeded in winning him back and putting her life back on track. Ada, on the other hand, had given birth to a daughter, adored her on sight – and then had to watch her tiny child die from a series of inexplicable fits.

Bouncing her own bonny baby on her knee, Lilla must have felt for the first time that life was being less fair to Ada than it was to her. Perhaps, also for the first time, she was emotionally the stronger of the two. Managing to pull her marriage back from the edge of the abyss had given her a new confidence. If she could do that, then she could do anything. But Ada had found her own experiences so painful that she said she could not face having another child.

What Lilla couldn't have told Ada then was what she had had to do in order to come out to India so soon after Ernie. And if she didn't tell Ada, she didn't tell anyone else. For the next eighty years she must have kept the secret buried deep inside her. Hidden under her ebullient exterior it must have gnawed away, a constant reminder that she had done something terribly, terribly wrong – something for which she might one day have to pay. And during the dark times to come, I fear she would feel that she was paying again and again.

In mid-November, before the snow cut off Kashmir from the rest of the world, Lilla headed north into the Himalayan winter. She and Ada would not be living in the same city but at least they would be in the same country – barely a week's travel and post apart. Lilla left the vast arches of muggy Bombay's gargoyle-and-stained-glass-ridden Victoria Terminal on the gleaming and sleek Punjab Mail train, which steamed up through the hot, dry plain to the large cantonment at Pindi, or Rawalpindi, the General HQ for the Indian Army in the north of the country. Here Lilla, nurse and child clambered off on to a dusty station platform.

Ernie was waiting for them. He and Lilla hadn't seen each other for eight months. Eight months of tear-filled letters and frantic, parsimoniously brief cables. They must have held each other on the station platform, Ernie's strong arms encircling Lilla's frame as she leaned against him, the polished brass buttons on his uniform imprinting themselves into her cheek. Lilla didn't burst into overemotional tears – Ernie described her as 'plucky' – but held her ground as if to say, right, I'm ready to go, we still have a long way to travel. Ernie may have given her a couple of moustachy slightly-longer-than-pecks on the cheek but a great long smooch on a public platform was not the done thing. In any case, it is always strange to meet a lover after a long time apart. Are they the same person that you said goodbye to? And if you can't spot any obvious differences, you wonder what alterations lie invisibly stitched beneath the surface. It can take a bit of time for the awkwardness to dissolve into easy repartee. And then Ernie and Lilla would have been wondering how things would turn out for them in this new place they were heading to. Everything had been fine – although only just – when he had left her back in London. But Kashmir? Would it still be fine? Or would their marriage start to crumble again?

For the following year of Lilla and Ernie's life, an unprecedented number of their letters were regarded as good enough to make it into his siblings' collection. This had not always been the case. 'Ernie, you must admit, does not rise to a very high standard,' his sister Laura had written the March beforehand, when she was trying to talk him out of leaving Lilla behind. But the details of his life in Kashmir were deemed interesting enough to include. And up until this point only two of Lilla's letters had been kept. Now, however, as Barbie told her, 'your letter of the 25th was a welcome surprise. It was a quite delightful letter & the family will not let you off, when they find out how you can write when you choose!' And from then until the following autumn, when the collection in Laura's long ballot box comes to an end, several of Lilla's and Ernie's scribbles are included, giving an extraordinarily detailed account of their life. And, for almost the first time, giving Lilla a voice.

Lilla and Ernie spent their first two days in the Pindi cantonment, staying with a Colonel Hawkins and his wife. Lilla charmed their hosts, and Ernie felt himself beginning to relax. 'She is a good little soul,' he wrote to Papa, and – fulfilling all the Howell criteria – 'so economical'. Then, taking a phaeton, they set off on the long journey up into the hills. The idea was to travel quickly during the day but stop every night. Ernie, a logistics officer to the core, had planned every detail of the trip, booking them into lodgings at each stage along the way.

The first day on the road went smoothly. But on the second afternoon, Ernie wrote, his careful arrangements began to disintegrate when one of their two horses died. With just one horse to pull them along, their pace was painfully slow. By the time they arrived at that night's lodgings, their rooms had been taken – by one of Ernie's senior officers. Lilla must have sensed that, frustrated by his inability to turn the situation around, Ernie's short fuse was priming itself to blow. Abandoning their beleaguered phaeton and the exhausted single horse, she darted back into the street and flagged down a tonga. She piled in Ernie, nurse and child and ordered it back along the road that they had just driven down. Three miles back they found a government rest-house – one of a chain of bungalows every ten to fifteen miles – with free rooms. The next morning, Ernie set about getting another horse sent down from Pindi. He was grumbling at the prospect of a three-day wait – a day and a half for the messenger to reach Pindi and another day and a half for the horse to arrive – stuck in the middle of nowhere, when Lilla started to produce 'food of all sorts out of a surprisingly small basket'. I imagine her, Mary Poppins-like, magicking up meal after meal of cold meats and cheeses, laced with quince and redcurrant jelly, out of a bottomless picnic basket. It was more than enough to last them three days. A sated Ernie settled down and began to enjoy the wait: 'we were perfectly happy and most comfortable'.

Two days further up the road, Ernie had to leave Lilla. He had found a wire waiting for him and within half an hour was on the back of the overnight mail-cart to Srinagar, where he froze for 'twelve long hours' before spending a day resolving whatever logistical problems had called for his attention. At 9.30 in the evening, he set off with some trepidation for Baramullah, a day's journey on from where he had left Lilla. He had arranged to meet her on a houseboat he kept there.

The Maharajah of Kashmir, fearing, as Jan Morris puts it, 'an influx of retired British officials into his arcadian State', had banned Europeans from owning land there. The British, however, had simply resorted to building houseboats that could take advantage of Kashmir's abundant waterways and lakes, and be moved wherever extra accommodation was needed. Kashmiri houseboats were peculiar craft. They looked, says Morris, like 'little Thames-side chalets mounted on hulls, with dormer windows and shingle roofs' – as if Bray or Marlow were

Lilla and Ernie's cottage in Bandipur, Kashmir, 1904.

transplanted from the banks of the Thames to the middle of a lake in the Himalayas.

It was two in the morning by the time Ernie arrived at the houseboat, and he crept aboard the silent vessel, 'fearing it empty'. To his surprise, he found Lilla, Mrs Desmond, the nanny, and Arthur 'comfortably asleep and quite snug'. They all spent two more days on board while Ernie finished some administrative work at Baramullah. Finally, they set off for the home he had prepared for his family twenty miles up the Kashmir valley from Srinagar, in an area called Bandipur, known to the British for its excellent trout fishing.

Ernie's house in Bandipur was far from grand. It was essentially a summer fishing hut and not an obvious place to spend the winter. Still, it was far better than his flooded lodgings in Srinagar. The descriptions of visitors and even Ernie and Lilla themselves range from 'hut' and 'match-box' to 'rat-palace' and even 'queer little hutch beside a raging torrent'. Photographs show a ramshackle single-storey cottage, its walls a jigsaw of whitewash, redwash and unpainted board, its roofs a medley of carved wood and slate, punctured by square brick chimneys that look as though they have been designed to weather far greater storms than the house could ever withstand. On the other side of the whitewater river that charges along the edge of its lawns, a similarly sized shack teeters on the shore in ruins, a stern reminder of what the vagaries of the Kashmiri weather can do to a home.

Kashmir is an imposingly beautiful and heartlessly cruel country. Its Himalayan summits rise up through the landscape like Olympian gods looking to the sky. In between their ridges and peaks the ground falls away precipitously, its cliffs eventually softening into rocky tundra that in turn flattens out into grassy slopes, tree-filled pastures and round-bottomed glacial valleys. Down here, meadows amble beside a water-garden of rivers, streams and lakes. Dotted alongside, Kashmiri shacks, cottages and houseboats sit as if in the lap of the gods. In the summer, these pastures fill with flowers, larger, brighter and more abundant than seems possible in real life. But, when winter comes, the temperature falls far below freezing and snow buckets out of the sky, its blizzards wrapping themselves around each building, each tree, like a great winter coat, and in the lap of the gods is exactly where the Kashmiris are.

Lilla brushed aside Ernie's concerns about the house, declaring it 'quite snug and cosy' in her letters. When they arrived there in late November, it probably was. The vast mountain walls that surrounded the valley were already iced white, but the heavy snow wouldn't spread across the low ground until January. However, when the winter proper came, it would be tough. In summer Bandipur may have been a welcome retreat from Srinagar but, apart from the local Kashmiri village, in winter Lilla and Ernie risked being cut off from the outside world. Lilla, however, viewed this impending onslaught of the elements as a challenge. Making a home against the odds was exactly what she knew how to do, longed to do. And in so doing, she must have thought, she could win Ernie round irrevocably.

She had a month before the snow arrived.

The house at Bandipur had just four rooms, and Lilla, Ernie, Arthur and Mrs Desmond were likely to be confined to this space for the best part of the winter months. The snow would be too deep, the temperature too low, to wander outside much. In any case, there wasn't anyone to go and visit. Lilla's first priority was to create a civilized living area for Ernie and herself. 'I have made the front room my drawing-room,' she wrote to her sister-in-law Ada Henniker, so thrilled to have a home of her own at last that she gave her every detail of the house — 'at last I am able to write and tell you how comfy we are in our little hut'. Next door was a room leading on to an L-shaped veranda, which she made their bedroom. On the far side of the house she put Arthur and Mrs Desmond in a bedroom and nursery, 'the latter is *so* nice, that I am sure many a nurse and child at home would envy'. It was hardly a separate wing, but it would at least give her and Ernie some space of their own. In order to keep out some of the cold, she had the veranda outside Arthur's bedroom boarded up: 'it makes a splendid hall'.

Ernie's camp furniture had been replaced by some bought by his sister Ada Henniker and her husband Fred when they had stayed on a houseboat in Srinagar over the summer. True to Howell form, it wasn't the most comfortable of furniture, but Lilla had to do what she could with it. She dug through the trunks and boxes of their possessions that had been sent up from Calcutta. Two years after their wedding, she was now unwrapping some of their two hundred and fifty wedding presents for the first time. Unravelling great bandages of yellowing tissue paper from delicately painted china plates. Heaving great silver bowls and candlesticks from dust-covered crates and arranging them around her 'drawing-room', their grandeur charmingly out of scale with the cottage rooms. Finding swathes of silks and cottons brought from China that she draped over the awkward furniture. And from the bottom of one of the boxes, she unearthed a heavy silk cloth covered in embroidery that Ernie recognized as his trophy from when he had ransacked the Forbidden City with Toby after the Boxer Uprising. Lilla sewed quilting on to the back and turned it into a thick bedspread for their bed. At night, they snuggled together under this constant reminder of his military prowess. 'She has made this hut so comfy,' wrote Ernie, glowing with husbandly pride.

Shortly after Christmas, the snow began to fall. Its heavy flakes curled around the house, turning their view across the valley into a fuzz of grey. Over the first few days, the morning sun melted it into slush and mud that froze back into an ice rink at night. And then, as the earth hardened, the frost spreading down through its layers, Bandipur turned white. The nearby lake froze over, first slowing into an eerie, viscous calm and then great patches of white began to spread across it, the last glimpses of dark water eventually sealed away beneath the smooth sheet of ice. The snow deepened. Foot after foot was dug away from the sides of the house and, finally, the falls seemed to ebb. The weather had done its work. The valley was still. Most of its creatures had burrowed themselves away against the cold; even the black Himalayan bears had vanished until spring. The cries of the few birds still darting from one white-limbed tree to another were muffled by the snow. Even the raging torrent at the bottom of their garden had slowed into a stiff, icy flow. Winter had come.

Inside their cottage, Ernie and Lilla settled into snow-bound domestic bliss. Ernie was besotted with his busy little son, accrediting all his achievements to Lilla: 'he has inherited his mother's cheery disposition'. Arthur charged around the house in the long, frilly white skirts and dresses that babies and toddlers of both sexes wore then. 'So plucky,' boasted Ernie in his letters to his family, 'bangs of all sorts he administers to himself but not one whimper.' From time to time, Arthur slept in his parents' room. 'He sleeps always on his face as I do,' wrote Ernie. 'He awakes I don't know how early but Lily has taught him not to make a sound until the bearer knocks at the door at 7am' when 'the little chap jumps in

his bed & says "atcha" or "over" or "oh dear".' Upon
hearing his son, Ernie would leap up and rush over to the
cot to 'take the little monkey into our bed'. And in an
astonishing gesture that would still score points for new-
manliness today, he changed him. 'I usually pull off a
mass of sodden garments – how he can stick them I don't
know.' And if anything irked Lilla, she didn't show it.
She is 'always good-tempered', Ernie wrote to his
mother.

Day and night, Lilla kept fires roaring in each room,
and the kitchen churning out steaming dish after steaming dish of poultry and game, plundered from the
'farmyard' of turkeys, geese, ducks, pigeons, fowls and
cows kept around the house and occasionally bagged by
Ernie himself on snowy forays with a shotgun. The only
other source for provisions – the villagers had little to
spare – were deliveries, weather permitting, from
Srinagar. At first she would have kept Ernie's food
simple, familiar, and stuck to dishes that she knew he
would like. Roasting pheasant coated in fatty rashers of
bacon. Stuffing long-necked wild duck with sage and
onions. Simmering sausage-filled wood pigeons in thick
tomato soup and claret. Stewing or baking tiny rabbit
joints with sultanas. Jugging hare, steaming it in a sealed
earthenware dish for hours on end.

Once she sensed that she had lulled Ernie into a steady
rhythm of expectation and gluttony, she must have begun
to branch out, spicing the dishes up into the curries he
had professed to miss in London. Bit by bit she would
have added new ingredients. Her recipe book is full of
surprising dishes that put bananas into savoury sauces
and mix stir-fried peanuts with chicken to make a pilau.
Then the pilaus slide from Indian to Chinese, Lilla
shredding the chicken, pulping the rice and coating the
dish in the Worcester sauce that she used instead of soy.
Ernie must have wolfed it all down, showering praise

over the chopped duck and sliced chestnuts and strips of chicken strewn with dark mushrooms. Making Lilla feel that, at last, she had him entranced.

After dinner, Lilla played the piano to Ernie and sang, even persuading him to join in. Ernie agreed to let her teach him the violin. He was not a natural musician, but he tried his best. 'He is now learning the violin obligato to my song "O dry those tears," it really sounds quite grand,' wrote Lilla. The two of them practised together every evening and Lilla – perhaps with a touch of womanly deception – clearly made Ernie feel that he was rather good. 'I am much interested in it,' he wrote.

Engulfed in a haze of roaring log fires, music, paternal pride and mouthwatering food – 'she feeds me so well' – Ernie fell completely under Lilla's spell: 'It was really the best day's work I ever did when I proposed to her. No man has ever had a nicer wife.' Stuck up on the Kashmiri mountainside, his old prejudices melted away: 'There is no mistake she is not rich but money will not buy her charms, her natural grace, perfect figure, perfect teeth & complexion.' And Ernie even seemed to realize, in his own way, that their future happiness was in some measure up to him: 'I must do all I can to make things easy for her. She must find Bandipur a great change from Bedford.' And even Lilla herself felt in charge. '[Ernie] was certainly run down before, but now he is a different boy, and enjoys life, and does not worry *one bit* – I hope there will be no necessity for me to leave him again, as it does him no good to be alone.'

And for a precious few months, Ernie even stopped referring to Lilla in the double diminutive of 'little Lily'. 'Lily', once Lilla had acceded to it, was there for good. Perhaps she sensed that Ernie was happiest thinking of her as smaller than him, given that he wasn't a very tall man himself. And, unlike his father, who took an extremely active interest in his daughters' education,

Ernie's view of women, with the exception of his sisters, was that of most men of his generation – they were lesser creatures.

Despite the new lease of life in his marriage, Ernie was still deeply frustrated at being snowed in. 'I hate this weather,' he wrote. Regardless of Lilla's best efforts to keep him entertained, he prowled around the house like a wounded tiger, bemoaning the difficulty of walking through the several feet of snow that surrounded the house, until at last the sleigh they were having built in the village was finished. Then, leaving Mrs Desmond to wheel Arthur up and down the boarded-up veranda – only his eyes were visible 'as he was so wrapped up in rugs etc.' – they set out nearly every afternoon to go shooting on the frozen lake. These trips, however, rapidly turned out to be more amusing than practical. 'There are thousands of birds,' wrote Lilla, 'but they know the gun too well and fly away before we can get near them.'

Ernie was not to be put off his prey so easily. Determined to bag some geese, he cobbled together what he called a 'mitrailleuse' from ten Brown Bessies – 'medieval weapons with which the Kashmiri troops are armed'. He tied the guns into a rack on a wheelbarrow and camouflaged himself in one of Lilla's nightdresses 'to match the snow'. He loaded the guns with a 'double charge of powder and buckshot', attached all ten triggers to a single string and crept towards the birds. When he had managed to manoeuvre himself within eighty feet of them, he pulled the string. The resulting bang sent the wheelbarrow careering into his chest 'and made me roar with pain'. But he had a goose.

Still wearing her nightdress, he returned to Lilla triumphantly, clutching the dead bird. It took three hours to roast. She turned the giblets into gravy, pounded some of the autumn's apples into a sauce and presented Ernie with a feast of his spoils.

By April, the snow was beginning to melt. While the rest of India began to heat itself to boiling point, a gentle spring settled on Bandipur. Lilla and Ernie's family life moved outside. Arthur ran around with the animals and on the lawns. Lilla and Ernie showered him with presents. At barely one and a half, he had a pony, a puppy, and even a goat-cart in which he sat, still in white frills, with a tent of a sunhat and parasols to shield him from the sun, clutching on to the reins. As soon as it was warm enough to sleep away from a fire and before so much snow had melted that the rivers had returned to raging torrents, Ernie and Lilla escaped from their little hut and into 'camp' on another Kashmiri houseboat. They ambled down the rising rivers, visiting waterfalls and springs, old temples and ruined palaces, sometimes abandoning the boat to camp in tents in the hills for several days at a time, listening to great spring avalanches roar down the mountains at night. When they returned with the rare birds that they had shot, Lilla had them stuffed and sent back to Ernie's sister Laura and her husband Sidney. Now, Lilla could do no wrong. Every one of Ernie's letters to his family was packed with praise for her. And by joining in Ernie's family tradition of collecting rare species of plant and animal, and following the instructions she was given to add to Laura's letter collection back in England – 'when you have a good many of our effusions, send them home in a packet' – she was showing them that she could do far more than just run a house and cook. Lilla even managed to take the upper hand in her relationship with her mother-in-law, writing to Barbie, 'give my fondest love to your mother and say, I *do* mean to write'.

But a single dark cloud loomed on the horizon. I had been wondering why Lilla had not pasted any snapshots

Arthur, Bandipur, Kashmir, 1904.

of herself in Kashmir into her album. Then, in one of her letters to Barbie, the answer emerged. Perhaps I should have guessed it sooner. After all, it seemed to be an immediate, inevitable result of any union, or reunion, between Lilla and Ernie. I must have been distracted by all the comments about Ada. By Ernie's amazingly indiscreet written whispers to his sisters not to '*say one word* about this awhile' but, 'in spite of all precautions', his wife's twin was 'in for an infant apparently to her great disgust'. By thinking that Ada's 'disgust' must have been masking a fear of having to watch another child die. And all this while there had been not one murmur about Lilla herself. But she was pregnant too, just a month behind her twin.

Ada's baby was due in July, Lilla's in August. Ada must have conceived during Lilla's visit, and Lilla within days of seeing Ernie again.

For all her enthusiasm, her passion, for Ernie, Lilla was not happy to be pregnant either. 'I wonder if you will be very much surprised,' she wrote to Barbie, 'to hear that I am in the "family way" again. Oh dear dear poor little me. Such is life – well, it can't be helped and I am trying to make the best of it.' At least, unlike Ada, she didn't have to go back to England for the birth in a desperate attempt to keep the child alive. But her memories of life immediately after Arthur had been born would still have been raw. And after what she thought she had done to her last baby, she must have been terrified that some great hand of fate would wreak revenge.

As spring turned into summer, social life in Bandipur took off. The British in India who were free to leave their posts flocked north to Kashmir to escape the baking heat in the rest of the country. Once there, they toured the countryside, and Ernie and Lilla's cottage became a stopping place along the way. 'We have been very gay,'

158

wrote Lilla on 1 July, 'this last week having people to nearly every meal, in fact the whole of June we have had guests.' Yesterday, she continued, 'we had two ladies to breakfast, for lunch and tea a Captain Steepnagle & the nurse who went to Gilgit. For dinner some R.A.M.C. [Royal Army Medical Corps] man, this sort of thing is my daily program.' Luckily, perhaps, for Lilla, they had no spare bedrooms and their visitors were limited to meals that, even seven and a half months pregnant, she could still produce – by ordering in ingredients from Srinagar, twenty miles away – with a flourish.

The odd visitor, however, did stay the night. A 'Prince Pedro of Orleans', wrote Lilla, turned up late one evening on his way back through the mountains to Gilgit. He collapsed at the door, too ill to move. Lilla put him up in a tent for two days until he could travel to a doctor. After the isolation of the winter, Lilla found all these visitors diverting but hard work, and looked forward to being snowed in with Ernie once more – 'I shall be quite glad when the autumn comes and we are by ourselves again.'

Summer brought more work for Ernie, too. 'This is my busy season,' he wrote. Throughout the winter he had made occasional forays to Srinagar. Now, in addition to organizing any official visits, he had to make the most of the warm weather to check the passes and trails north through the Himalayas towards Russian-occupied Afghanistan. India was a prized possession of the British Empire, a vast wealth-creating machine envied by the world's other great nations – especially by imperial Russia, whose own vast empire stretched from the Baltic to the Pacific in one solid block, whisking tantalizingly close to India itself. For decades, Britain had feared a potential Russian invasion through the Himalayas. And while their two armies had faced each other across the mountains, young British and Russian heroes had galloped around the Central Asian mountains and deserts in disguise, gathering information and seeking to convert local tribes to their cause in a glamorous escapade known as the Great Game. A game in which Ernie was now playing a very minor role.

Ernie's task was to work out the best way, if any, to take an army through the mountains. He set off on one expedition to Gilgit with a team of Kashmiri guides, donkeys and ponies. They climbed a thousand feet at a time, along paths so narrow that when one pony knocked into the overhanging cliff and stumbled it disappeared down the hillside to its death. He crossed torrential rivers on terrifying footbridges, making the mistake of looking down at the water swirling beneath him: 'I had to turn back.' The party climbed to 14,500 feet and, even in July, the slopes were covered in thick snow, through which they skidded their way down, unloading the animals and rolling the bundles down the hill. When he returned, his hands and face had been sunburnt a deep red.

At the end of July, Lilla spent a few days in Srinagar visiting the vacant Assistant-Resident's house, where she would give birth the following month. In a postcard to her cousin, Lulu Covil, she still sounds upbeat. 'Awfully hot,' she scribbled. 'Just seen the house we are going to next month, lovely place – best love yrs L.H.' A few days later, Ada Elderton gave birth to another girl in England. 'All Ada and Toby can knock up between them is another petticoat,' mocked Ernie from one of his mountain camps. 'I hope my Pilili will be man enough to knock out another man.' But, after gritting her teeth and barely uttering a whimper through her hours of labour – leading Ernie naively to write 'never was there a child born with such ease' – Lilla gave birth to a girl in the last week of August.

Ernie could scarcely conceal his disappointment. His

marriage had seemed to him so perfect that Lilla's failure to give him a second son knocked him for six. 'Lily is satisfied and so I don't like to grumble,' he confided to Barbie. 'I want the child called Esmé,' he added. He lost out, however, even on this. Lilla overruled him, calling their daughter Alice after her mother. And hot on the heels of this came another blow. He received orders to move. His time in Kashmir was over.

Ernie must have begun to curse his luck. First a daughter. Then her being named after his mother-in-law, of whom, however his feelings for Lilla had changed, he can scarcely have been fond. Now Kashmir – the posting of a lifetime – cut short. To make matters worse, he would have felt that he had only himself to blame. Throughout the past year he had been plagued by a recurring eye infection that, at times, had led Lilla to write his letters for him. Then, unable – despite Lilla's best efforts – to face another claustrophobic winter in the hills, he had asked for two months' leave over the following January and February. The response from headquarters had been brief: move to a new post. And at the beginning of October, as soon as Lilla's confinement was over, she found herself packing up their little fishing hut in Bandipur and heading south to the desert city of Lucknow.

8

THE TABLES TURN

Lucknow, India, October 1904

IT IS NOT OFTEN that lovers swap roles. Usually the pattern formed at first, one person chasing, the other aloof, sticks fast. Just as you think that a change is about to happen – the lover drawing back for once, the beloved starting to fuss around – some small circumstance takes a turn and they both revert to type. The beloved clambers back on to his or her pedestal, reprising a moody gaze at a more appealing horizon. The lover scurries around, picking up the debris, trying to transform the broken this and that into some pretty object that will make the loved one smile.

Not so with Ernie and Lilla. In England, Ernie had decided to give his marriage another chance. In Kashmir he had fallen in love again. And, even though he and Lilla were now being hustled out of their mountain paradise and down on to the hot, dusty Indian plain, Ernie found himself increasingly dependent on the wife he had once tried to abandon.

As Ernie's spirits sank, Lilla swept him up under her wing, soothing his injured pride at losing Kashmir with comfort food. She could conjure up the smoky atmosphere of an English gentlemen's club by smearing anchovies on to hot toast dripping with melted butter. She knew how to keep cheddar on a high shelf in their larder until it was stale enough to darken and crack, then melt it into browned onions to make cheese on toast with a rich, earthy tang. Surrounded by mountains of Indian rice, she could curry sardines and rice together, spooning the fishy, mushy, oily mixture on to a bed of fried apples. She chopped ham, hard-boiled eggs and parsley into tender cooked rice, tossing the sizzling ingredients into a creamy kedgeree. She simmered long-grained Patna rice and tomatoes until it softened into an Italian risotto. And so she lulled Ernie's anger with himself, with his eyes, with the system that had sent another man to take his coveted place in Kashmir, in a smooth, rich, buttery haze of food.

Lucknow made as stark a contrast with Bandipur as India could provide. Instead of nestling among the cool, clear pinnacles of Kashmir, Lucknow sits surrounded by the flat horizons of the vast Ganges plain. Even in winter the temperatures are as hot as a northern European summer and between April and June the heat can soar to a stifling fifty degrees centigrade. And unlike remote, peaceful Bandipur, Lucknow was a former Muslim capital of India. Its buildings were a riot of golden domes, turquoise arched ramparts and ivory-inlaid mosaic. As Rudyard Kipling puts it in his novel *Kim*, 'No city – except Bombay, the queen of all – was more beautiful in her garish style than Lucknow.' Embroidered silks were piled up inside the doorways of its shopping streets whose air was thick with a rich, intoxicating perfume – a perfume that carried with it deep memories of unrest.

For all the order that the heavy British garrison imposed upon the town's surface, underneath it quietly seethed with rebellion against its imperial invaders. Half a century before Lilla and Ernie arrived, Lucknow had cut the deepest wound that the British had suffered in India. In the midst of the Indian Mutiny of 1857, the mutineers of Lucknow had besieged the British Residency, which was crammed with no fewer than three thousand British and loyal Indians. The siege lasted for eighty-seven days and the squalor, disease and starvation far outstripped what the Boxers later achieved in Peking. When British troops eventually came to the rescue, just one thousand – a third – of those besieged had survived. The building still stands almost as it was found by the British troops in the autumn of 1857, a charred ruin, its walls peppered with cannonball holes.

When Ernie and Lilla arrived in the autumn of 1904, the same mutinous spirit still bubbled through the city. Not that Lilla would have been expected to come into much contact with it. For, unlike Bandipur, where they had lived more or less by themselves – their closest neighbours the local Kashmiri villagers, who were happy, as Ernie had boasted, 'to do anything' for Lilla – in Lucknow they found themselves part of the rigidly ordered life of the British cantonment.

Cantonments in India were a little like foreign concessions in China. They were dwelling, shopping, schooling, worshipping and socializing areas for the British, fenced off from the gritty reality of India. They were designed to be a self-sufficient world, their green lawns and wide tree-lined avenues a utopia to comfort even the most homesick souls. But there the similarities ended. For while foreign concessions in China were a base from which to explore if not the countryside then at least a flavour of the real China and other foreign concessions, the cantonments in India made themselves as inward-looking as they could possibly be. And as the Indian heat stifled the British residents' bodies, dampening their skin under their tight-fitting clothes, the cantonment way of life carefully starved their minds of the reality of the India outside. There were parks for the children to play in, polo fields for husbands to play on, and social clubs that still managed to convey an air of condescending exclusivity even though they were basically open to any white-skinned face.

Lilla can have hardly noticed the sterility of her environment when she arrived. Ignoring her own exhaustion so shortly after having a baby, she had carted two children and a grumpy husband down from the Himalayas and hundreds of miles across the Indian plain. By the time they reached Lucknow, the children were not at all well. Whereas, back in Kashmir, Arthur was so rosy-cheeked that one lady who saw him said, Lilla wrote, 'he was the healthiest & most English-looking chap she had seen in India, it pleased me very much to hear that', now things were quite different. 'Arthur's little face is half the size,' she wrote, and baby Alice was far from thriving. Lilla and Mrs Desmond had tried to feed her 'every food under the sun', eventually having a go with 'milk & barley water with mellius [a honey mixture]'. Lilla was desperately worried to see her two-month-old daughter so sick. Every cell in a new mother's body is programmed to obsess over how much her newborn is eating and how much weight he or she is gaining. Even today, mothers with robustly healthy babies can feel helpless if their child skips a meal. Back then, in India, as Lilla knew all too well – from the deaths of little Jack Henniker and her twin's child – the stakes were high. 'It makes me so unhappy to see them, with little white faces,' wrote Lilla, all her maternal instincts painfully sharpened and wondering, perhaps, whether she didn't deserve to lose a child, too.

No sooner had Lilla started to settle her ailing family into their new home than she was told that they had to move – 'to make matters worse we have to turn out of our house – to think of packing once again, it makes me sick – I am so weary of it all'. At least this time it was only to another house in the cantonment. For several exhausting days Lilla scuttled from one house to the other, repacking the boxes that she had just carefully emptied in the first and organizing the cleaning and preparing of the second. Then at last, at the end of October, they moved into an imposing house that could not have been less like the beloved fishing hut she had had to leave behind. Her new home was a grand villa with a semi-circular veranda that bulged out from its stone façade, supported by half a dozen fat classical columns.

Lilla, like Ernie, would much rather have stayed in Kashmir – but for very different reasons. Ernie missed the great outdoors, the expeditions, the shooting and fishing. He also missed the independence and autonomy of being posted outside the chain of command. In the army lists for Ernie's Supply and Transport Corps, Kashmir is entered in whispery italics hinting at the subterfuge and derring-do of the Central Asian spying wars between Russia and Britain. In Lucknow, Ernie was an accounts clerk, jammed behind a desk all day with a host of superior officers to bark orders at him. One in particular seems to have given Ernie such a rough time that as he left India he wrote to apologize for being such a 'hard task master'.

What Lilla missed about Kashmir was the cosiness of their cottage and the roaring fires. The evenings spent at the piano while Ernie tried to accompany her on the violin. The snugness, the togetherness, of their life high up in the hills. Not having to worry about anyone else. For Ernie, Kashmir had been a physical adventure. For Lilla, it had been a romantic one. Looking around her new surroundings, the carefully manicured lawns and gardens, the rows of pasty expatriates trying to live for the greater good of empire, she must have realized that she was going to have to create a brand new type of adventure for Ernie and herself. And within the corniced walls of her grand stone villa, she started to construct a grand Raj life for her family.

Three years on from Calcutta, Lilla was a master of conversation with other expatriate wives. She had two children to discuss – who, thankfully, had fully recovered – and the kudos of having spent a year in Kashmir. She also had her own house, which doubtless she arranged with considerably more style than most of her neighbours – the limitless heavy Chinese silks and miniature-stitched embroidery sent over by her mother, who had returned to Chefoo, raising a few envious hackles around the cantonment. She dressed Alice in frills and Arthur in immaculate short frocks with starched sailor collars and sometimes, as if to make his connection to the Scottish Andrew Eckford real, a kilt. Even Mrs Desmond joined in the show. There were surprisingly few English nannies in India – most people made do with Indian ayahs. Mrs Desmond, whom Lilla called 'Nurse', paraded her status in great constructions of hats that looked as if they were better suited to a medieval play than the Asian sunshine.

And Lilla could certainly entertain. She loved entertaining. She'd grown up weaving her way between the guests at the Eckfords' endless parties. In Kashmir she had managed to produce great feasts by sleight of hand. But here in Lucknow she had time to think and plan properly. She and Ernie were, as ever, fighting to live within the budget of his wages. Still, she would have made sure that the food she served was among the best. When the meat wasn't good enough for an English roast, she had a dozen curry recipes up her sleeve. At the back of her recipe book is a section on housewife's tricks. One of these is a recipe for 'mock' pâté de foie gras conjured up by mashing cooked chicken livers or 'liver sausage' with stock, lemon juice, seasoning and — if possible — truffles. Lilla completed the disguise with hard-boiled eggs, pastry and aspic jelly.

Next to this section are pages and pages of menus for dinner parties. Fruit, soup, sole, chicken then rum omelette for those who still had room. Roast duck followed by strawberry ice cream, my favourite. A traditional mushroom soup, stuffed veal and apple meringue. Lobster salad, mmm, sheep's tongue 'boiled with brain sauce' (thank God for the change in modern tastes) and rhubarb charlotte, an indulgent mixture of cake, stewed fruit and cream. The ubiquitous prawn cocktail, followed by beef with fried bananas and pine-apple mousse that sounds like an early form of fusion cuisine. After dinner, Lilla played the piano and en-couraged her guests to sing — hopefully sparing Ernie on his novice violin.

By flinging her family into a full-blown cantonment life, Lilla was disguising the air of unease emanating from her husband — 'I do wish Ernie would cheer up,' she wrote to her sister-in-law Ada Henniker. But Ernie's career was flagging. Staying healthy was crucial to success in India. Hordes of diseases lay in wait for the weak. Medical problems didn't just keep a man in bed for a couple of weeks, they bestowed a stigma of not being up to the job. Ernie's problems with his eyes — which had flared up within months of returning from a prolonged sick leave in England — were enough for the powers that be to shove him on to a back burner in Lucknow and let him simmer gently while his juniors were promoted beyond him. As his self-esteem drooped, so his temper flared. This time Lilla could rise above her husband's bad moods. She could stand firm in the face of his explosions and busy herself with the house, the children, and a thousand other things she found to do. Of the two of them, she was the one making a success of their respective roles in life. And, inch by inch, she must have felt the gap between them growing.

It is at this point – in the late autumn of 1904 – that the collection of Howell letters comes to an end. Maybe Laura had come to agree with Barbie that it would require 'an elastic-sided bungalow . . . I always feel compunction in tearing up letters but really I don't know what else one could do with them – even one's descendants could not enjoy such vast piles as would accumulate.' Just between the Howells themselves – ignoring their various husbands and wives – there were six children and two parents, all writing to each other once a week. That makes around fifty letters a week, well over two thousand a year.

For the next ten years, I tracked Lilla through a handful of letters that emerged from a range of albums and drawers. Some were from Ernie's superior officers, kept, I guess, for the praise they bestowed. Others fell out of the bottom of files lurking in attics, that nobody had bothered to throw away. Then there are a mass of photographs that put Lilla in various places on certain dates – photographs that popped out of Lilla's own albums, or other dusty family tomes hidden at the back of cupboards, photographs archived away in the bowels of libraries or, like those from Toby and Ada's albums, flown to me from across the world. I pored through the old Indian Army lists in the British Library and worked out where Ernie was posted when, and as what.

And then there were the stories I have grown up with. Above all, the one about Lilla falling out of love.

Lilla and Ernie stayed in Lucknow for a couple of years, punctuated by summers in the hill station of Naini-Tal, to which the Lucknow cantonment decamped to escape the hot weather. It is a mountainous region scattered with so many lakes that it has earned the nickname the 'Switzerland of Asia'. But it wasn't Kashmir. The steep tree-covered hillsides leading down to the water had been carved into the manicured lawns of the cantonments down on the plain. And, transplanted several hundred miles north and a couple of thousand metres up, cantonment life continued as before – Ernie's frustration at his crawling career manifesting itself in increasingly frequent outbursts of temper.

When eventually they moved on it was to a drier and duller posting in Meerut, a town that the clipped British voices called 'Merit'. Even a long-overdue promotion to major had left Ernie still spending his days burrowing through mounds of paper behind a desk – bringing only a brief respite from his dark moods. And here, Lilla's enthusiasm began to fade. The family photograph albums whose pages she had so meticulously filled with pictures of their life in Kashmir – and even Lucknow – simply petered out. It was as though, barely twenty-four years old and just five years into her marriage, she knew that it was no longer something she would wish to remember. As Ernie's sister Laura had so neatly written to their youngest sibling Evelyn, living in India 'is an awfully hard life for a woman ... you need an awfully good husband to make it worthwhile'.

When she needed to, whenever she found reason to, Lilla visited Ada in Bombay. Once there, she wouldn't have complained about her life with Ernie. Not even murmured that anything was wrong. The pressure for any siblings, let alone identical twins, to keep up with each other can make it hard for them to admit something may not be right. But then twins don't always have to use words for a message to be read loud and clear. Despite Lilla's eulogies of cantonment life, what a wonderful husband Ernie was, how well he was doing, Ada would have known – maybe even guessed from Lilla's letters, without seeing her face to face – that all was not as it might have been.

Ada's troubles were different. In sharp contrast to Ernie, Toby was going from strength to strength in the navy. He was rapidly establishing himself as one of the great and the good. Successful and confident, he was easy to love and found it easy to love in return. Ada worshipped him, and he adored her. But even this love couldn't keep their babies alive. Their second baby girl – the one for whose birth Ada had gone to England – had started having fits and Ada had had to watch this child die too. She had returned to India to be with Toby and, like Lilla, would have been pretending that nothing was wrong. Given Toby's position as Principal Officer of the Bombay Dockyard, she had plenty to do socially. She probably claimed that she had hardly the time for children in any case. But, again, without a single word being uttered, Lilla would have known that this wasn't quite true.

On more earthy matters, Ada was frank. The confidence that had been ingrained in her as the elder twin, and by having Toby, made her open when it came to the practicalities of life. She claimed she always read *The Times* while Toby was 'in the act', as if attempting to make light of her childlessness and so lessen the pain. But, within the family, she was widely assumed to be frigid. It may well have been the case. There can hardly be a greater disincentive to making love than the fear of having another child and watching it die. Understanding as Toby was, at times he found Ada's physical coldness hard to bear. As the years passed, his after-dinner stories would begin to include increasingly sexual innuendoes – with more than a hint of desperation at their heart.

Enjoying their time together, however, Ada and Lilla would have pottered around Bombay, going for dress fittings, shopping for Ada's house, the two of them giggling at tea parties, and at home bustling around the kitchen, organizing Ada's bemused Indian cook into making spring rolls and chow mein. At times it must have seemed that they had wandered back half a dozen years and were just nineteen again, buffeted only by the sea breezes in Chefoo. As though, as long as they were together, nothing bad could happen to them.

And when they parted, it was Ada's turn to feel a wrench. That postcard of Ada's from Bombay says it all: 'Lilla and children left today for China. Sorry cannot write.'

In China, Lilla's photographs pick up again. At the end of 1907, a long-awaited great hand reached down from the sky and plucked Ernie from his dusty desk in Meerut, posting him back not just to China but to his old military station in Tientsin, which was about as close to Chefoo as a British soldier could be. And, instead of languishing behind a desk in the middle of an unhappy chain of command, he was now Chief Supply and Transport Officer for the forces in China. Snow-covered panoramas of Peking, the Summer Palace, the Forbidden City, fill up entire pages of Lilla's album. I can remember my grandfather, Arthur, showing me one of him, Lilla and Ernie, standing in the snow outside the Forbidden City in Peking. But Arthur, dear Grandpa, died when I was ten – years before his mother – and I can't find it now.

As Lilla moved back to China, she must have felt the blood pump faster through her veins. Like Calcutta and Bombay, the centre of Tientsin was packed with towering colonial edifices. But the streets that ran between them could hardly have felt more different. Tientsin was smaller than Shanghai, but just as cosmopolitan. Instead of the colourless monopoly of British fashion, British food, British drink, British parties, that reigned in the cantonments and the cities of the Raj, Lilla was once again surrounded by the styles, tastes and smells from every corner of the world that made her blossom. Ernie probably thought a little blindly that it was he who was pleasing her and puffed his chest out to match, reckoning this was a long-overdue chance for their relationship to take off again. But Lilla can hardly have noticed. Her smiles, the lightness of her step, would have come not from her husband but simply from being in China. Whether it was the tiny stitching on its embroidered coats, the reservation of its tea ceremonies, the miniature hedges, ponds and waterfalls of its formal gardens, the delicacy of the detail in its carved roofs and painted murals, the perfection of each pinched parcel of dim sum, it was all small, perfect, neat. And it was the world she knew. It was home.

Yet almost as soon as this life in China was handed to Lilla, it was snatched away again. In April 1908, barely four months after Ernie had arrived and just about the time when Lilla was planning a glorious summer in Chefoo, Ernie was suddenly posted back to India, as a result of unspecific 'changes in the system of administration'.

But when Ernie left, Lilla didn't go with him. Instead she pressed ahead with her plans to take her children to her family in Chefoo.

From then on, she would no longer feel a need to wed her movements to his.

On Ernie's return to India, the tide that had begun to turn in his direction in China continued to flow. Within a month of arriving back, he found himself in the position of purveyor of fine wines and spirits to Lord Kitchener, the commander-in-chief of the Indian Army, on his tour of the summer hill stations. Ernie tracked down the cases of alcohol, bought them at a good price and sent them up whichever hill the thirsty Kitchener was perching on. 'The chief is most grateful for all you have done,' wrote FitzGerald, Kitchener's aide-de-camp. He must have been. By August Ernie had been moved to Mandalay, in what was then Burma, and put in command of his own mule corps – the soldiers in charge of loading, driving and protecting military mule-trains, the principal means of transporting supplies over usually tricky non-railway territory in pre-motor days.

After four long years of dragging his heels, Ernie was once again bursting with energy and confidence. He proudly forwarded his letters from FitzGerald to Lilla in China.

How ironic that would turn out to be. Kitchener was the man who invented one of the great scourges of the twentieth century – the concentration camp. He first used them to imprison Boer women and children after burning their farms in the British war against the Boers of 1899–1902. I wonder how fondly Lilla remembered those letters when, thirty years later, she found herself locked up in just such a camp by the Japanese.

But by the time the letters reached Lilla back in 1908, it would already have been too late. In an almost childish way she seems to have loved Ernie most when he wasn't interested in her. Once she had not only won him round but found she was the one keeping his head above water, I think she discovered that there was not much lasting love there. Or maybe she simply outgrew him. In any case, although hurting each other from time to time can be part and parcel of a loving relationship, I don't think you can ever really forgive someone for trying to leave you in the way Ernie had tried to leave Lilla. For the rest of her life, Lilla would feel scarred by Ernie's behaviour back in England – the wound manifesting itself primarily as an obsession with having some money to leave to her children and grandchildren so that their husbands and wives wouldn't want to leave them too. And later it surfaced to spur her to write her recipe book. As if, when her life was again turned upside down four decades on, she still automatically felt a need to show what a good wife she could be.

But now, the little remaining love between them must have been eaten away by half a decade of Lilla covering up Ernie's failures and putting up with his near-constant grumpiness at home. She was still proud of her husband, still pleased at his success – she always was, even when she spoke about him to me seventy years on. And she was still prepared to play the role of a loyal army wife, even if it was duty, rather than desire, that made her do so. But it was clear to everyone back then that she wasn't in love with him any more. Clear enough for the story to have reached my young ears generations later, forming an early impression that what you should do and what you might want to do were not always the same thing.

Nonetheless, in August 1908, Lilla didn't follow Ernie to Burma. She followed Ada to England.

Ada and Toby had had another child, a boy called Alan. He was alive but ill, and Ada and Toby had taken him to England, where the doctors had advised them to stay. Toby had decided to resign from the Indian Navy and transfer to the Royal Navy in order to be able to do so.

Lilla booked Arthur, Alice and herself on a boat to England. Her excuse was easy. Arthur was almost six. It was time for him to begin the long separation from his parents and go to boarding school in England. Ernie approved and didn't blink. Lilla would settle Arthur into school, leave Alice in the care of Ada, and return to India the following year. And she did.

I am surprised that Lilla went back to Ernie. I know that, back then, duty played a larger role in people's lives than it does now. I understand that she may have been

Lilla sailing for England, August 1908.

trying to make the marriage work, or simply hoping to hide the fact that it wasn't. But Lilla could easily have stayed with the children for a few years without raising any eyebrows at all. Maybe she felt that she had to go back because being in the same place was the only relationship she and Ernie had left. Still, I struggle to imagine how she could have left her children behind in England, and why she chose to play the role of wife to a husband she was no longer in love with rather than be a mother to them, whom I know she loved very much. But of course, being stuck in England with the children was precisely what she had once fought so hard to escape.

I have to keep reminding myself that this was another time, almost another place. 'The past is another country,' wrote L. P. Hartley in *The Go-Between*, 'people do things differently there.' And they did. Lilla wasn't being a neglectful parent by leaving her children in England. She was simply doing what, back then, everyone thought was best. Once children reached school age out in the British Empire, they were sent Home. Not just to escape disease, not just for an education but, in a slightly sinister way, to ensure that they grew up 'British'. Unless their parents chose to separate, their mothers remaining in Britain while their fathers pursued some greater good or ambition abroad, the children of the British Empire barely saw their parents between the age of about five and adulthood. Their upbringing was handed over to a combination of relatives – often maiden aunts – and the English public school system that turned them into the same empire-building stock as their parents. Arthur used to tell me time and time again how he remembered sailing away from India as a small boy and barely seeing his parents for years at a stretch.

For the next five years, as she rounded the corner from her twenties to her thirties, Lilla seems to have scurried between Ernie in India and her children and twin in England as much as she could, continuing her Indian adventure by playing an officer's wife to the hilt. I can picture her bounding with exaggerated enthusiasm for his mule corps. Admiring the polished belts and boots of the soldiers' uniforms – 'w-w-w-wonderful, d-d-darling' – the long line of beasts with gently rounded bellies, and the punctiliousness with which they arrived at each port of call and left again. In the evenings, she would have welcomed her husband with open arms, the simmering of a feast to come prickling her soft, freshly washed skin. And then, as soon as was decent, she was off again back to England, back to close whatever painful gap had opened up since she'd last seen Ada or her children. Still, these gaps could be long. In a letter I found at the bottom of a tin box in my father's study, Arthur's childhood scrawl reads, 'Mummy is coming home next year.'

But Lilla, and the hundreds of other empire wives like her, were not the only people rushing from pillar to post at the beginning of the twentieth century. In a strange way, Lilla's busy handling of her own domestic politics – struggling to keep both her husband and children happy – mirrored the political and diplomatic manoeuvrings of the great military powers of the day. Almost ever since Russia, Japan, Great Britain, France, Austria, Italy and Germany had joined forces to quell the Boxer Uprising – ever since Lilla had met Ernie – their ambassadors had been scuttling from court to government to court in a merry dance as they frantically tried to keep war between them at bay. The imperialist expansion of the nineteenth century had already painted almost the entire globe the colour of one empire or another. Nonetheless, the first decade and a half of the twentieth century saw a great surge of rearmament. Germany vied with Britain to have the largest navy. France decided to increase the size of its

A rare picture of the family together: from left, Arthur, Ernie, Lilla and Alice.

army. And each power made every effort to introduce the latest technology into its fighting forces. Even Ernie found himself ordered back from India to England in 1913 for a course in the 'mechanical transport' that would one day put his mule corps out of business. Upon his return to India, he was promptly promoted to lieutenant colonel.

All this left the armies all dressed up with no place to go.

By the summer of 1914, a vast bonfire had been laid in Europe. A great pile of tinder packed with kindling.

All it needed was a match.

On 28 June 1914, the heir to the Austro-Hungarian throne was assassinated in the Serbian city of Sarajevo. And, within a few weeks, the world was at war. At its start, the war was expected to last three or four months and to be over by Christmas. But of course it lasted over four years and saw a loss of human life on a scale never before envisaged. France and Germany lost about two million men apiece. Australia and Canada, even India, suffered huge losses. Britain lost half a million men under the age of thirty. Russian losses remain uncounted, but ran into millions. By the end, even the United States, who only entered the war in 1917, had lost over a hundred thousand men.

Life in the battered world that eventually emerged from the war in 1918 had changed irrevocably. War had become something to be avoided at almost any cost. The old European empires would never recover and, from now on, the world would increasingly dance to America's tune. The hitherto mainly patriarchal societies evolved into democracies as – after having been asked to fight in such a terrible war – every man, regardless of wealth or social status, was given the vote.

One of the most dramatic developments that the First World War set in motion was the changing role of women in society. During the war, women had famously stepped into the jobs of the men who were away fighting. Women had been working in munitions factories, farming, ferrying food around the country, running the railways and even on active service in the auxiliary forces. The years that followed the war saw them shed their corsets, win the right to vote, and make the most of the advances in technology that war always seems to bring. As increasing numbers of labour-saving devices – ovens that you could turn on and off instead of stoking all day, and vacuum cleaners, fridges, and even washing machines for the lucky few – made their way into homes, women gained both time and freedom.

But Lilla's freedom was to come in another way.

Ernie was in Quetta, right up on the North West Frontier, when war broke out. In April 1915, an Indian Expeditionary Force was raised to venture up through Mesopotamia – modern-day Iraq. Trained up to the eyeballs in 'mechanical transport', Ernie was dispatched with it.

Britain had already taken the chief city in southern Mesopotamia, Basra, from its Turkish occupiers in the first months of the war. This had been a vital strategic move as Turkey had entered the war on the German side and the port of Basra lay next door to the island of Abadan, where the Anglo-Persian Oil Company had its refinery. This refinery supplied oil to Britain's newest and fastest 'Dreadnought' ships and if Turkey had cut off the oil supply a substantial proportion of the Royal Navy would have been brought to a standstill. But Britain now had its eyes on a greater Turkish-held prize – the city of Baghdad, and Mesopotamia itself.

The Expeditionary Force's plan was to travel by boat.

First north up through the flooded southern Mesopotamian plain, and then up the river Tigris to Baghdad. A veritable floating army of machine guns and field guns was assembled, spread over hundreds of local river craft – rafts, tugs and barges. For a logistics and transport officer like Ernie, the Persian Gulf Expedition, as it was called, must have been dream and nightmare rolled into one. At first the going was good. The army cruised north from Basra, the Turks scattering before their prows. Within a month, the British boats claimed a heroic victory over their first target of Amara, a hundred miles upriver and about a third of the way to Baghdad, when their field commander Major-General Townshend charged ahead and captured the city with a corporal and twelve men.

The price of such heroics was organizational disaster. To the frustration of Ernie's logistics corps, Townshend's river dash had left an army running out of supplies trailing behind in his wake. Southern Mesopotamia was an unromantic, forlorn mudflat. In May and June, when the British were rowing their way north, the temperature and mosquitoes were at their height. And the flooded plain that they were sailing on was a vast sewer pullulating with disease. Any food left was rotting and there were scant medical supplies with which to tackle the raging dysentery and paratyphoid. Townshend himself was shipped back to India on sick leave. When Ernie fell sick he was sent to England.

Lilla was waiting for him there. A couple of years before-hand, Andrew Eckford had retired to England leaving the firm in the hands of Lilla's brothers, Vivvy and Reggie. Shortly afterwards, he had died. But Lilla's mother Alice was still living in a sprawling semi-detached villa on the outskirts of London – Number 4, Crystal Palace Park Road – which must have realized all the Howells' fears of suburbia. Lilla nursed Ernie for five frustrating months. A professional soldier, Ernie must have been aching to return to battle before it was all over. His old Indian boss, Lord Kitchener, had become Secretary of State for War and his face was looming down from posters throughout the land. 'Your country needs you,' the drawing bellowed, his outstretched arm appearing to point straight between the eyes of anyone who stopped to look. By the end of 1915, more than a million volunteers had signed up – for war was still regarded as a glorious opportunity for adventure. Those who hadn't were receiving anonymous white feathers of cowardice in the post. When, in December, Ernie was pronounced fit to return to action, he must have raced to book a passage back east. He might not have been heading for the still-glamorous and sought-after centre of the action in the trenches on the Western Front – the full horror of this war had yet to reach its climax, let alone the eyes and ears of those still at home – but he was going to play his part.

Shortly before Christmas 1915 he boarded the SS *Persia*, a passenger liner, to return to the East. As Lilla bid him farewell, I don't think it occurred to her that she might never see him again. The journey had its risks. Just seven months earlier, the *Lusitania* had been sunk by a U-boat, killing 1,200 passengers. But this had caused an outrage. As a rule, a U-boat was supposed to surface in a gentlemanly fashion and give a warning to an enemy civilian ship, allowing those on board time to clamber into lifeboats and, if necessary, taking them on board the U-boat itself for their own safety. Only then would the vessel be sunk with a gun mounted on the U-boat's deck. In any case, U-boats could carry only half a dozen underwater missiles at a time, and they kept them for when the gun wouldn't do.

Lilla and Ernie's parting was probably not so different

to any of their other separations. A firm enveloping hug, broken off brusquely enough for Ernie to maintain his dignity in front of his fellow passengers. A final peck on the cheek. A promise to meet up again as soon as possible when the war was over, surely in no more than a few months' time. And Lilla, now thirty-three and with thirteen-year-old Arthur and eleven-year-old Alice standing on either side, would have waved him off.

Ernie's trip promised to be comfortable. The passenger list shows only 185 passengers on board, and there was a full crew of almost 300 to look after them. His fellow passengers included a few couples, several families both British and Indian, an infant or two unnamed on the register and a smattering of military men like himself. Among them was a colonel whom Ernie befriended, Lord Montagu of Beaulieu. Montagu was a motoring fanatic and in the late 1890s he had been one of the first people in Britain to own a motor car. On the *Persia* he was, amid some scandal, travelling with his mistress, the actress Eleanor Thornton, whose curvaceous figure was the model for the 'Spirit of Ecstasy', the six-inch silver figurehead that still adorns the bonnet of Rolls-Royce cars today. Montagu had been appointed inspector of all mechanical vehicles in India. Ernie, a logistics lieutenant colonel trained up in mechanical transportation, must have had a great deal to talk to him about.

By the time the *Persia* reached Marseilles, the passengers reckoned that they had passed the most dangerous part of their journey. The ship's captain was less convinced. He had been given detailed instructions as to the exact course he should take through the Mediterranean and how he should destroy the ship's documents were the worst to happen. With this in mind, he held the ship at Malta until precisely 10 p.m. on Tuesday 28 December so that its journey through the U-boat-infested corridor between Crete and North Africa would be made under the cover of night. The following day, before the ship reached Crete, there was a lifeboat drill. Comfortingly, with the memory of the *Titanic* still fresh in every sea-traveller's mind, the boats were only half full. That night, as the *Persia* crept past Crete, the crew were tense, jumping at every sound or flicker on the horizon. But, as dawn broke on the 30th, a wave of relief swept through the ship. The worst was over. They were now within twenty-four hours of the safety of Port Said, in Egypt.

Even in midwinter, the sun off the North African coast can be strong and the weather distinctly, almost claustrophobically, warm. By mid-morning the ship's main saloon was becoming stuffy. The passengers began to clamour for the portholes to be opened. Given the calm weather, in peacetime this would not have been a problem. In wartime, however, it was strictly forbidden as open portholes could rapidly sink a listing ship. As the temperature rose, the passengers' protests grew. Eventually, permission was given for the portholes to be opened.

What they didn't realize was that the *Persia* was being tracked by U-boat 38 of the Imperial German Navy, in the hands of the U-boat ace Max Valentiner. In just five days in August 1915, he had sunk thirty ships. Valentiner had two attributes that marked him out from other U-boat captains. One was the ability to sneak right up to a ship unseen. The other was enough ruthlessness to open fire on civilians, which he had recently done when the passengers on an Italian vessel had failed to follow his orders to disembark – the scandal of this event filling the newspapers as the *Persia* set sail.

According to his diary, Valentiner was not convinced that the *Persia* was a civilian ship. He wrote that he believed it was a troop transport – maybe he saw Ernie wandering the decks in his uniform. But I'm not sure that this mattered. A few weeks previously he had searched a British civilian ship and discovered sealed orders for all British ships to attack U-boats, and this, in his view, made all British ships fair game. And as the *Persia* had a gun on its deck, it would have been impossible for Valentiner to surface without imperilling his U-boat and crew.

Shortly before one, the luncheon gong on the *Persia* was rung and the passengers poured into the saloon. But as they lifted their knives and forks to their first course, Valentiner's U-boat, hovering under the waves just a few hundred yards from the *Persia*, let fire a precious torpedo.

At ten minutes past one Valentiner's torpedo exploded in the *Persia*'s hull. As the ship began to list, its engines continued to steam away, propelling it forward at some speed so that it took in more and more water as it went. Within three minutes, the main saloon was underwater and the sea came pounding in through the open port-holes. The ship's decks started to fracture and the stench of explosives began to rise up through the cracks. By now the tilt was making it impossible to lower the starboard lifeboats, and the passengers and crew who had managed to reach the deck flocked to the port side. The situation there was not much better. The few boats that were making it into the water were being smashed by the on-going speed of the ship. As the water gushed in, the *Persia* turned on its side. Those who could, clambered back across the ship's near-vertical deck and leaped from the rails as the ship went under. At 1.15 p.m., just five minutes after it had been hit, the *Persia*'s funnels disappeared beneath the waves.

Ernie made it off the ship into the water. He was lucky to do this. Most of the three hundred-odd lost, including seventeen of the nineteen children on board, were trapped below decks – many on their way back to their cabins to retrieve their life jackets after the drill the day before. The cheaper your cabin, the further you had to walk from the saloon. As the ship went down, it pulled many of those in the water into a whirlpool of wreckage that knocked them about. Ernie went under and then, pulled up by his life jacket, rose to the surface as the sea cleared. Montagu told Lilla that he had last seen him in the water after the ship sank, 'looking dazed and confused as we all were but otherwise all right'. At that stage, Ernie still had a life jacket on. Montagu managed to reach one of the five lifeboats that picked up more than 150 survivors. Ernie somehow did not, despite the broad sweep for survivors made by the lifeboats. Nor, as it happens, did Eleanor Thornton. 'You will easily understand how much I sympathise,' wrote Montagu to Lilla.

Years later, my aunt Jane, Ernie's granddaughter, was accosted at a party by a lady who swore that Ernie had saved her mother's life by handing her his life jacket. He had claimed to be a strong enough swimmer to cope.

Poor Ernie. It must have been very cold in that water. And he hated the sea.

Lilla was doing her hair, her always perfect hair, when she heard that the *Persia* had gone down. The announcement made on New Year's Day by P & O, whose ship it was, simply stated, 'Most of the passengers and crew lost. Four boats got clear.'

I imagine her, motionless with shock, gazing into her dressing-table mirror, its wings showing her cheeks whitening almost to the colour of the tiny diamonds in her ears as she thought of Ernie floating cold and lifeless beneath the sea.

It was two days before the first list of survivors emerged. The story was splashed over the front of *The Times* on the morning of Monday, 3 January 1916. It named those who had already been taken off the lifeboats. Lilla must have read and reread the list several times. Ernie's name wasn't on it.

Lilla didn't know whether her husband was dead, or whether he was still paddling some lifeboat to shore. Another boat carrying survivors did make it to shore a few days later. But Ernie wasn't on board that either. As the weeks passed and no more boats appeared, Lilla must have felt suspended between marriage and widowhood. Between Ernie and an empty space. Between a life in India and another future. Wondering what life would hold for her now.

The telegram came on 24 January. The postmaster's pencilled scrawl covered two pages: 'The King and Queen deeply regret the loss you and the army have sustained by the death of your husband in the service of his country their Majesties truly sympathise with you in your sorrow Keeper of the Privy Purse.'

Ernie's family were, naturally, extremely sad to lose him. Some time afterwards, his sister Laura wrote in a family history of the 'very bitter irony of fate that he should be drowned' after having given up being a sailor years earlier. Papa had died in 1911, but Mama – who survived until she failed to recover from a gallstone operation in 1919 – posted a movingly simple tribute in the memorials column of the papers: 'In loving memory of my darling son, Lieut. Col. Ernest Russell Howell, I.A., lost in the S.S. *Persia*, off Crete, Dec. 30th, 1915.'

But Lilla's feelings were not so clear cut. And as the words on the telegram sank in, she must have felt a strange combination of relief and despair. It had been decided. Officialdom, the powers that be, had drawn a line through her husband's name. She should think him gone.

Yet it must have been hard to feel certain. There was no eye-witness account of his head sinking beneath the waves, no body to bury, no guarantee that somewhere, somehow, Ernie hadn't clambered ashore and was living, breathing, still. All Lilla had was a note telling her that somebody thought, to the best of their knowledge, that Ernie was sleeping somewhere beneath the cold waves of the sea.

Nor would she have felt certain that she wanted to cry.

PART II

Peace

USEFUL ICE CREAM HINTS

If the ice cream is required quickly a
small amount of gelatine helps the
mixture to freeze more smoothly. The
cream should be beaten until quite
stiff before being added.

The mixtures that ices are made of
vary greatly in richness. They may be
made of cornflour or custard powder,
sweetened & flavoured to taste, or egg
custard & fruit puree. To make the
foundation ice cream, beat the eggs &
sugar together & pour on the warm milk.
When cold, add the cream. Ice cream can
be served in glasses with a sauce or
fruit. It can also be served with
sponge cake, the middle taken out &
replaced with ice cream. A handle made
of sponge can be placed on top thus
forming a basket.

9

AN ALMOST HUSBAND

England, 1916

LILLA PLAYED AT BEING Ernie's widow just as she had played at being his wife. As the war ground its way through 1916 and 1917, guzzling hundreds of thousands of fresh young lives in a great sausage machine of battles with names like the Somme, Verdun and Passchendaele, mourning became a way of life in Britain. Turning the dead into heroes helped to dignify the slaughter.

Lilla flung herself into the national mood. 'She went around weeping,' and set about gathering mementoes of Ernie's triumphs. Letters of praise from his superiors. Photographs of him looking stern in his new lieutenant colonel's uniform. Photographs of the grander houses they had lived in. Newspaper clippings of his mini-obituary and descriptions of him as a 'well-known passenger' on the ill-fated *Persia*. Even his certificate of Mechanical Transport training. She bought a small black album and, on page after page, pasted them in.

Her son, Arthur, copied her. In between endless photographs of the old stone buildings and playing fields of his boarding school – in his own black album – are dozens of copies of a stern portrait of his father in uniform. It was as though he didn't know how else to mark or feel his death. Didn't have anything else to remember him by. He'd barely seen him since he was six.

And, until I started to write this book, those formal photographs were almost all I knew of Ernie, too. There was one hanging in the drawing room in one of the houses Lilla lived in when I was young. I think it must have been the same photograph I later found my father hanging on the wall in our house the day after Lilla's funeral. The gruff-looking moustached head and shoulders staring out from the wall made the stories of his filthy temper feel very real. Lilla used to point to it and say, 'That was my h-h-husband. He died in the First World War.' I remember gazing at it and struggling to reconcile this terrifying image from a time that seemed as far back as the Pyramids with the vibrant and delicate creature shimmering in black beside me.

She had worn black ever since, she said. After Ernie's death she had even taken an emerald-and-diamond brooch that he had given her to a jeweller, who ripped out the coloured stones. I can remember her still wearing it sixty years later. Its empty settings gaped as though something very precious had been lost. Now I realize that these extravagant gestures were designed to hide her lack of real grief.

And here Lilla's story parts company with the Howells'. She strikes out on her own, still quite young at thirty-three and now free and single. She kept in touch with Ernie's siblings – after all, they were her children's family too. She even stayed with one or two of them from time to time. However, from now on, Laura, Barbie, Evelyn, Ada Henniker and the less loquacious Auberon fade into the background. An old family tree I was sent shows me that they all had children who married – even Ada Henniker who, ignoring her doctor's orders, went on

Arthur in his scholar's gown, and his desk at Winchester.

to have two more children after Jack died. And they must have gone on to have grandchildren and great-grandchildren too, creating a vast web of Howell cousins.

But I can think of only one or two whom I have ever met.

Lilla's official grief lasted just three years. She had, after all, been a little younger than I am, as I write this, when Ernie died. And I think that I'm just starting out on life. So I suppose it would be strange to expect Lilla to shut up shop romantically and decide, well, that was it, she'd had a husband, a few adventures and a couple of children – now it was time to sit back and watch them grow up. Still, that was exactly what many young women did in those years after the First World War. Some hadn't even married. Lost their boyfriends, their fiancés, at the bottom of some sodden trench. Their true love had gone, and there was not much hope of finding a replacement. A whole generation of British women found themselves growing up with no prospect of marriage – the only career that they had been brought up to follow. But, having worked during the war, many had acquired a taste for independence. And they would gradually meta-morphose into the first great wave of women teachers and doctors, who married a career instead of a man.

Not so with Lilla. As the war ended and a victorious but exhausted Britain began to pick itself up again, Lilla found that being a widow was rapidly losing its glamour. Ernie had left her very little money and the war had brought the family business in China more or less to a halt. That left Lilla, as is still recounted, having to lean her bosom over Arthur's headmaster's desk and whisper that, now she was a poor widow, she had to find a scholarship for her son. And thus Arthur, never destined for a university career, found himself a long-gowned scholar at Winchester College. I think Ada must have

Toby, Ada and Alan outside Buckingham Palace.

paid Alice's school fees, leaving Lilla resentful of her dependence upon her sister. The imbalance between them that, for the first time, had shifted in Lilla's favour in India seemed to be swinging back into the old pattern. Ada now had a son – Alan had survived and flourished – and a daughter, Betty, too. And an adoring husband, whom she was still in love with. And plenty of money. Even more grating, I'm sure, was Toby's continued success. The year after Ernie died, Toby was awarded a CMG – made a Companion of the Order of St Michael and St George – for distinguished public service. Ada had gone with him to Buckingham Palace to receive it. Ada had met King George and Queen Mary. Lilla would have been pleased for Ada but so jealous that she could barely speak about it. It was becoming clear that she needed a husband, too. Preferably a successful one. However, in an almost bachelorless country the odds were not good. Lilla, however, was now not a woman to be deterred by odds.

Hidden at the back of Lilla's black memorial album to Ernie are photographs of another man. Another lieutenant colonel. His name was Malcolm Rattray. From his picture he looks a taller, thinner version of Ernie. Upright, uniformed, terribly Britishly proper, with a neatly divided moustache, its ends waxed into upturned points, giving him a slightly surprised expression. Malcolm was a surgeon in the Royal Army Medical Corps. And a highly decorated soldier – a bearer of the Distinguished Service Order.

Ugly gossip claims that Lilla chased Malcolm all over the place. Well, maybe she had to do the running. Malcolm was hardly a ladies' man. He'd reached fifty without a wife in sight. What a challenge for the feisty Lilla. I can imagine her fussing around him as she'd fussed around Ernie. Tempting him with rich gravies that disguised the stringiness of post-war meat. Making up for the lack of butter and cream with liberal splashes of brandy, rum and claret that warmed his stomach. Concocting sweet puddings from spoonfuls of jam and cupfuls of flour. Plying him with more and more food magicked out of a larder gaping empty like the rest of Britain's kitchens. His stomach shrunk by the wartime shortage of food, Malcolm must have eaten until he was ready to explode, and had little choice but to sink into one of the high-armed chairs dotted around Lilla's drawing room and drift off into a deep, hypnotic sleep.

Still, it was not easy to prise him out of his bachelordom. Malcolm did not appear to be driven by the same impetuousness that had rushed Ernie to propose. And they were older. Lilla was a widow, which meant that they could spend time together, walking through London's parks, without too many eyebrows being raised. Lilla cooked and cosseted, walked and waited. Eventually, in the autumn of 1919, Malcolm was posted out to Basra, Mesopotamia, which was still held by the British in order to protect their oil interests and where they were trying out a new military tactic of using aircraft to bomb the local tribes into submission. This enabled them to reach targets far inland without having to send in the army. But by then Malcolm was hooked. Clearly unable to tear himself away from the comforts of Lilla, he proposed.

However, Lilla no longer needed a husband quite so badly. As the months had passed, business in China had begun to pick up and Lilla's brothers Vivvy and Reggie were again in a position to send her an allowance. She could now afford to rent her own home, pay her daughter's school fees and live not extravagantly, but resonably well. Still, she had set out to marry Malcolm, and marry him she would.

And she was more than a little hooked too. 'It was a

love match,' Lilla's daughter Alice told her own children. And it probably was. Malcolm looks like the sort of man who had eyes that sparkled with surprised gratitude each time Lilla did even the tiniest thing for him – cooked for him, accompanied him on some trip, straightened the buckle on his army belt. Nobody, he must have blurted out in clipped tones, had ever looked after him like that before. His profuse thanks would have sent a warm glow pumping round Lilla's veins. Ernie had eventually told her she was wonderful, but still had somehow taken her help for granted. Malcolm, on the other hand, must have made her feel like a luxury, gazing at her like a large faithful dog, utterly dependent, and leaving Lilla firmly in charge.

She accepted his proposal, packed up her house and, leaving Arthur and Alice at their boarding schools in England, followed Malcolm out to Basra to marry there. I can see her skipping up the gangplank of her boat like a teenager, blissfully unaware of what was about to happen.

It would be hard to describe Basra in 1919 as a romantic place. It sits at the top of the Persian Gulf, in the same fetid marshlands in which Ernie's war expedition had floundered. The photographs in the back of Lilla's little black album show a port fringed with palms, giving it a deceptively escapist air. Behind them, however, a city of mud appeared to have oozed up from the hot, wet flat-lands, ready to sink back into oblivion at a moment's notice. Even the British jetty had a hopelessly ram-shackle, temporary look to it, a mess of criss-crossed timbers bound together under a crumbling roof. In every direction the horizon was depressingly flat, the un-cannily straight line of the sky pressing down on the mud, as if squeezing the life out of anything trying to breathe.

Lilla arrived on about 17 November 1919, probably on a ship called the *Varsova*. In the album there is a photograph of it pulling out of the port, taken from the top of a building nearby. Either Malcolm or Lilla or maybe, giggling like a pair of somewhat overgrown schoolchildren, both of them must have clambered on to the roof to take it. The earliest date for the wedding would have been two weeks away, to give time for the banns to be read. It would hardly be a white wedding as Lilla already had two almost grown-up children. But Lilla would still have stitched some Chefoo lace on to her hat and suit, begun to search out flowers from the town, started to prepare Malcolm's army quarters for their life together after the wedding.

Only the wedding never happened. Ten days after Lilla's arrival in Basra, Malcolm was dead.

I can't tell you how he died. Records from that time are thin on the ground. There is no consular register for deaths before 1920. Nor does Malcolm's name appear in the hospital death lists. He must have died suddenly, before he could be moved into a cast-iron hospital bed. I rather wonder whether, having been plied with so much rich food by Lilla, his heart simply packed up.

Lilla must have reeled with shock, the fetid Basran air sticking in her throat. The picture she had dreamed up of her life with Malcolm – a soft fusion of grand garden parties and tender moments – crumbled in front of her eyes. He'd been snatched from her, and in the outrage that real grief brings Lilla must have shaken with anger against her invisible enemy. She was only thirty-seven, and both a husband and a fiancé had died on her, abandoned her. And probably still burning with a chemical combination of shock, anger and grief, a few days later she found herself following a funeral

RATTRAY.—On the 27th Nov., at Basrah, Mesopotamia, Lt.-Colonel Malcolm MacGregor Rattray, D.S.O., R.A.M.C., second son of the late Andrew and Susan Rattray, of Portobello, Midlothian, aged 50.

cavalcade instead of stepping up an aisle clutching a bouquet.

Malcolm's coffin perched on the braided shoulders of four colonels. A three-hundred-strong guard of honour – far larger than the one that would have welcomed her and Malcolm as they left the church after their wedding – walked ahead. It was a formidable procession. Perhaps the grandest moment of Lilla's life. And the most tragic. When they reached the dusty cemetery, Lilla would have seen that the crosses marking the rows of dead from the war were already beginning to weather. Malcolm was placed in the next empty space, a mound of crumbling earth piled on top of him. A white marker was plunged into the earth at his feet. Peering at the picture of it in the back of Lilla's black album, I can just make out the number 17F scrawled at the top.

And that was all that was left of the man whom Lilla had so wanted to be her husband.

Lilla must have been bundled on to a boat back to England shortly afterwards. I imagine her wandering the decks, numb with grief, old rancid-tasting memories bubbling back, remembering how she had bounced up and down on that bed, the pain, the miscarriage, and that searingly guilty feeling of relief as she had headed out to Kashmir. Was that it? Had she brought all this on herself? No no no, she must have wanted to scream. Life wasn't like that. You couldn't just give up and say nothing would ever work. You had to go on. Go on she would.

But the pain from Malcolm's death was far from over.

Back in England, Lilla would have gone straight to her mother's house in Crystal Palace. And it was there that she must have learned that Malcolm – who had already changed his will in her favour before leaving for Basra –

had left her the substantial sum of ten thousand pounds. Today this would be worth two hundred thousand pounds. But it would have felt like a lot more than that back then.

Lilla wasn't poor, but this would certainly make life easier. And she wouldn't have to depend on her brothers quite so much. It must have made her feel that Malcolm hadn't been snatched from her quite so abruptly. That, in a way, she had managed to marry him first.

Then, just as she was coming back to earth, steadying her feet, planning how she'd live alone, Malcolm's family contested the will. It was all, they claimed, a mistake. There was no way that he could really have intended to leave his money to this woman he hadn't married. She was just some upstart from China who had clearly been after Malcolm's money, and should be stopped.

The rejection, I'm told, cut through Lilla like a knife. She must have felt herself shrinking back to the nervous nineteen-year-old cowering upstairs in her in-laws' house in Kensington Gardens Square. She hadn't been good enough for the Howells. Now she wasn't good enough for the Rattrays. But Lilla had come a long way since she had married Ernie and however much it hurt she wasn't going to let herself be made to feel small again. Summoning every ounce of inner strength that she could find, she shot back at the Rattrays: 'Take the money if you want it. It's not how *I* want to remember him.' Refusing to discuss the matter further, she signed the money over. And, as if running from her emotions, she took to the road.

It wasn't easy to track Lilla through the next decade. There were no momentous events, no more collections of letters. Just an endless pitter-patter of anecdotes and childhood sightings by her nephews and nieces who are still alive today. One remembered Lilla telling her off for being rude to her governess in Shanghai. Another remembered Lilla bringing her daughter Alice to stay in Tientsin, the same summer that a typhoon had nearly swept them all away on the beach in the seaside resort of Peitaiho. Then there were recollections of Lilla coming to the rescue when her younger sister Edith started to go blind. Lilla escorted Edith and her two children back to England – via North America. There was Alice's wedding in England in 1925 – to a man called Havilland de Sausmarez who had nine sisters, not a single one of whom ever married amid the dearth of bachelors after the First World War. Lilla must have been in Britain then. And there are photographs: Lilla in India, Lilla in France, Lilla in England.

Lilla spent these years, like the world around her, in a frenzy of perpetual motion. The West was bouncing back from the horrors of the First World War and the Twenties were beginning to roar, and Lilla roared with them. Her feet barely touched the ground. Perhaps she was trying to keep up with Ada – the pictures I have often show Lilla standing beside her twin – as Toby was posted to Malta, then Constantinople, in increasingly grand naval roles. And when Toby wasn't working, he took Ada to Biarritz, where they rented a house, and entertained and gambled and danced in considerable style.

Or perhaps Lilla was trying to move so fast that she couldn't be compared to her twin. So fast that nobody, not even she, had a chance to notice she had neither a home nor a husband. At times it seems as though she was even trying to outpace time itself. Time that was nudging her past forty towards fifty. Time that would – if she let it – make her feel old when, as the post-war world boomed and charlestoned its way through the Twenties, Lilla's photographs show a woman who felt she still had a lot of life to live. She had abandoned her widow's weeds and rib-clenching corsets for the new and

Lilla in the 1920s.

liberating fashions of long cardigans, wraparound dresses and knee-length skirts that for the first time showed off those amazing legs. Still in black, with a few splashes of white à la Coco Chanel, she posed coyly, wearing long strands of pearls waiting to be twisted in her fingers. She had 'men around her like butterflies', her nephews and nieces said. And in every city, treaty port or cantonment, she found a new admirer, a lonely old widower or bachelor drifting through the expatriate routine. She promised to write, and did. When she wasn't on the move, she was at a writing desk dashing off girlish letters to dozens of men all over the world. 'My letters keep them alive,' she used to whisper.

When Ernie's youngest brother Evelyn became Resident in Kashmir and made Arthur his aide-de-camp, Lilla followed. Instead of a fishing hut in Bandipur, this time she stayed in the rambling mock-Tudor Residency in Srinagar surrounded by lawns just too bright and vegetation far too lush to carry off the intended illusion of living in England. They went upcountry to the Kashmir Lilla remembered. They picnicked by lakes and on hills. Lilla waved Evelyn and Arthur off over the same craggy white mountain passes that Ernie had crossed. When they had disappeared from sight, her mind must have wandered back to her time there with Ernie. To that time when she had an adoring, if flawed, husband, and a perfect little fishing hut of a home.

In 1927, Toby was posted to China as principal sea transport officer of a twenty-thousand-strong naval-based Shanghai Defence Force. The failure of the Boxer Uprising of 1900 had set in motion a great struggle of ideas among the Chinese of how best to turn their country into a modern nation state. A series of anti-imperial uprisings had culminated in the 1911 overthrow of the five-year-old Puyi, China's 'last emperor', and the trademark red walls of the imperial palace – the Forbidden City – were symbolically repainted a violent blue.

The following year, a thoughtful-looking young Western-trained doctor called Sun Yat-sen, who had masterminded most of these anti-imperial uprisings from abroad, declared himself the first, and provisional, president of the Republic of China, and set about organizing elections. But within a few months, his National People's Party, the Kuomintang, had been over-thrown by the head of China's army, General Yuan Shih-k'ai. Unlike Sun Yat-sen, who came from a poor family and had been educated in mission schools, the pugnacious-faced Yuan came from a long line of senior government officials. At the age of twenty-one he had followed the practice of sidestepping the taxing traditional examinations to become an official by buying himself a position.

Yuan's visions for China included developing an in-dependent judiciary as the best means of bringing an end to the deeply irritating extraterritoriality of foreigners, and economic reforms such as improving agricultural yields and low-interest loans – all under his own dictatorial rule. But within three years he had died of kidney failure and China fell under the rule of an ever-changing sequence of local warlords – many of them Yuan's former henchmen – who had little desire either to reunify or to modernize the country.

The effect of all this on the treaty-port community had been minimal. Bearing in mind the anti-missionary campaign of the Boxer Uprising, as a precaution, missionaries in the more distant outposts were called back to base during the 1911 revolution. But after that, as Frances Wood puts it, 'the uncertainties of warlord rule were, for foreign residents, not very different from previous uncertainties'. And most treaty-porters bothered about only their local warlords.

But by the 1920s, things had changed. In 1919 it was revealed that plans for the Versailles peace treaty included handing over China's Shantung province to Japan. And on 4 May of that year, the Chinese mounted widespread demonstrations against the proposal. They felt particularly aggrieved as they had sent tens of thousands of men to dig trenches on the Western Front, and this term of the treaty seemed an exceptionally poor way for the Allies to show their gratitude. Perhaps because Japan had been occupying the former German concessions in the area since the outbreak of the war, the Allies went ahead with the award, and thus earned the enmity of the Chinese. Then, at the Washington Conference of 1921–2, perhaps equally unwisely, the Allies proceeded to alienate Japan by taking Shantung back. If they had deliberately tried to incite war between the two countries, they couldn't have done it any better.

Sun Yat-sen had then started to reconstruct his dream for a unified, modern China, setting up a Kuomintang, or Nationalist, government in Canton, in the south of the country. This government had the support of the newly formed Communist Party and, perhaps remembering all too clearly how his previous attempt at holding power had ended, this time it exercised military rule. The force backing it was known as the National Revolutionary Army, whose leader was an ambitious man called Chiang Kai-shek, who, like Yuan, had been born into a wealthy family. Instead of purchasing an official title, at the age of twenty-one Chiang had gone to a military academy in Japan. A photograph of him in military uniform, taken as he rose to power in his mid-thirties, shows him long and lean, with the steady gaze of a man utterly confident of his own ability.

Sun Yat-sen didn't live to see his dream realized. In late 1924 he fell ill and the following March he died of liver cancer. Just two months later, a series of Chinese worker protests and strikes against their foreign employers provided the encouragement the Nationalists needed. And in 1926 the new leader of the Nationalist Party – perhaps unsurprisingly its military commander, Chiang Kai-shek – started to lead his troops out of southern Canton in a move to unify China known as the Northern Expedition.

This time, the treaty-port residents were worried. They fled as Nationalist troops approached, not from fear of any direct attack upon themselves, but because they had no desire to be caught in the crossfire between the Nationalists and local warlords. And in late March 1927, as the Nationalists neared the city, the treaty-port powers amassed the Shanghai Defence Force. With it came Toby Elderton.

As Toby was saluted into Shanghai harbour on the prow of a battleship, Ada and her two children, Alan and Betty, went to join him. Lilla raced to catch up. She wasn't going to let Ada go back to China without her. Not when she was travelling in such glory, with Toby at her side. By the time Ada and Toby arrived in Chefoo for a visit, Ada's photographs show Lilla already there and with a brand new man on her arm. She'd met him through her elder brother Vivvy, and his name was Ernest Casey. He was one of the richest businessmen living in Chefoo and 'a sweet old thing'. He was unmarried, had no children and no relatives to look down on Lilla. In any case, he was far from grand. He wasn't even second- or third-generation treaty port. He'd simply pitched up out of nowhere and made his fortune himself. Casey – everyone called him that – was smitten. Lilla dragged him around with Ada and Toby, naughtily flirting with both men as if to show that she could keep up with Ada and have a husband, even Ada's husband, too. Toby took the bait and put an arm round each twin and called them 'my

Toby and his 'wives', Chefoo, 1928. Lilla is on the left.

The waterfront, Shanghai.

wives', raising a few eyebrows. Ada stood there, buttoned up in a double-breasted jacket resembling an ill-fitting uniform, looking uncomfortable with her twin's more open sexuality.

Casey asked Lilla to marry him. Lilla said maybe. And added him to her list of penfriends as she turned on her heels and left.

By the end of the Twenties, the place to go was France. The north-east of the country was still hopelessly trench-scarred, but although the post-war economic boom was running out of steam and the American stock market on Wall Street was about to crash, on the Riviera, it was said, the ladies were painting their toenails red. Ada and Toby announced that they were taking their two happy, healthy, nearly grown-up children, Alan and Betty, on a driving tour of the country. Lilla packed Arthur into an equally grand car and persuaded her eldest brother Vivvy and his wife Mabel to match Ada's party of four. Vivvy and Mabel were over from China, 'spending money like water', and throwing parties at the Ritz. The two groups met in Antibes, the twins, now forty-seven, wearing identical hats, driving identically shiny cars, each with three people in tow. Ada was keen to be off with her family. Lilla pretended to be too occupied with her party to care. When they returned, she encouraged Arthur to paste together a commemorative album of their trip, to show how grand it had been.

Then Lilla stumbled again. Arthur had followed his father into the army, where he was employed to hunt three days a week, compete in horse trials on another and attend grand parties at the weekends. At one of these he fell for a girl dubbed 'The Princess of the City' by the gossip columns, the scion of a grand industrial family who accompanied her father around town. Her name was Beryl Bowater. She was a dashing huntswoman and lived with her parents and a multitude of servants in a grand house in Chester Square, at the heart of Belgravia, still London's most expensive residential address. Arthur was a handsome man, with regular features, sandy hair and a twinkle in his bright blue eyes. He rode like a centaur and had even won an army boxing championship. And Beryl fell for him too.

Although encouraged by Beryl, Arthur's first attempt to raise the question of marriage with her father, Sir Frank, was met with ridicule. 'You couldn't afford to keep her in silk stockings,' he bellowed, kicking him out of the house.

Indeed he couldn't. Compared to the Bowaters, Arthur was penniless.

Beryl pleaded with Arthur to try again. She pleaded with her father. How could he deny his darling daughter what she wanted?

The wedding was in London, in April 1931, in the grand church of St Margaret's, Westminster, which nestles between Westminster Abbey and the Houses of Parliament. It's a strange place to marry as the crowds of tourists outside assume that they are watching some kind of royal wedding – some of the royal family do marry there – and line up along the paths to cheer the guests and the quaking bride. I remember my heart pounding as I cleared the twenty-yard stretch between bridal car and church door myself another April, almost seventy years later. I can see from my grandparents' wedding photographs that the crowds were just as thick back then. Perhaps fewer tourists in those days than locals up to see the sights. But I doubt that Beryl was as overawed as I was. The great and the good were there for her wedding. And that's pretty much what she would have wanted.

As Lilla entered the church through the onlookers outside and saw the pews stacked with grandees she was

Vivvy, Lilla and Mabel on the road to Paris.

Ada (left) and Lilla in Antibes, 1929.

bursting with pride. But when she was taken to her seat she found herself, as she still used to say years later, 'stuck behind a pillar'. As soon as she and Sir Frank finished their procession out of the church, he slipped away. And worse was to come. The reception was at Claridge's – still just about London's smartest hotel. When Lilla tried to join the traditional receiving line of the bride and groom and their parents, all welcoming the guests, she was pushed away. The Bowaters turned their backs. They were not, even if she was the groom's mother, going to introduce her to any of their friends. For years afterwards, Lilla's daughter Alice and her husband, Havilland de Sausmarez, fumed, their daughter tells me, about how badly Lilla was treated that day, at her own son's wedding. And Lilla herself swore that she'd heard the Bowaters mutter 'that yellow woman' under their breath.

It must have brought back everything Lilla thought she had overcome. It wasn't just the Howells and the Rattrays, now it was the Bowaters too who regarded her as a second-class citizen. Lilla was still just a foreigner from China, the offspring of one of the thousands of British families who had gone to better themselves abroad. A colonial whom people like the Bowaters – who had been wealthy enough to remain in Britain – didn't want to see coming back.

Lilla turned to the trick that had worked before and took off. She ran. Tried to outpace the humiliation by rushing from visit to visit with her relatives and acquaintances around the globe. But as soon as she had picked up enough speed to start to forget, she was brought to a shuddering halt.

Throughout the Twenties, the Eckfords had been spending money almost as fast as they made it. Edith and

Dorothy – as Andrew's only real children – owned the firm. Vivvy and Reggie ran it for them on fat salaries. Toby could look after Ada. The brothers passed money on to Lilla and their mother, Alice. Alice was still living in the house in Crystal Palace with two servants, a driver and a shopping habit of buying a dozen of everything she liked.

But as business was flourishing, it didn't seem to matter too much what anyone spent. The political situation in China was as stable as it had been at any time in the twentieth century, which was not very. Chiang Kaishek's Northern Expedition had been more or less successful – he had managed to keep an army together over thousands of miles, and for many months. But almost as soon as his Nationalist troops had taken Tientsin and Peking in late 1928, things began to grow rocky. Various Nationalist factions had split away. Chiang's somewhat shaky alliance with the Communists had fallen apart. The latter were now regrouping in opposition to him. Meanwhile the warlords whom Chiang had brought under control on his way north kept changing alliances.

Nonetheless, there was still enough of a Nationalist government to begin discussing changes to the treaty-port system and the abolition of the Chinese bugbear of foreigners' extraterritoriality. But, in 1931, these discussions were suddenly interrupted when Japan, still aggrieved by the decision of the Washington Conference of 1921–2 to remove Shantung from its control, invaded Manchuria.

None of the other foreign powers made a fuss about this move by Japan. And what a mistake that would turn out to be. Perhaps, at the time, they were so grateful that the Nationalist government's efforts had been diverted away from the treaty ports that they decided, with shortsighted self-interest, to avert their eyes. And, of course, the Westerners in the treaty ports were on very friendly terms with the Japanese in China. They were, to some extent, their colleagues. I have a photograph, taken around this time, of Vivvy and a dozen other Chefoo businessmen at the end of what had clearly been a long evening with their Japanese hosts. Half-empty plates, bottles and cushions are strewn over the floor and low tables. The guests are all men. One of four Japanese women in make-up and kimonos – perhaps they are geisha? – is laughing as she refills Vivvy's glass to the brim. The Westerners appear slightly the worse for wear, Vivvy perhaps most of all. The Japanese are strikingly composed.

A few months after they had invaded Manchuria, the Japanese explained politely to the British and American press in Shanghai, over caviar and champagne, that they needed to defend Japanese civilians in the city's Chinese residential district of Chaipei. That very night, Japanese troops mounted machine guns on their motorbikes to spray the streets with bullets. And the Westerners – some dressed in evening clothes – quite literally stood by and watched. The next day, the Japanese bombed the area. Over the following couple of months, several thousand Chinese civilians were killed.

However, after that relations between the Chinese and Japanese seemed to calm down. For a while the Chinese boycotted Japanese goods, but that came to an end and trade picked up – without any resumption of talks over extraterritoriality.

Cornabé Eckford was only one tenth the size of vast houses such as Jardine's and Swire's that together dominated the China trade. Even so, as a shipping agent for Jardine's, Asiatic Petroleum – now known as Shell – and P & O, the firm was a substantial concern. Cornabé Eckford itself shipped frozen eggs to America in brand new refrigerated ships and exported every type of straw

*The Japanese entertain the Westerners, Chefoo,
mid-1930s. Vivvy is in the front, second from the left.*

braid under the sun. The braid was woven by peasant families in the Chinese countryside and sent to the nearest Cornabé Eckford office. Vivvy and Reggie used special measuring devices to determine its grade – ladies' hats, straw boaters or rope – and had neat rolls of it packed into wooden crates to be sent off to milliners, gentlemen's outfitters and shipyards around the world.

Cornabé Eckford made hairnets, too. The local Chinese grew their long plaits to cut off and sell. And one hundred more of them sat in a factory in Chefoo sterilizing the hair and weaving it into hairnets to ship to New York.

The most glamorous trade was silk. Rolls of unbleached silk already woven into a soft fabric known as pongee were hurried across the Pacific to Vancouver on three-funnelled Empress boats that could shave a couple of days off any other crossing – vital to keeping down the high insurance on silk shipments. The silk rolls were then bundled on to long, slinking freight trains. These sped across North America with such urgency that passenger services were held up to let them pass in order to meet the tight price deadlines set by the futures markets in New York and Montreal.

The least glamorous trade for the Eckfords, as it would turn out, was peanuts.

What happened certainly wasn't Reggie's fault. Reggie had spent the past thirty years moving around China expanding the firm. By the 1930s he had settled in Tsingtao, a German treaty port a couple of hours' drive across the Shantung peninsula from Chefoo and still famous today for its beer. Over the years, Tsingtao had been slowly expanding to overtake Chefoo in both size and trade. Reggie ran what was by then the largest Cornabé Eckford office and had become British vice-consul in the port.

It was Vivvy, as the elder brother, who ran the old head office in Chefoo. Or rather he didn't. He spent most of his time painting and drawing, constructing backdrops for the regular amateur theatricals in the Chefoo Club. He was a keen golfer, and built Chefoo's first and only golf course – playable only at low tide. He was head of the local freemasons. Larger than life in both character and physique, he was a bon viveur and a sportsman. He was everything that didn't require him to while away the hours behind a desk in the Cornabé Eckford offices.

Nonetheless, the business seemed to be running itself quite happily. Whenever there was a particularly large shipment that meant the firm had to borrow the money to buy the cargo, somebody nipped down to the Hong Kong and Shanghai Bank and brought Vivvy the chit to sign. The money would be handed over to the firm's comprador, the Chinese buyer who went inland to find the goods. He then sent them to the Cornabé Eckford warehouses in the new port of Weihaiwei, an hour down the road from Chefoo. On an appointed day, a ship came and picked up the cargo. In due course Cornabé Eckford was paid, and the firm pocketed the profit over and above the bank's advance.

When a large order for peanuts came through, Vivvy thought nothing of it. He signed the chit, gave the money to the comprador and went back to the golf course. But when the ship arrived at the warehouse to pick up the cargo, the loaders pulled back the tarpaulin – imaginatively strewn with a few peanuts – to find nothing underneath. And the comprador had vanished.

The scandal rocked the treaty ports. The Eckfords' betrayal by their comprador cut right to the heart of the Westerners' existence in China, exposing just how precarious it was. If the traders couldn't rely on their compradors, their key employees, the most trusted of the Chinese that they dealt with, then whom could they rely on? Who would turn on them next? The news must have sent shivers down the spines of those whose businesses depended on their compradors – the high walls around the foreign concessions in the treaty ports beginning to feel paper thin.

For the Eckfords, however, the consequences weren't simply unnerving, they were disastrous.

The Hong Kong and Shanghai Bank called in the loan. The firm couldn't meet it. Vivvy couldn't meet it. Nor could Reggie. Nor could anyone. The firm's and the Eckfords' own assets were frozen. Reggie's attempts to wire his children's school fees to England were stopped midway. His children were shipped back to China with their grandmother, Alice, whose house in Crystal Palace was sold to meet part of the debt. 'In any case,' says one of Reggie's daughters philosophically, 'we were all called Chinks at school.' Reggie and Vivvy were turfed out of their grand houses in Tsingtao and Chefoo and their possessions auctioned. For years afterwards, the family would go out to dinner to find their old ornaments on other people's mantelpieces.

The bank's decision was regarded as financially harsh but justifiable, given the way in which Vivvy had been failing to run the Chefoo office. It was unforgivable, I'm told, that nobody, neither Vivvy nor either of his two sons who worked for him, Erroll and Rae, had been to the warehouse to check on the cargo. Still, Vivvy went to the British consulate to beg for help. The consul did what he could. Another Chefoo trading firm, McMullan & Co., agreed to take on the bankrupt rump of Cornabé Eckford 'on very generous terms'. There were jobs for Vivvy, Reggie and as many of their sons as wanted them. But there wasn't any more money for Lilla.

Ernie had left her barely enough to live on. Both Arthur and Alice were struggling with young families. Alice's husband had hardly a bean. Sir Frank Bowater was pleading poverty and Lilla saw that Beryl and Arthur needed more help than he was providing. She knew what she had to do. Ernest Casey's offer of marriage – kept fresh by Lilla's I'm sure gently teasing correspondence – was still on the table. He even promised to leave everything to Arthur and Alice. Right now, that seemed very important.

Lilla followed the rest of her family back to China.

10
GOING HOME

Victoria station, London, autumn 1934

LILLA WENT BACK to China 'via Siberia', as she put it, in October 1934. The Trans-Siberian Express was a tough way to travel but far quicker than the boat. Lilla still hated to waste time and it meant she could be in Chefoo in thirteen days instead of seven weeks. Concertinaing the distance between China and her children and grandchildren in England in this way made it feel less of a wrench to leave them behind.

At Victoria station she met up with her nephew Rugs, one of Reggie's sons. At just seventeen Rugs was being prematurely parachuted out of the protection of an English boarding school and into a job in China with McMullan & Co. Lilla had offered to escort him out. On this trip in particular, she must have welcomed the company. She scooped him up and bundled him on board the heaving steaming train to Europe. He still remembers the journey well, and this is what he told me.

It took two days to reach Berlin, hauling on and off a cross-channel ferry, the rails clattering through the night. Hitler had become Chancellor of Germany the year before. A few months later he had managed to seize absolute power in a country hungry for self-respect. Germany had been politically and militarily humiliated by the terms of the Treaty of Versailles, which fear of starvation by the victorious Allies' continuing blockade had forced it to sign. The treaty had required Germany to give up its navy, its air force, almost all of its army and its precious territories in Silesia, West Prussia, Alsace and Lorraine. The country had then been devastated first by runaway inflation in the early 1920s and then, barely a decade later, by the worldwide economic depression that followed the Wall Street Crash. This had left Germany's population hungry and unemployed. And, amid a general fear of the revolutionary Communist movements growing in Europe, Hitler's Fascism had swiftly gained huge appeal. By the autumn of 1934, when Lilla and Rugs reached Berlin, his Brown Shirts were already marching the streets and the Nazi flag was flying from every building. Lilla must have found the combination of fear and efficiency with which even the station porters were hauling cases from platform to platform slightly eerie. She'd grown up surrounded by Germans – Chefoo's Shantung province was the main area of German influence in China. She spoke the language. She and Ada had been sent to finishing school in Darmstadt, a small town near Frankfurt – an episode marked by page after page of postcards pasted into one of Lilla's photograph albums. But here, now, in Berlin, the people she thought she knew must have seemed suddenly quite foreign – both disturbing and comforting her. It wasn't just her life that was changing, everyone else's was as well.

Lilla and Rugs spent a brief night in a hotel. In the morning, they boarded the train for Stalin's cold grey Communist Moscow. The Moscow that had frightened Italy into Mussolini's Fascist hands before scaring

Germany into Hitler's. That had murdered its way to domination of the dozens of old Russian Empire states that spread from the Pacific to the Baltic. And which was now looking to nudge its borders further west into central Europe. Here the swastikas were replaced by a blood-coloured field of red flags, yellow hammers and sickles glinting in their corners. It was easier for Lilla to lay a finger on what was wrong. The treaty ports in China were packed with White Russians who had fled the revolution and Communist takeover of their own country. Governesses who spoke the perfect French they had learned in their families' grand apartments in St Petersburg now found themselves conjugating verbs in schoolrooms instead of hosting literary salons. Doormen whose upright shoulders were used to the heavy braid of a cavalry officer's armour. Cleaning ladies whose ear-lobes still hung low from the weight of the diamonds they had once worn. The stories that these Russians had brought with them to China had made the treaty-porters' blood run cold. A few hours in Moscow was enough. Then Lilla and Rugs steamed east out of town on the Trans-Siberian Express.

The journey through the ice took seven long days. The train stopped and started dozens of times each day. Sometimes in wooden-chaleted towns that reminded European travellers of the Alps. Sometimes at snow-bound villages, where it was hard to imagine anyone could survive the winter. Sometimes at just a collection of broken-down shacks, where Lilla and Rugs heard orders being barked, the click of rifles being primed, as unwilling passengers were hauled off the other end of the train. At these stops, they found themselves sitting in silence until the train had pulled away.

For hundreds of miles the track was enclosed on either side by an interminable beech forest. Lilla must have felt that she was being swallowed up by a long tunnel that would spit her out on the other side of the world, into a new existence. The train rattled on, the heat from its wheels melting the ice on the rails. Even inside the train it was so cold that they had to wear gloves to stop the skin on their hands sticking to the brass rails as they clutched their way to the dining car. Vast piles of black caviar served as casually as butter overflowed from bowls in the middle of the table. Other than that, the fare was barely edible. They wandered on out of the first-class section of the train to find the other carriages packed with passengers crammed upright on to wooden benches, their heads bouncing off their neighbours' shoulders as they tried to sleep.

They staggered back along the swaying train to their berths, where Lilla opened a suitcase that she had packed with food, just in case. I can just see her sitting there in the rocking carriage, an open bag on her black-skirted lap heaving with flour-dusted salami and wurst picked up in Berlin. With hard cheddars and soft smoked cheeses, kept fresh by the refrigerating temperature on the train. With freshly ground coffee and loose China tea. Tins of pâté, peaches in syrup and chilled chocolate bars that it took an effort to break in two. Lilla and Rugs pressed their noses against the steamed-up window panes, straining to catch a glimpse of the snow-ridden forest and magnificent lakes outside. And they nibbled their way to the Manchurian city of Harbin.

Harbin is one of the most northern cities in China. Even in summer it can be a desolate place. But when Lilla and Rugs arrived there was, as in Berlin, a deeper chill in the air. Ever since it had invaded Manchuria three years before, Japan had been piling a vast army into the north-eastern province – a force far too large for the province alone. But the soldiers had kept on arriving, the rumble of their feet shaking the windswept Manchurian wasteland. Harbin's streets must have felt ready to overflow with neat, sharp, uniformed faces waiting to have somewhere else to go.

Still, Lilla would have found this less worrying than what she had seen in Berlin. For the past twenty years Japan had been trying to secure a foothold in China. And, so far, it had made little difference to the foreign residents of the treaty ports whether the Nationalists, warlords or Japanese were in control of the surrounding countryside. There was always something or other going on out there and, as one former treaty-porter told me, people were 'so used to trouble' that they ignored it – 'it never even hit us'.

Perhaps, if your life was in China, if that was where your home, your business, your family and friends were, it was simplest to see things that way.

What Lilla, the Eckfords, Casey and everyone else who stayed may have underestimated – or perhaps chose to close their eyes to – was quite how deep-seated the veiled Japanese resentment of the Western powers' presence in China was. If the USA had Latin America, France had North Africa and Britain had India, then Japan felt that China should be theirs and theirs alone. And just as Lilla was taking her life back to China, to settle down in the only place that she had ever felt was home, the Japanese Army in Manchuria was poised, waiting for its moment to pounce.

From Harbin, it was just two more days to Chefoo. One day on the Manchurian train to Dairen – a port near Port Arthur on the Liaotung peninsula that hovers over Chefoo in the Yellow Sea. A final night in a hotel. Then a few hours by boat to Chefoo.

Chefoo in the 1930s was a far busier town than the quiet port that Lilla had left thirty years earlier. The full-time foreign population had grown to about a thousand. And, according to Chefoo's entries for those years in the

China Directory, an annual handbook of facts, figures and firms in the treaty ports, there were now over thirty trading firms, half a dozen missions including the flourishing mission schools, three banks and a building society, the *Chefoo Daily News*, a delicatessen, an old-style German restaurant and a brand new amusement park. Chinese Customs were still battling with the inevitable smuggling around Chefoo's rocky coastline, bandits still roamed the countryside and, although an area was still nominally recognized as international, the residents had handed over the running of it to the same Chinese committee that ran the Chinese part of the town. The old city was now a labyrinthine market with entire streets selling just silk, just livestock, or only padded clothes. There were even dedicated markets for thieves and prostitutes – those who managed to sidestep the Chinese authorities. The local government was still executing convicted criminals like cattle on Second Beach. They carted them through the town in bamboo cages wearing dunces' caps on their heads and, with the aid of the modern gun, managed to kill fifty at a time in ten minutes flat.

The sea was bustling. Sampans idled off the main beach as fishermen dived for octopuses on the seabed. Basking sharks drifted in through the reef and, at night, the bay glowed with phosphorescence. On the other side of Consulate Hill – many of whose former consulates were now occupied by wealthy trading families – the harbour was crammed throughout the summer months. The US Navy had begun using Chefoo as a base from May to September each year. A huge local building boom had started, to try to accommodate the sailors' families that followed the ships. But some of the US Navy still came alone. At four o'clock every afternoon the sailors flocked ashore on 'liberty boats' to enjoy the cabarets that moved up from Shanghai for the summer. The bars along the waterfront were packed to overflowing, the girls and their madams leaning over the low garden walls beckoning to potential customers.

Chefoo's slightly more old-fashioned pleasures were still on offer, too. There were mule rides and rickshaw rallies for picnics up at the dragon temple on Temple Hill. There were carriage drives along the avenues between the mulberry orchards that were the local silk-worm factories. Lunch at the Chefoo Club started with a gin and tonic at noon. Its visitors could choose from a men's bar, billiard room, mixed cocktail lounge, mixed tea lounge, a ladies' lounge and the terrace overlooking the beach. After the offices closed at four, Chinese players waited on standby at the tennis courts for foreigners who turned up without a partner. Later, there was bowling in the old wooden alley in the club's basement.

Girls with bound feet on their way to work in a hairnet factory.

Business, on the other hand, was changing. The global economic depression had almost killed off the old hair-net and straw-braid markets – boaters and bonnets were luxuries that were not being replaced. And as soon as people again had money to spend, they wanted something quite different. The new fashion seemed to be for embroidered bedlinens and table napkins, simple, pretty, feelgood items that helped lift the grey gloom that had descended on people's homes. And that is just what Lilla's fiancé, Casey, made.

Casey & Co. was a large building right on the waterfront overlooking First Beach. It was at the harbour end, about a hundred yards from the club, which was tucked into the bottom of Consulate Hill. An L-shaped brick building with flashes of red and white lightening up the predominantly grey stone, it curved in a great colonnade of arched windows along the ground and first floors. Inside sat rows of Chinese women. Many of them had to be brought to work on wheelbarrows as they couldn't walk. According to Chinese tradition, whether rich or poor, women had their feet tightly and agonizingly bound in early childhood – usually at around the age of five – to stop them growing any further. Claire Malcolm Lintilhac, who worked as a nurse in Chefoo and examined these grotesquely crippled feet, describes the binding process in her memoirs:

It had to be done very carefully if serious
complications such as gangrene were to be avoided.
Slowly but firmly the four small toes were folded
under, gradually embedding them into the ball of the
foot leaving the big toe free. As the foot grew longer,
so the instep was bent under and back, giving the foot
its abnormal arched appearance. Bathing, powdering
and rebinding had to be done at careful intervals. But
as long as the foot was still growing, the intense pain
was always there.

Although this barbaric practice had been officially abolished with the end of the Chinese imperial dynasty in 1911, it was many years before it stopped – perhaps because it made girls more attractive to their future husbands. It certainly prevented them from running away, or even leaving the home alone. Going to work in a factory was one of the few ways in which they could go out at all.

Once there, these women spent all day sewing tiny, neat stitches into lace-fringed tablecloths and handkerchiefs. Delicate flowers seemed to spread across the linen under their fingertips. Miniature pink lilies, their petals falling open as they died to reveal the suggestive folds within. Bright blue cornflowers with orange centres and pure white daisies. White globes with yellow lips and great headdresses of scimitar-shaped petals, strewing leafy twigs and red and black berries in their path. As I run my fingers over the cross-stitches, straight stitches and little French knots on the linen that Lilla gave my mother and me, I remember Lilla's enthusiasm still bursting through that stutter, years after Casey & Co. had gone: 'They are j-j-just so p-pretty. B-b-beautiful, aren't they?' Lilla loved Casey's embroidery. She was so keen on it that, when she arrived in Chefoo, she didn't marry Casey straight away. She made the most of the way in which the world had changed since she had grown up and went to work in his business.

Even fifteen years after the end of the First World War, surprisingly few women were working. The worldwide depression had both cut the number of jobs available – and those that existed tended to go to men – and dampened the adventurous mood of the Twenties. According to Mary Taylor's social history of women in the twentieth century, even fashion seemed to push them back into more traditional roles: 'in keeping with the more subdued times, the 1930s saw a return to a new

231

femininity. The androgynous look of the 1920s disappeared as longer hair became fashionable and women claimed back their curves. Clothes were more restrained and skirts lengthened.' And 'women, with a few notable exceptions, seem to have disappeared', either 'eclipsed by economic problems' or 'hidden behind net curtains'.

But Lilla was not one to hide. Instead she became one of just three European businesswomen in Chefoo. Another, Miss Weinglass, worked at the ICI (Imperial Chemical Industries) office, and a Mrs Rouse ran a mail-order company for embroidery and silk. Lilla did much the same thing. She helped choose the patterns and colours for new designs. She layered samples in boxes overflowing with tissue paper and sent them to prospective clients in the new markets of Australia, South Africa and the Netherlands. She helped look after the women in the factory. And Casey made it clear to everyone that she had the authority to sign for the whole firm.

But, after everything that had happened – the bowing and scraping to Arthur's headmaster, the problems with the Rattrays over Malcolm's will, the collapse of the world economy and then of Cornabé Eckford – Lilla was no longer going to put all her eggs in one basket and rely on Casey alone. She was determined, absolutely determined – would be until the day she died – to have her own money to give to her children and increasing numbers of grandchildren.

So, for the first time in her life, as well as working in Casey & Co., Lilla went into business on her own. Earth was being flattened and foundations laid on every square inch of spare land in Chefoo. Ninety years after the first treaty ports were opened, ever-increasing numbers of foreigners born in China were reaching retirement age. Many of them were choosing to retire to the seaside at Chefoo – perhaps for the scenery, perhaps for the air, or perhaps because they felt safe in the shadow of the great American warships that loomed offshore for half the year. And, as the American naval presence swelled, there was a never-ending stream of wives and children looking for homes to rent. Now that she was earning a living at Casey & Co., Lilla decided to take the small amount of capital that Ernie had left her and join in this property boom. Houses, she clearly thought, were a safe investment. Bricks and mortar couldn't vanish or become worthless overnight as so many stocks and shares had done in the Wall Street Crash. When rented out, the houses would provide an income, and they might also increase in value, giving her something substantial to leave to Arthur and Alice.

It didn't occur to her that the treaty ports might simply cease to exist.

The development that Lilla chose to invest in was called the Woodlands Estate. It was at the far end of First Beach from the club, beyond the boarding schools, on a slope called East Hill that overlooked the bay. She could afford five houses. She bought one that was already there and four plots of land upon which to build. She threw herself into the project with pride. 'My little houses', she called them in her letters back to England, as though they were her children. I still have her photographs of the completed buildings. Their architecture was a curious fusion of East and West. Each house had an Eastern single storey but dormer windows poked through the roof. The roofs themselves were tiled and square-chimneyed, yet their ridges fell into an oriental upward curve. The windows had both glass and shutters and were a mixture of traditional English triple bays and ornately corniced tall twin rectangles. Even the garden walls weren't flat but curved up into gentle ramparts, hatted with single stone slabs, a miniature version of the walls around the Casey compound.

'My houses at Chefoo': Lilla's property empire.

Lilla clearly thought through what her tenant families might need. The photographs show that, on the outside, each house had a veranda on which you could sit in the shade and look out over the beach, the lofty rooftops on Consulate Hill and the string of green islands beyond. In front of the veranda and to the side was a little lawn for the children to play on. Beyond this, a flower bed, filled with the plants that would grow best in Chefoo. Coming in and out on short leases, her tenants wouldn't have a chance to build a garden of their own. And most of them would be too busy with young children. Inside, she packed the houses with almost everything practical she could think of. The lists of contents I found at the bottom of an old briefcase in my parents' attic include flower stands and brass vases, hatstands and newspaper racks, bridge tables, candlesticks, linen baskets, hot-water bottles, waste-paper baskets, jelly moulds, champagne glasses, cake plates, card trays for visitors' cards, ashtrays for smokers. Lilla even hung pictures on the walls.

When the houses were ready, Lilla welcomed the first families in. She helped mothers find amahs to look after the 'young ones'. She showed them where to buy the best food. And how to bargain for a good price.

She would still have remembered how much that could matter.

Lilla married Casey on New Year's Day, 1935. She didn't think it was right to marry in the church in Chefoo again, especially not another Ernest, a man with the same name. So they went to Shanghai and stood in front of the altar in the grand British cathedral there. Not a young bride and groom in the first flush of love but a couple with lives already ingrained in their faces. Casey was in his sixties. Lilla was fifty-two. She was beaming from ear to ear – with the contentment of a woman who had finally drawn all the strands of her life together.

The hall, Casey and Lilla's apartment, Chefoo.

None of her family believed her when she said she was in love with Casey. She felt obliged to justify it time and time again. He gives me everything a woman could want, she told them. Well, they didn't doubt that. She even tried the argument that he needed her: 'Poor lamb . . . If anything happened to me, I simply don't know what would happen to him.' That too was true. Casey had been the epitome of a lonely bachelor before Lilla had swept back into his life. Admittedly he had been looked after meticulously by Chinese servants who seemed to know what he wanted before he did himself, but even that was nothing compared to having Lilla around.

Casey's home was an apartment along the seaward side of the Casey & Co. building. Lilla moved in and started to wave her magic wand. Instead of the long row of hessian-shaded windows that marked the factory, the arches in front of the living quarters had been opened into a shaded cloister. Behind this, a long hall ran the length of the building. When Lilla found it, it must have felt like a waiting room – a few uncomfortable chairs in a draughty corridor. Without a moment's hesitation she transformed it into a miniature version of one of those old-fashioned galleries that run long and wide through English stately homes and were the centre of family life. She lined the walls with side-tables crowned with flower arrangements, ornaments and plants exploding from their pots. She hauled in armchairs and sofas, creating different corners in which to chat, read or even sew. On the window side, beneath the sunlight that poured in off the sea, the furniture was wicker. On the apartment side, and against the wood panelling at the far end, it was warm dark wood. She threw carpets and rugs down on the floor, hung paintings at a tilt out from the high walls so that you could enjoy them sitting down, stuck silk-shaded standard lamps in the dark corners and hand-painted Chinese lanterns around the bulbs hanging from the ceiling.

Once Lilla had sorted out Casey's home, she started to organize his social life. She found the best chef in Chefoo and lured him over to work for her. Together they prepared weekend lunches famous throughout the town. Lilla constructed her lunch parties carefully, Rugs tells me. Never more than eight guests and, phone call by phone call, she painstakingly built up a crowd that she knew would work well together. She draped her long dining table in Casey's beautifully embroidered table-cloths and folded those flower-strewn napkins at each place. Down the centre of the table stretched pretty objects, silver dishes, flowers low enough to talk across. Every silver knife, fork and spoon shone so brightly that Lilla could see her own reflection in them, clear as day.

The meals began with soup. Then something light. Salt and pepper prawns in lettuce so crispy that it dissolved on your tongue, leaving the fresh flesh of the prawns – hauled out of the Chefoo sea that morning – to fall away between your teeth. A main course came next. Sometimes a British roast, more often a great sizzling Chinese dish, a jamboree of just-cooked slivers of beef or duck and thin slices of still-crunchy pepper whose skin had just begun to bubble under the heat and which melted at the end of each bite. Sauces that were an intriguing combination of sweet and salty. Sauces that coated the food but were still light enough to run off the edge of a spoon.

Then came the sweet courses. First a steaming pile of treacle, stewed fruit layered into biscuit and cream, towering, wobbly jellies and blancmange, or even a baked Alaska carried triumphantly into the dining room, its meringue crust still cooking but the ice cream inside deliciously cold. As soon as this was swept away a row of intricately laced sponge and sugar baskets containing sweets and crystallized fruits appeared along the table, each rising curl a noodle-thin strand sculpted into shape

238

and coated with sugar before baking. Finally, with the coffee, came the cake. In any case, by now it was teatime. 'If you sat down at one,' says a regular guest, 'you'd have been hard pushed to leave by six.' And so, before they'd had a chance to haul themselves up from the lunch table, Lilla would be tempting her guests with lightly buttered scones and jam, pastry-encased fruit tarts, the slices of strawberries, gooseberries and peaches fanning out from the centre of each tiny cake, and alcohol-soaked raisin breads and sponges that pinned you to your chair as their vapour engulfed your eyes and nostrils.

I have a photograph taken in the courtyard of Casey & Co. after one such lunch. Lilla is smiling. Not a just-for-the-camera sort of smile but a smile that has taken over her whole face – her eyes, her eyebrows, her cheeks – and body. Her head is up, her shoulders are relaxed, her arms by her sides, the fingers of her left hand loosely clasped in those of the right. She is standing between Casey and Mabel. Vivvy is behind her. Rugs is at the end of the row. They are all grinning away as though they are still laughing over the last joke, still savouring the last glass of wine or brandy, the last cake. I think this was one of the happiest times of Lilla's life.

She was making beautiful things to sell. She had her own little business as well. She organized. She entertained. She played her Steinway. She served tantalizingly delicious food out of her own kitchen. She was driven around the town and countryside in a shiny black sedan that Casey had given her and which was certainly as smart as anything Ada owned. And, even if she may not have been madly in love with her husband, even if she didn't tremble at his every touch, she found his love for her hard to resist.

From the moment they met, Casey had adored her wholly, without reservation. 'He doted on her.' Casey's love was one of the few things in Lilla's life that she

After lunch at Lilla's, Chefoo, 1938: from the left, Mabel, Lilla, Vivvy, Casey and Rugs.

hadn't had to fight for. He made her feel the most precious, valued, loved woman in the world. 'Such love,' she wrote, 'no man has given to a woman.' He needed her. When she was away, with her brother Reggie in Tsingtao, with friends in Shanghai, or if she had dashed back to England on the Trans-Siberian Express to see her children and Ada, Casey took care of her little houses himself, cleaning them in between tenants. His attempts were not always successful, but the mere fact that he had tried so hard on her behalf meant a lot to Lilla: 'The poor lamb did his utmost . . . & felt very proud.' But when the tenants went in, they said it was dirty – 'his disappointment!!! So it shows you,' she wrote to her son Arthur, as houseproud as ever, 'that *my presence* is necessary – as no tenant that goes into my houses when I am there says it is dirty!!! I look into *every corner* . . . of course I will tell him, he did very well indeed.' And I think she found looking after him surprisingly fulfilling. On the evenings when they were alone together, I can almost hear him reading aloud to her in a soft, lilting, unclipped voice and telling her how fabulous she was.

And the love that grew out of this mutual caring, this holding-hands sort of love, would prove to be stronger and more constant than any Lilla had known before. It was a love that would survive all the terrifyingly high hurdles yet to come.

Just as Lilla started to build her new life in Chefoo, the wheels that would ride it into the ground were already beginning to turn. For a couple of years the area around Chefoo remained peaceful, but in the rest of China civil war was raging and Chiang Kai-shek's Nationalist Party, still nominally in power, was losing popular support. One of the reasons for this was that, rather than retaliate against the Japanese violence of the early 1930s, Chiang had ignored it and focused on trying to eliminate his rural Communist opposition instead. By the mid-1930s support for the Nationalists was at such a low ebb that, in December 1936, Chiang was taken prisoner by a local warlord in Sian. A few months later he was released but he was weakened by the humiliation – he had been captured wearing only his pyjamas – and Japan saw the moment to invade.

In July 1937, Japanese soldiers swarmed south from Manchuria along China's prosperous eastern coast and took Peking and Tientsin, their bayonets stopping only at the gates of the foreign concessions in the latter. In August and September they were locked in battles over Shanghai. And, although the Japanese again avoided entering the international settlement, several foreigners – and several thousand Chinese – were killed in their bombing raids on the main shopping streets. December that year saw one of the worst atrocities in modern warfare with the Japanese 'rape' of the city of Nanking, where Chiang Kai-shek's fragile government was based. The Japanese Army ran wild through the city with a mind-numbing, inhuman viciousness. Chinese women were gang-raped by soldiers and bayoneted like pincushions. Others were simply shot or sliced to pieces. Few survived. The lucky ones managed to take their own lives before the soldiers reached them.

Again the foreigners were carefully sidestepped. Yet, in the treaty ports, a chill began to set into expatriate bones. Until recently, the Westerners argued among themselves, the Japanese had been their colleagues. To an extent, they still were. The Japanese would never, they thought, dare do anything like this to Westerners. What they missed, or simply didn't want to see, was that to the Japanese the key difference between the Westerners and the Chinese was not race but the strength of their governments. Two decades earlier, the Japanese had waited for the Germans to find themselves at loggerheads with the rest of the

Japanese troops enter Tientsin as Westerners look on.

With Japan bombing the Chinese areas of Shanghai, the residents flee into the international settlement.

treaty-port nations in 1914 before slipping into their place and taking over their Chinese territories. And, as Lilla herself had seen, back in Europe, in those countries to which so many of the treaty-port residents were supposed to belong, trouble was already brewing.

Having digested Peking, Tientsin and Shanghai, the Japanese Army reached Chefoo in the last days of 1937. At first, the Westerners were relieved to see the red-and-white flagged vehicles rolling in. As news of the Japanese advance swept through the country, the Nationalist Army had destroyed the infrastructure in Japan's path and broken up the Japanese-owned factories and warehouses. It then fled towards its new headquarters in Chungking in the west of China, which the Japanese chose to ignore. The treaty ports were left with no semblance of law and order and at the mercy of rioters and looters encouraged by the damage that had already been done. The damage in Chefoo – where there were few industrial units, for even Casey & Co. consisted of seamstresses rather than heavy machinery – was minimal. Still, Lilla must have felt very vulnerable. Casey & Co. was one of the largest buildings in the centre of the town. And anarchy is terrifying. The crowd was attacking the Japanese today. Tomorrow it could be the British.

In industrial Tsingtao, just a couple of hours from Chefoo, the looting was so bad that, on New Year's Eve, Lilla's brother Reggie organized a force to try to keep control until the Japanese arrived. Not only had a large number of sites been destroyed, but the departing Nationalists had aggravated the situation by releasing a couple of thousand criminals back on to the streets. Ignoring the growing tension between their governments back home, the British, Americans, White Russians and Germans clubbed together to form the Tsingtao Special Police. The doctors were German, the drivers and intelligence officers Russian, and the British and

Japanese marines enter Tsingtao.

Alice Eckford, Tsingtao, 1938.

Americans wielded the 'sticks, pieces of board, anything available' that they could find. They charged the crowds of rioters that they found attacking waterworks, Chinese villages and foreign property. The Tsingtao Special Police held the town for ten days. On 10 January, Japanese marines began to land. In a formal ceremony, Reggie handed over Tsingtao to Japanese Rear-Admiral Shisido. In return, Shisido handed Reggie a delicately engraved and painted china urn. 'It was absolutely beautiful,' says Rugs, who had been fighting with the Tsingtao Special Police too – as though the very beauty of it, the extent of the Japanese gratitude, should have alerted them to what was to come.

The Tsingtao Special Police was disbanded, each member clutching a picture of its extraordinary commemorative coat of arms – a shield quartered into the Union Jack, Stars and Stripes, Russian flag and swastika. A sword rose up through the middle. On the shield were the words 'Tsingtao, 1938'.

There is something about this picture, the sight of the British and American symbols so closely intertwined with the jagged black Nazi cross and that date, which makes the hair stand up on the back of my neck.

As the Japanese took over the treaty ports, order returned. Lilla, her brothers and sisters and Casey all welcomed the peace. The factories were repaired. Business started up again. The cricket matches resumed. Inside the larger treaty ports, such as Shanghai and Tientsin, it was almost as though nothing had changed. Hardly a Japanese face was seen within the clearly demarcated foreign concessions. Even in Chefoo, where there were no concession gates for the Japanese to wait outside and the Japanese Army had taken over every street and alleyway, stopping only at the foreigners' front doors, cocktails reappeared on the terrace at the club and life seemed to slip back into the same easy rhythm as before.

It was about this time, in 1938, that the indomitable Alice Eckford died. Over eighty years old, she was still pinning up her skirts to show off her knees. She could still pretend, just, that everything was almost as it had always been.

Just.

At first the only noticeable change was that the Chinese policemen who had been directing the traffic had been replaced by exceptionally courteous Japanese soldiers. Then the Japanese began, ever so slightly, to clamp down. They closed the Yangtze river – supposedly a British domain – to all but Japanese ships. They made all foreigners in Tsingtao have cholera jabs every six months – you had to show your cholera pass at checkpoints throughout the town. Even in laidback Chefoo, they began to run the treaty port with alarmingly proprietorial efficiency. Fortifications were built on Second Beach, beyond the school. All signs in Chinese were torn down and replaced with Japanese characters. Leaflets were distributed describing the 'New Order' in Asia. The red suns of the Japanese flag seemed to rise over almost every corner of the town in an unearthly dawn.

Even from inside the thick stone walls of the Casey compound, Lilla began to wonder what might be coming next.

PART III

War

SUKIYAKI

This is a Japanese dish.

Put into a frying pan, which contains plenty of fat, the following.

Thin slices of meat, sliced onions, sliced cabbage, mushrooms, bamboo shoots, and spring onions.

Put all this, or some at a time if a large amount is required, into the frying pan. Add some Worcester sauce and a little sugar. Mix well for the meat to cook properly. The fat must be piping hot for rapid cooking.

Rice must be served with the Sukiyaki, and placed into individual bowls. Then the desired quantity of Sukiyaki is placed on top.

11
WAR

1939

IT TAKES A GREAT DEAL of fear to make a person who loves the life she has pack a bag and run away. People don't give up their homes, their property, their friends – everything they have – unless they are extremely scared. Scared they might be humiliated, imprisoned, tortured or killed. And, back in 1939, Lilla as yet feared none of these things. In any case, if she and Casey left China to run away from the Japanese, they would lose everything they had. And where would they go? They wouldn't have enough money to retire comfortably in England – where all they would ever be was a couple of pieces of imperial flotsam and jetsam, washed up by the tide. Casey, already in his late sixties, was too old to move to Malaya, India or Burma and start up a new business, a new life, all over again.

In any case, once the Japanese had raised their flags and laid down their regulations, nothing more seemed to happen. As 1938 rolled into 1939, little changed in the treaty ports. Business continued as before. The lunches, the parties, the picnics went on. If new trouble was brewing anywhere, it was back in Europe.

Japan and Russia were not the only countries looking beyond their own horizons. The old European conflict was rearing its head. This time it was fuelled by fear on both sides. The agitators — the Fascist governments in both Germany and Italy — were driven not only by a desire to expand their own borders but also by a long-standing fear of the Communism that had taken over the old Russia. The appeasers — France and Britain — were sufficiently paralysed by fear of another war on the same scale as 1914–18 that they didn't try to stop them until it was too late.

In the autumn of 1938, the British Prime Minister Neville Chamberlain and the French Premier Edouard Daladier met Hitler in Munich. By then Hitler had rearmed Germany, taken Austria and was threatening to invade Czechoslovakia. Still desperate to prevent another war in Europe, Chamberlain and Daladier agreed to split Czechoslovakia and hand the German-speaking Sudetenland to Hitler in exchange for his promise to leave the rest of the country alone. Chamberlain returned to Britain proudly waving the written agreement and claiming that he had secured 'peace in our time'.

Six months later, Hitler marched into Czechoslovakia.

Britain now responded by promising to go to war with any power that invaded Poland — as it was feared Hitler might. The following month, in April 1939, Italy seized Albania, galvanizing Britain into reintroducing conscription and at last rearming. In May, Italy and Germany joined forces by signing the Pact of Steel.

From then on, it was only a matter of when.

But just as war seemed inevitable, the drumroll towards battle paused, swords hovering in the air just a few inches apart. Europe held its breath. By the middle of July 1939, Lilla must have felt that the gap in warmongering was beckoning her back to England. If war did come to Europe, it could be her last chance to see her children, her grandchildren, Ada. She followed her usual route – a boat north from Chefoo to Dairen, and then the Trans-Siberian Express back to Europe.

The last leg of the trip, from Moscow to London, must have been extraordinary. The summer of 1939 in Europe was as oppressively hot as the region's politics. The train would have been baking, claustrophobic, the passengers fidgety, the waiters jumping at the clink of china. And at each long station stop in Eastern Europe, families – the parents white-faced, the children, as if sensing that something dramatic was happening, strangely calm – were heaving suitcases and brown-paper parcels tied with string on to bulging trains.

Arthur met Lilla at Victoria station and drove her to the house he was renting in Haslemere, in the countryside outside London. Under pressure from Beryl to make more money than the army paid him, in 1936 he had given up his commission and become a stockbroker in the City. But, still a soldier at heart, he had been watching events in Europe and speaking frequently to his former army colleagues. He knew, he'd been telling Lilla for years, that war was coming. A couple of years earlier he and Beryl had been on a driving tour of Europe: France, Italy, Austria, Germany. In Munich they'd seen teenage soldiers beating up elderly Jews wearing stars on their chests. They were spotted watching the scene in horror, and were arrested on suspicion of spying.

I still find it hard to imagine Beryl, my grandmother, being arrested. There has never been a less likely spy. Beryl was not a practical woman. When she married Arthur she had never been in a kitchen, nor did she know that butter came from cows. She spent the last decade of her long life with her mind back in the 1920s, in a whirl of finishing schools, debutante dances and society balls – the settings where she felt most at home.

After a few hours in a cell in a police station, they were released. Arthur, my grandfather, always said he knew then that war would come. Not if but when. When they returned home, he put the family's London house on the market and moved them out of the city.

Lilla spent a few days at Arthur's. My aunt Jane, Lilla's granddaughter, remembers her there. They sat in the garden. A perfect English garden on a hill, overlooking a deep valley and woodland beyond. In the garden, a rolling lawn, trimmed hedges, the last roses still out. Lilla watched the seven-year-old Jane teasing her three-year-old brother David, my father, as he stumbled about on the grass. Each time that Jane trespassed what Lilla regarded as 'a line', she called out to her. My father, wearing only a bathing suit – it was too hot to wear anything else – rode his tricycle into a great patch of stinging nettles and turned it right over. The rash spread all the way up his back, his arms, his face. He screamed as Lilla ran him a cool bath and emptied 'bluebag' into it – it made whites whiter and, curiously enough, also soothed burning skin.

Then it was off to Ada and Toby in suburban splendour in Norwood. It must have felt just as hot in England as it had been in central Europe. Everything, even the traffic around them, seemed to be waiting, suspended between a peace that had left them and a war that wasn't quite here. Ada had a new car. She would inevitably have asked Lilla to admire it, goading Lilla into reminding her that her own car, in China, was at least as good if not better. Casey had bought her a brand new one just the year before – a green 1938 Ford 85-horsepower DeLuxe Fordor Sedan. She gave Ada a photograph of the car, herself, Casey and their driver, as if to prove her point. In the heightened atmosphere, bickering was probably the only way to talk. And the question of who had the better car would have been left unresolved, perhaps deliberately, to crowd out other questions. Ones they didn't want to think about. Like how long it might be until they saw each other again.

From Ada's, Lilla went on to see her daughter Alice, her husband Havilland and their four children. All growing fast. Hard to keep up with who was doing what. Another week or so. Then back to Arthur. But now Russia had signed a non-aggression pact with Germany. That left Poland open for Hitler's tanks to roll in. And Britain had committed itself to fight if it did.

The war that they had been waiting for was about to arrive. But there was a chance, the papers said, that it wouldn't come. That Chamberlain's Anglo-Polish Alliance would deter Herr Hitler. Arthur disagreed.

Lilla, Arthur and Beryl spent the weekend in the garden again. I can see them doing their best to pretend that Lilla's visit was just like any other visit, in any other year. Lilla makes a plate of raspberry jam sandwiches. Wasps keep hovering over them. Lilla raises her arm to brush them away. The children are playing. Arthur gets up to go and make a pot of tea. Lilla fills their cups. And a warm, muggy wind that peels back the blades of grass one by one seems to hover instead of disappearing over the next hill, waiting – like everything else in Europe – for what will happen next. This wind bears the faint scent of armies on the move, thousands of tons of thickly greased gunmetal turning freshly harvested European plains to mud. It seems to drift right over the children. Jane raises her head inquisitively to a passing gust, sensing the slightly forced scene around the table a few feet away, then resumes her teasing play. But the grown-ups, despite the warmth of the air, shiver. Their bare arms – Beryl's white flesh and freckles, Arthur's clenched forearm, Lilla's skin that has known sharper, colder winds – prickle into goosebumps.

It was the next morning that the call came. Monday. Arthur had gone up to his office in London. When he heard the news, he rang home immediately. Hitler had offered to 'protect' the British Empire if Britain promised not to intervene if he attacked Poland. Britain had turned him down. Arthur was sure that Germany would now invade Poland. The war was, at most, a few days away. If Lilla was going to return to China, she had to leave immediately, he told her. And the Siberian way was already out of the question; she would have to take the long route round by boat. She should leave today if she could. If she waited until the German tanks rumbled over the Polish border, it would be too late to go anywhere. That is, if she really had to go.

The discussion had been rattling on all August, ever since Lilla arrived, says Jane. Stay in England with her children, her grandchildren, with Ada, but with war coming in Europe – and they could all remember the last one, no mistake. Or go back to China, her 'home', her husband? All your husbands have the same name, Ada would have teased her, a thinly veiled suggestion that Casey was hardly the love of her life. Why go back to him? But it was all right for Ada, she had her husband in England with her. Why shouldn't Lilla be with her husband as well?

And Lilla wasn't going to do what Ernie had tried to do to her and leave Casey on the other side of the world when things weren't going so well. It was too late now for him to join her in England. She had a fortnight, Arthur reckoned, to make it through the Suez Canal before the war closed it – and Casey would never be able to get there in time if he was coming from China.

Still, Arthur tried to tell her that she was mad to go.

Even though they all knew what Hitler wanted to do in Europe, nobody was fooled about what the Japanese were already doing in China. What would happen to her there?

But now Lilla was going. She was leaving straight away. She was up and packing her cases in her room. Jane remembers her moving quickly, those elegant legs almost skipping along, her black hat already on her head. This time she knew she wouldn't be returning to England for a long while. 'I hope the children won't forget me,' she wrote on her way to China.

Lilla left England that day, 28 August, and took a train straight through France to Marseilles. On 30 August she boarded the French ship the *Félix Roussel*, bound for Shanghai. The following day, Hitler invaded Poland. Two days later, Europe was at war. Five weeks afterwards Lilla wrote to Arthur and Beryl as she approached Shanghai, describing her journey. Her visit to her family was already a long, long way away. 'It seems years & years since I left London. And what a lot we have gone through since.'

The first eight days at sea were the most frightening. France, too, was at war with Germany and the *Félix Roussel* was trying to make its way through the Mediterranean unseen. The ship crept south, under a complete blackout. A single cigarette light could betray them to the slender, invisible eye of a U-boat periscope and not even a candle was allowed on board after dark, leaving the passengers 'creeping around' in darkness. 'I shall feel funny having light again,' wrote Lilla, 'especially going to bed.' At night, the ship was sealed up. Every crevice, every chink that might let out a forbidden glimpse of light, was stuffed with blackout lining. And for the first, worst stretch, from Marseilles to Tunis, the ship was overcrowded. Packed to the brim with every

last desperate family that had clambered on board, trying
to escape the tanks and guns that were on their way. A
worried Lilla counted the lifeboats. 'Not one of us could
have been saved.'

After Tunis, the ship turned east. Past Sicily, then
Malta, right over the spot where Ernie's ship had been
hit. Lilla must have wondered if he was still down there.
Somewhere on the seabed under a thousand tons of salt
water, trying to make good soldiers out of the fish. I
wonder if she lay awake at night, barely able to breathe
in her sealed-up cabin and starting each time a large
wave thudded into the ship's hull, thinking she was
about to join Ernie in the cold black water outside.

The *Félix Roussel* reached Suez and then crossed into
the Red Sea, where the heat 'was awful'. The most
dangerous part of the journey was over, but the blackout
remained and with it the ever-present fear that this clunk
or that rattle was something far worse than a chain
sliding back on to the deck.

The morale of the other passengers waned. They barely
bothered, even the ever-so-chic French, to change out of
their pyjamas. The men wandered the corridors in their
dressing gowns until noon. The women flung on the
clothes that they'd left on a chair the night before, faces
bare of make-up and, to Lilla's horror, having 'not even
dressed their hair'. When Lilla asked them why they had
given up making an effort, they replied, 'We might be
drowned any moment, so why bother?'

Lilla was shocked. In her view, letting oneself go was
as good as allowing the enemy to win. She dressed in the
half-light every morning and spent twenty minutes
arranging her hair. In times like these, what you looked
like was one of the few things over which you still had
control. She walked down the corridor with her head
held high, and sat in the salon and flirted with the
Frenchmen on board. They flocked around Lilla, almost

the only woman prepared to go on playing the game of real life. *'Très élégante,'* they crooned, Lilla boasted in her letter. *'Très élégante.* Your children must be so proud of you being so brave, so *courageuse.'* I can see her beaming from ear to ear. 'You wouldn't believe,' she fluttered back, 'that my children are thirty-seven and thirty-five.' *'Mais non,'* her admirers replied, *'c'est impossible.* You have not more than forty-five years yourself.' So it went on. But as dusk fell, conversation ground to a halt. The passengers fumbled their way through the blackout back to their cabins alone, the darkness reminding them of what was going on in the world outside.

At Colombo, a Mrs Wheman came on board. She was a widow from Surrey, moving out to Peking, and her mother was going to follow her from Canada. Lilla marvelled at her decision. 'She says she wants to go back to Pekin [*sic*] and die there.' And 'she proposes taking a house in Pekin & learning Chinese to give her occupation & an object to achieve'. And she was doing it now, come what may. Lilla sat with her and they talked about the wonders of China, the colours, the silks, the art, the people, the food.

At Saigon nearly everyone disembarked, leaving only a dozen passengers in first class. 'If anything happened now,' wrote Lilla, 'we could have a lifeboat each.' Nothing did happen, but the lights stayed out. And, at last, Hong Kong's junk-filled harbour made her heart leap with joy. 'Oh what a lovely sight it was.' The *Félix Roussel* stayed in the harbour for six hours and Lilla darted on shore with Mrs Wheman. 'She felt like a schoolgirl. The Chinese, the junks & everything connected with China she loves.' The two of them must have scuttled through the market stalls and up the alleyways, unfolded heavy silk fans and tiny paper parasols, wrapped embroidered shawls around each other and unwound great rolls of uncut chiffon, draping it this way and that. They would have walked past stalls laden with strangely still shark fins, stepped around pails groaning with writhing, sinewy green snakes that made occasionally successful bids to escape a fate of soup or stew, and felt the steam from a thousand baskets of rice settle on their skin, leaving a thin, pasty film. At last they were back in China.

When the *Félix Roussel* sailed out of Hong Kong harbour that evening, the lights in the city seemed to shine like 'millions and millions of stars'. And as the ship moved further out to sea, the harbour searchlights followed it playfully, setting the whole ship 'ablaze with light'. To Lilla, the 'utter darkness' of the past month was over.

Little did she realize how much darker things were to become.

For the first few months, China felt a long, long way from the war back in Europe. Over there, the Germans were the enemy. In China the Germans were allies, and the enemy was Japan. Briton and German, American and Italian, sat drinking side by side, bemoaning the Japanese blockades around the foreign concessions – in place to prevent the Chinese escaping from the cruel Japanese rule into the foreign territory of the concessions. The blockades meant that the streets outside the concession gates in Tientsin, Shanghai and other treaty ports were clogged with hundreds if not thousands of Chinese trying to push their way through. Taking a car out meant crawling through a narrow tunnel of waving arms and shouting faces, small hands pulling at the doors, trying to open them and clamber in. And although no Japanese soldier even so much as peeped an invasive toe into foreign territory – that would have been an outright declaration of war – they had ceased helping people and provisions make their way in and out. Inside the concessions, food supplies thinned. Business began to slow. But the parties, the tea dances, the cocktails, the treaty-port way of life went on as if almost nothing were awry.

In Chefoo, however, where the Japanese had long been in control of the entire town, things were slightly different. As the autumn of 1939 dissolved into the winter of 1940 and the foreigners' home nations became increasingly embroiled in the war in Europe, the courtesy that the Japanese had hitherto shown the other foreign residents in Chefoo melted away. The Japanese started to accuse the foreigners, especially the British, of assisting the Chinese rebels. They ceased to be a helpful traffic-stopping local authority and began to insist that the treaty-porters, like the Chinese, had permits to travel, permits to trade. Permits that became increasingly hard to come by. That old decision not to have official concession areas and gates, to let easy-come easy-go Chefoo spread as it wished and be run by the Chinese themselves, had come back to haunt the Chefooites.

In these first few months of the war in Europe, as Japan was tightening the thumbscrews on the treaty-porters in China, Lilla at least knew that her daughter Alice, Ada and the grandchildren were all safe back in England – the terrible civilian bombing had yet to come. Arthur had rejoined the army, going straight back in as a major, and Lilla longed for him to become a general. 'I won't die happy until I see my son General Sir Arthur Howell,' she had written on her way back to China. Much to Lilla's frustration she believed that if his wife hadn't pushed him out of the army and into the City just three years beforehand, 'it could have materialised'. But now it was extremely unlikely and, she had hastened to add, 'whatever you are, your mother loves you'.

However, whatever Lilla's hopes for Arthur, by the spring of 1940 she had no idea where he was. All troop movements were highly secret and every soldier's letters home were checked by army intelligence. Any references to, or descriptions of, surroundings were heavily crossed out so that no intercepting enemy spy or talkative relation could know where the writer was. As a result, these precious missives often arrived with thick black ink deleting half the words. But, for the moment, as far as Lilla knew, her son was alive and she kept sending parcels of socks and underwear and home-made jam to his regimental address for forwarding – as though, as long as the parcels went, he would have to stay alive to receive them.

And then, in May 1940, Germany invaded France. The British troops were beaten into a shambolic retreat. Bombed on the beaches at Dunkirk as they scrambled for a space in the small boats that had come to rescue them. Britain gave up on China. The home country was too busy keeping itself afloat. The few remaining British soldiers were pulled out of the treaty ports, leaving the civilians to stare at the departing ships, wondering what would happen next. Then the Americans went. All of them – soldiers, businessmen, officials, missionaries, wives and children – were advised to go home and many of them did. But by that far into the war, anyone who had come from Europe either had no home left to go to or no means of reaching it.

The Japanese still didn't invade the foreign concessions in the larger treaty ports. But now that the Westerners had been abandoned by their governments, now that there was nobody to protest, the Japanese started to treat the foreigners in Chefoo like prisoners.

I have a letter from Lilla in front of me. It is dated 20 August 1941, several months before Britain and Japan were officially at war. The paper has yellowed, the ink faded to a dark blue-grey. And the only reason it ever reached England was because Lilla persuaded a friend with a permit to travel south to Shanghai to post it. By then, letters posted in Chefoo 'don't leave this port'.

Lilla's letter is a reply to one from her daughter-in-law Beryl. Beryl, who had muttered disparagingly behind Lilla's back that she looked as if she had Chinese blood in her. Beryl, whose family had regarded Lilla's – the Howells as well as the Eckfords, and God knows what they would have made of the Jennings story had they heard it – as poor nobodies. Beryl, who might never have been in a kitchen before she married but who by now hadn't seen her husband for two years, was spending her nights firewatching and, like every other mother caught up in the war, was desperately worried about getting enough food for her children. Beryl was begging Lilla for money because, she said, her father wouldn't help. The only reason the letter was brought to Lilla's door was because Beryl hadn't put enough stamps on it and the postman could therefore ask Lilla to pay the excess in cash.

'My darling Beryl,' Lilla replies. Darling Beryl? How could Lilla be so forgiving? Is that what war does to you? Was she that pleased to receive a letter? Or did Lilla simply remember how tough being short of cash had once made life for her? My darling Beryl, Lilla wrote back, 'your father is a rich man from our point of view, and surely he must realise that you want help.' But she still tells Beryl to ask Ada for a cheque for Jane's school fees: 'she has a few pounds of mine left'. And she tells her about life in Chefoo.

'I cannot tell you all dear child but what we are going through.' The firms had been locked up. The offices, businesses – the Westerners' very reason for spending their lives in China – were bolted up, chained, padlocked and guarded 'to see no-one comes in and no-one comes out' by those same Japanese soldiers who not long before had stopped the traffic for Lilla when she wanted to cross

the road. All bank accounts were frozen, leaving everyone to exist off a complex system of probably
unredeemable IOUs: 'some people were clever & saw
what was coming & got a few pennies in'. And, to Lilla's
intense frustration – 'Alas. Alas. We are not allowed to
receive letters or papers' – the post stopped
coming, almost cutting them off from life beyond Chefoo.
'The Post Office must be full up with letters, papers &
parcels from floor to ceiling I should think.'

The one connection with the outside world was the
radio: 'what a comfort and blessing it is to one & all'. But,
to Lilla, the hours between the radio news broadcasts,
'7.45 am London, 1 pm Shanghai, 6 pm London, 9.30 pm
San Francisco', loomed like a vacuum threatening to
devour her. And it was this gaping emptiness day after
day that she found hardest to bear: 'We must all occupy
our minds, as being prisoners is no joke.' Casey was filling his time going round the town trying to cheer up 'the
sick and nervy ones' by reading to them. Lilla was telling
them to 'Hang on. Perhaps after the war things may
change for the better.' Then she went to cut the grass and
weed the flower beds in the gardens of her empty houses
on East Hill. When she could mow and dig no more she
went to the church and knelt down by the altar, trying to
mend the embroidered altar cloth. But the satin was so
rotten that 'it can't stand touching' and it fell apart in her
hands.

It seems to have been Vivvy who gave Lilla the idea of
writing a book. He himself was working on a history of
Chefoo, 'the start to the present day', wrote Lilla, 'with
his own drawings, really quite good'. Maybe Lilla's
twinly competitiveness extended a little to her elder
brothers. Maybe 'labour lost' being 'the end of all things',
as Lilla put in her letter to her daughter-in-law, she
leaped upon an activity that would produce something

she could keep as well as fill the empty days. Or perhaps the reason was simply that given the futility of writing letters that would never arrive, especially those daily notes to Ada, she turned her urge to write towards something that didn't need to be posted.

It had to be a recipe and housekeeping book. It must have been the only book Lilla felt she could write. In any case, just as Vivvy clearly regarded the history of Chefoo as his area of expertise, Lilla knew that hers was food. The buying of it, the preparing of it and the serving of it – and making a home a place where you wanted to be. And good fresh food – the food that the treaty-porters had taken for granted – was fast disappearing from Chefoo's shops. Or at least the Chinese seemed too frightened of their new rulers to offer it to anyone with a Western face. Vivvy's book about Chefoo was his way of keeping the old treaty-port life, the life that was vanishing, alive. Writing about food would be Lilla's.

And there was something else, too, that made Lilla want to write a cookery guide. An instinctive drive lurking deep in her subconscious. Although she reveals it herself in her letter to Beryl, I don't think she was aware that this force was driving her.

But, even four eventful decades on, Lilla clearly still felt the scars of Ernie's attempt to abandon her in England with their baby. As her world was turning upside down again, she found herself automatically talking about the misery of living with mothers-in-law, as a couple in Chefoo were doing: 'The rows that go on, and now they have decided to part company – what a pity, as it will leave a bitter feeling for always now – why didn't they have their own little houses from the first . . .' Lilla was desperate to convince her old Howell sisters-in-law of how optimistic and brave she was being. 'I have written to Auntie Bob and Auntie Ada Henniker lovely long letters, worth printing,' she wrote, frantically adding at the top, 'In case the Aunts Bob & Ada H haven't received my letters – give them my news will you – I know many letters have been lost.'

And longing to show what a good wife she could be.

The book she started to write wasn't just a recipe book. It was a guide for new housewives, with sections on economical dishes, economical menus and how to make sweets to sell 'when a little extra pocket money is needed'. Advice on how to shop wisely. And scattered throughout, tips to keep household costs down.

Although Lilla might not have managed to erase what had happened to her forty years beforehand, it was through this weakness, this old ghost, that she would now find the strength to survive.

Then the anti-British demonstrations began. The Japanese hauled every single Chinese man, woman and child out into the streets and marched them up and down the seafront, chanting and brandishing banners bearing anti-British slogans. The mood darkened. Lilla stopped wandering around the town unless it was strictly necessary. She and Casey huddled together inside their apartment, watching their former factory and office employees march past their windows.

She began to write.

12

RICEPAPER RECIPES

Chefoo, late summer 1941

LILLA FOUND A TYPEWRITER in the apartment. One that had somehow made its way across from the locked and guarded office. It must have been a portable, as she later managed to carry it from camp to camp. I have an old typewriter on my desk. One made in the 1930s, as Lilla's surely was. It is a portable, too, although it weighs over six kilos. Another grandfather used it to type up his secret reports to Churchill on the information he had gathered on expeditions behind enemy lines in Greece during the Second World War. It is the only thing of his I have. Unlike Lilla, he didn't make it back from his last trip.

The typewriter I have is an Imperial. A 'Good Companion'. It's unlikely to be exactly the same model that Lilla used, but it can't be very different.

It sits on a board about thirty centimetres square. Its black enamel gleams back at me, reflecting the light from the lamp hanging over my desk. The keypads are small, round – about a centimetre across – and seem to hover in the air. But underneath, each is connected to its corresponding printing arm by a slender, almost invisible, dark

267

metal lever. The printing arms themselves spread out in a semicircle in between the keyboard and the ribbon that sits over the roller. Their ends thicken into the carved letter-stamps – ink-stained grey metal wedges resembling a sinister mouthful of teeth.

Typing on this machine is as difficult as carrying it about. Nothing short of a finger-numbing determined thump produces an imprint on the page. Far from the long-fingered elegance of electronic typists today, typists back then must have had knuckles of steel. And the shift key actually shifts the entire rear half of the machine back half an inch, so that the capital letters hit the inky ribbon instead of the lower-case characters.

Lilla was not an experienced typist. She had typed the occasional letter for Casey, filled in the odd rental form for her houses. She had never been able to close her eyes and let her fingers fly across the keyboard as though lost in some sonata – although it's hard to imagine who could on one of these machines.

The first line she typed was a row of capitals. I can see her sitting bolt upright at a table, her left forefinger pressed firmly down on the shift key to hold it back, and typing each letter in turn with her right. I-N-T-R-O-D-U-C-T-O-R-Y. Then she went back and underlined each one with a dash, as if to make the task fill as much time as possible.

As she sat there listening to the jeering of the demonstrators fade into a heavy silence, broken only by the occasional asthmatic chug of a Japanese armoured car, did Lilla have any idea how long she would have to write?

The war proper came to China in December 1941. It was early on Monday 8 December in China – the difference in time zones making it a day ahead of Hawaii – when the news of Pearl Harbor rang through the radio. Japan had gone over the edge and there would be no turning back. That was it. War. In Shanghai, in Tientsin, the Japanese stormed into the concessions and the foreigners poured down on to the streets among the Japanese signs and flags, tanks and megaphones. Trying to reach home. Trying to reach somewhere. Trying blindly to grasp the hand of a loved one that was being pulled away by the force of the crowd.

In Chefoo, Lilla and Casey spent the day in their apartment. They went from room to room, following the Japanese order to make an inventory of every item they possessed. Their grand piano. Their lacquered tea tables. Their gramophone. One big clock. One hatstand. A bronze Buddha. A chrome bathroom table. Their glasses – an astonishing four dozen tumblers, four dozen claret glasses, four dozen port glasses, four dozen champagne glasses, four dozen cocktail glasses, four dozen liqueur glasses – showed just how much they entertained. And so it went on. I still have the list. It reads like a goodbye. As though they already knew that they were about to lose the lot.

A couple of days later, there was a knock at the door. A group of Japanese soldiers stood outside, their steel helmets and knee-high boots glinting in the sunlight. They'd come to take Casey away for questioning. I'm sure Casey told Lilla not to worry as they led him off. Not to worry? He was almost seventy years old. How could she not worry? I can see her fighting back the tears as he stumbled away.

The soldiers left Lilla clutching a red armband instead of a husband. It read B for British. B and a number by which, she was told, she was known to the Japanese authorities. She was not to go outside without it on.

Casey didn't come back that night. One by one, the

Japanese were locking up every British or American businessman still in town in the Astor House Hotel on the seafront. Even the headmaster of the Chefoo school was taken. The rumour was that they were interrogating them long into the night, accusing them of anti-Japanese business activities, although nobody, not even the interrogators, can have been quite sure what these might be.

For the first time in her life, Lilla, usually fearfully proud of her tiny business empire, must have been grateful to be overlooked.

The next day the soldiers came back. They came back to every house they had taken a businessman from to see if there was 'any incriminating evidence', wrote Gladys McMullan Murray, whose husband and brother were both being interrogated. I can just see the soldiers in their helmets swarming through the dusty Casey & Co. factory that had been locked up for months. I can hear their boots rattling down the empty aisles between the seamstresses' benches. Hear the flutter of paper as they turned the office drawers inside out, looking for evidence that didn't exist. Hear glass splintering as they knocked Lilla's photographs off the side-tables in her apartment, off the Steinway, to check whether documents were hidden inside. The crash of her bedroom drawers as they were turned upside down on the floor, strewing her silk underwear about the room in a mêlée of lace and bayonets. I can see Lilla standing there, yearning to rush around tidying everything up but finding her limbs frozen in fear. As she watched the soldiers pile up bundles of customer orders, details of fabric weaves and shipping bills, she must have wondered what they were asking Casey about. Would he remember each customer order, each fabric design? Give the right answers? If he didn't, what would the Japanese do to him?

The soldiers came back and back, writes Murray in her autobiography. They 'kept coming in . . . They removed the telephone. All our private papers were burned and all valuables taken.' Murray hid a few things in her young daughter's soft toys, hoping that they at least would not be bayoneted. I can see Lilla perched on a chair, her head bent over the dresses and coats in her lap, using the light of a reading lamp to stitch her jewellery into their hems.

Each morning the businessmen's wives and families, all wearing their armbands, would walk past the Astor House Hotel to show the prisoners that they were still alive and well. We 'dared not stand still', writes Murray, 'but only walked slowly past'. The prisoners stood at the windows, staring out to sea, unable to speak.

I can picture Lilla and Mabel meeting on the beach-front, near the hotel. Mabel, Vivvy's wife, who was looking after her eighty-six-year-old mother, Josephine Lavers, nonetheless with her gloves neatly ironed and her hat pushed back into shape. Lilla's hair arranged, her diamond earrings in her ears, looking as good as she can to show Casey she's all right. They walk past the hotel as slowly as the cold and the Japanese guards allow, hoping to glimpse their husbands through a window.

And when she had done this, Lilla must have returned home, sat down at her typewriter and started to type.

It can't have taken Lilla long to finish her 'Course of Cooking', that first dozen pages of tips and hints. Then she was on to stocks and soups. A great long list of soups. Recipes she had in her head. Recipes she found in books, had cut out of magazines and newspapers. Recipes given to her by friends. Something, at least, they could still chatter about. Some sound familiar: asparagus soup, leek soup, mushroom soup. Others bring a sigh of relief that I wasn't born fifty years earlier: bone soup, giblet soup, kidney soup, liver soup, ox-foot soup and sheep's head soup. A few take me back in time, to that comforting, fuzzy glow of television costume dramas: beef tea, mutton broth, Scotch broth, mulligatawny soup. The names evoke nursery teas and old-fashioned kitchens. Warm, cosy images a galaxy away from Lilla alone in her apartment, trying not to think about what would happen next. Trying to keep herself immersed in a world where there were still the leftovers of great joints of lamb, pork and beef to make stock from. A world in which these had not long since vanished from the market stalls. Where the men hadn't vanished from their homes. And where she could keep on hoping that everything would be all right again.

The sheer flimsiness of the paper Lilla was typing on seems to emphasize how tenuous these hopes were. After the first couple of pages of blank paper Lilla ran out and turned to typing on ricepaper receipts, torn from a blank book left behind by the soldiers. The ricepaper is so thin that I can see right through it. It is hard to believe that it has survived the shifts and stamps of an old-fashioned typewriter.

But Lilla was gentle and neat. I imagine her edging the paper in, typing slowly, easing the machine forward and back, from side to side, and winding it out without a single crease.

On Christmas Day 1941, as a gesture, as if clinging on to the idea that this was an honourable war, the Japanese let the businessmen go home briefly. Just long enough for a church service and Christmas lunch. Lilla, Casey, Mabel, Vivvy and Mabel's mother – Lilla's family in Chefoo – would have eaten together. Vivvy and Casey would not have uttered a single word about what they were going through in the hotel, not wanting to worry their wives any more than necessary. But, looking at their husbands' pale, wasted faces, Lilla and Mabel would

272

have known without asking that something awful was happening to them.

I am trying to imagine their meal. Lilla must have been living off peas, beans, lentils and peanuts, as everyone else in Chefoo was doing at the time. 'Just as nourishing as meat,' she later wrote, 'especially if suet dumplings, bacon or fried bread are served with them.' But on Christmas Day Lilla must have managed to lay her hands on at least a chicken, its flesh lean and taut from age. Her chef long since gone, she would have basted it again and again in its own thin juice, kept it well covered, not allowed a drop of moisture to escape. Still, it can't have been the same as turkey or goose. They must have chewed through their mouthfuls, pushing a smile on to their faces between each bite. Trying to have a normal Christmas conversation, talking about anything they could think of except the war. If they could think of anything else at all. Then they would have exchanged presents. Something small, a token. A favourite piece of embroidery. A drawing. A card. It was hard, almost impossible, to find anything new, so, like everyone else in Chefoo, they circulated their own treasures. Then tried to sing, Casey and Vivvy mustering all the enthusiasm they could, with Lilla accompanying them on the piano, striking chords.

When the soldiers came back that afternoon to take the men away again, they took Lilla's car with them. The car she'd boasted about to Ada. The car in which she and Casey had gone on so many picnics and dashes across the peninsula to see her brother Reggie in Tsingtao. Or even just out at night, when it was too cold or wet or far to walk. By Christmas 1941, there hadn't been any petrol for over a year. Still, the car had been sitting in the garage as if one day soon she'd take it out again. As the Japanese soldiers drove it off, they took that hope away too.

* * *

273

A few days later, after going to wave to Casey, Lilla picked her way around the ice on the road over Consulate Hill and walked up to the Japanese consulate, a large concrete block overlooking the harbour, to deliver a letter. Everyone else, she'd heard, had been given a receipt for their cars, as though they'd be able to claim them back in a couple of months' time. Another gesture. A hopeful one. But any straw was worth clinging to. Honoured Sir, she wrote. Would you kindly allow me. I should be so grateful. With many thanks. Yours faithfully. She took the letter right to the door, addressing it to the commanding officer, Colonel Shingo.

After two attempts, one of her letters came back with a reply. I have it in front of me. Lilla's letter is written on thin, semi-transparent, almost shiny paper. As if to emphasize her straitened circumstances, she has used both sides rather than run to a separate sheet. The Japanese reply is on imperiously thicker paper. I can almost feel the roughness of the weave. It is just four lines long but the sheet is double, leaving three grandly empty pages that shout out to the recipient that Japan is very much in power. This is followed by a part-printed, part-written Japanese ricepaper receipt. Lilla must have wondered how this could be all that was left of the great metal hulk of her car.

At the end of January, Casey came home. As the UN War Crimes Commission charge number UK-J/C.24 spells out, he and the other businessmen imprisoned had by then spent several weeks being 'subjected to protracted interrogations on the suspicion of espionage, conducted by Sergeant Keichi Ohga of the gendarmerie'. No details of the methods of questioning used are given. But, as though they were trying to break the spirit remaining in those who could still walk after being interrogated, the Japanese then paraded several of their shattered prisoners – most of whom were as elderly as Casey and Vivvy, everyone else having gone off to fight – through the streets of Chefoo. And, every few hundred yards, they brought their miserable captives to a halt and made 'derogatory speeches' intended to humiliate them.

Casey came back to Lilla a shadow of the man who had stumbled out of the apartment in December.

Vivvy, relatively impervious to his surroundings or at least good enough at pretending, came home too. The one man who didn't come back was Vivvy's boss, Bob McMullan, who'd taken on the busted rump of Cornabé Eckford and given everyone in Lilla's family a job a decade beforehand. Now the biggest taipan in town, and Grand Master of the Masons as Vivvy had been, McMullan had been sent to a jail in Tsingtao. 'These things,' wrote Gladys McMullan Murray, Bob's sister, 'seemed to make him more suspect.' Three long months later, in April, his wife was at last told he was being released. But on the day he was supposed to return, as she was putting up the balloons, the ribbons and the welcome-home signs, a passing Japanese soldier casually called out to her that her husband had died in jail. It was later said that he had been locked in a cell too small to stand up in and slowly poisoned to death.

After that the anti-British demonstrations returned with vehemence. The marches up and down the seafront continued. From time to time the Japanese authorities set up vast outdoor cinema screens and herded hundreds of Chinese in front of them to watch films proclaiming the 'New Order in East Asia'. Reel after reel showed villages and towns being occupied by lorryloads of immaculate Japanese troops, skies full of gleaming aeroplanes and Japanese flags flying from every post. The Chinese were left in no doubt as to who controlled their fate. And as the Chinese fear of their Japanese occupiers grew, so the pitch of their anti-Western shouts heightened.

Rumours flew of former servants selling 'information' to the Japanese. Japanese official after official – naval, consular, military – turned up at British and American 'enemy national' doors. They measured up the premises and gave the inhabitants form after form to fill in before departing with a different warning of evacuation or eviction each time. And at night, Lilla and Casey had to bolt and shutter their doors and windows against the starving Chinese who viewed the new status quo as an invitation to take what they could.

But Lilla still didn't want to leave China. Her possessions, her houses, her businesses, the legacy that she had built up for her children, everything was in Chefoo. She knew that if she and Casey left now, they would never see any of it again. So, when they were offered places on one of the diplomats' boats that left Shanghai for England in August 1942, they turned them down. Lilla must have somehow still been telling herself and everyone around her to 'Hang on ... things may change for the better.' In any case poverty in an England which, at that stage of the war, might still have been invaded can't have seemed a much better proposition than staying in China. And, as I have to keep reminding myself, back then Lilla had no idea how long the war would last. Or what was about to happen.

It must have been just after the diplomats' boats had left that the rumour first surfaced that all 'enemy nationals' were going to be taken into a camp. Locked up together like cattle so that the Japanese could swarm into their homes. Panicking, some of the Westerners started standing in front of their houses like the street hawkers they had once ignored, trying to turn baskets full of possessions – books, binoculars, photograph frames, candlesticks, furniture, anything – into hard cash that they could stuff into their clothes and take with them when they went. Others gave their belongings to their

German and Italian friends, who would not be going with them. Lilla gave some of hers to her houseboy. He'd kept on coming to help her even when she hadn't had anything other than a meaningless IOU to pay him with. He promised to take good care of everything. Especially her fur coat. She would need it, he said, for the winter, when she came out of the camp in a few weeks' time.

Nobody knew when or where they would be going but the moment Lilla knew she might be leaving she would have begun to prepare. I imagine her packing just as neatly as she did everything else, layering crinkling tissue between each item. Not as optimistic as her houseboy, she opens a suitcase and folds in warm clothes, furs, cashmere, hats, gloves, stockings. Pairs and pairs of thick stockings. Long underpants for Casey. And shoes. If they ran out of shoes in camp – she would have thought this through – they'd be barefoot. Bedlinen, towels, tea towels. In between the layers of clothes, she slides photographs. She sews her jewellery into the lining of the dress she will wear when they depart and works out how to tie bundles of cash around her and Casey's waists. Then come Casey's books, her recipe book and the typewriter – her hope-creator in the greying world around her. She wedges spare ribbon into the corners of a suitcase and searches the apartment for every last scrap of paper to take with her. And food. The greatest picnic she would ever pack. A picnic that might have to go on for longer than she cared to think. A picnic of everything she could squeeze in or carry and that would last. Tinned meats, fish, fruit, vegetables, rice pudding. And cooking implements. A mixing bowl. A wooden spoon. A saucepan. Sugar. Salt. Pepper. Spices that might turn whatever they were given into something they could swallow. Then, a few pretty things. Small pleasures that could still make her smile. A couple of prints. Some of

Casey's embroidery. Make-up. Hairpins. A sewing kit. Lace. Soap.

It was only October when the knock at the door came, but it had already snowed. A deep, early snow that heralded an exceptionally bitter winter. Lilla opened the door to find a group of Japanese soldiers blocking her in. She and Casey were to be taken to what the soldiers euphemistically referred to as a 'civilian assembly centre'. They had one hour to prepare and could take a single suitcase each. They were told that they would be able to return in a few days' time to collect anything else they needed. In a few days' time, after the looters had had the run of the place. Lilla knew that anything she left behind now she would never see again. She fixed her hair and make-up, changed into her jewellery-laden dress and threw on an extra overcoat too bulky to pack. She bundled Casey up in his coat too.

Lilla must have made a final frantic dash around the apartment, her home. Was there anything else she should take? Anything else she could take? The apartment was still overflowing with dozens of precious objects that she had collected over the years. Each piece of furniture arranged just so. Every lampshade, every curtain, carefully chosen. And as she walked out the door, Lilla, like everyone else, was forced to leave her home open 'to anyone who cared to enter', writes Murray. 'Looters were encouraged by our captors.'

Lilla and Casey's bags would have been very heavy. Maybe, like many of the other Westerners staggering along the streets that morning, they found a wheelbarrow to struggle with. If they were lucky, they would have been allowed to pay for a rickshaw to take their suitcases.

In a straggling column, the 'enemy nationals' walked past the harbour and through the crowded, narrow lanes of the old Chinese city. The Chinese stopped and stared at their former princes turned into paupers, whispering in Chinese, says Murray, 'O, they will eat much bitterness now. They have nothing but bits and pieces.'

They walked for a couple of miles. Up Temple Hill to the American Presbyterian mission compounds that lay between the hospital and the temple pagoda at the top. Temple Hill, where Lilla had been for so many picnics as a child, as a Heavenly Twin, as a grand hostess in Chefoo. Now she was going as something altogether different. The high stone walls of the compounds were surrounded by great rolls of barbed wire. Smaller pieces were strewn about the ground to catch anyone who approached. There were guards at the gates. Stepping carefully along the path, Lilla filed in.

13

EATING BITTERNESS

Civilian Assembly Centre, Chefoo, late October 1942, ten months after Pearl Harbor

THERE IS SOMETHING particularly terrible about being forced to leave your home. Its familiar walls bulge with memories. Each room has its own atmosphere – a hidden smell that stirs your senses into the right mood to eat, talk or sleep. It's where your roots have pushed their way between the gaps in the floorboards and the cracks in the bricks.

And when you are torn away, the roots remain, ripped apart and weeping.

Lilla was to find the next three years of her life so horrific that she would hardly be able to talk about them. Not even to the BBC camera crew who would one day come to interview her about her experiences as a prisoner, about how she'd written her recipe book. It was her opportunity for fifteen minutes of fame but she sat in a high-backed chair that stood by itself in her grand-daughter's drawing room, legs neatly crossed, unable to bring herself to say a word. To her family she occasionally let slip odd snippets of information about her time in camp. Fragments that betrayed some of the pain and indignity she had tried to erase. And I have her recipe book – a book of the memories that she'd wished she had instead.

But life in this first camp and in the second, worse camp that Lilla was sent to was so restricted, so unrelentingly focused around the basics of survival, that her fellow prisoners have been able to paint me a vivid picture of what happened to her. Each of them gives a different viewpoint of internment, a different camera angle, according to their age and gender and whether they came from the business or missionary community – the latter looking at the world through a softer focus. Gladys McMullan Murray came from a business family and was in her early forties when she was interned with her husband and four of her children, ranging from nineteen to four years old. Nearly all the others who have spoken or written about these camps were far younger than Lilla when they were imprisoned.

And if they are young enough to be still alive today, then they were too young to notice a grey-haired lady writing a recipe book in the camp. Also, to the young, like J. G. Ballard's semi-autobiographical Jim in *Empire of the Sun*, rather than curtailing their freedom, war and internment offered a great adventure. In the words of David Michell, who was a nine-year-old pupil at the mission boarding school in Chefoo when he went into the camp on Temple Hill with his sister, Joyce, who was then ten, 'What school child wouldn't jump at the chance of a Tom Sawyer-like existence, where nothing was normal, particularly school work?'

But life for the older people in the camp was far, far harder. Norman Cliff, at seventeen, should have been graduating from the Chefoo mission boarding school that year but instead found himself being interned with his two younger sisters, Lelia, fourteen, and Estelle, twelve.

He describes how 'the physical and mental strains of internment life' took their toll on the prisoners, 'particularly those over forty. There were mental breakdowns, workers collapsing on shift with fainting and low blood pressure.' Joan Ward, née Croft, is the only internee I found who remembers Lilla. She holds an image in her head of Lilla 'as a rather refined, elegant person walking down the street of the camp, her head up, bearing herself well'. She didn't know Lilla well enough to remember her recipe book but still describes with feeling how 'the hungrier we became, the more obsessed with food we were'. And, as Ward was interned with her parents, she was acutely aware of how different the experience was for young and old. One of the most painful things for the older people in the camp was that, right at the end of their working lives, when they had just saved up enough to retire, they suddenly found themselves penniless. Like Lilla and Casey. 'Losing everything in your sixties, as my father did, was torment,' Ward told me. Particularly when you had no idea whether you would find work, or still be physically capable of doing it, when you were released.

The mission compounds on Temple Hill contained several spacious detached family houses – spacious, that is, if a single family were living in each – a church, a hospital and a couple of schoolhouses. All were built, as the drawing I have shows, in a fusion style of Italianate arches and pagoda roofs. They spread over a broad swathe of the Temple Hill slopes that led out towards the sea on what was, looking from the Chefoo Club on First Beach, the far side of the harbour. To convert the compounds into an internment camp, the Japanese had encircled three areas, each containing one or two family houses, with barbed wire. As Lilla arrived with the rest of the business community – all the Chefoo enemy nationals who were not part of the mission boarding schools that still stood at the far end of First Beach – they were directed towards the houses next to the church, on the seaward side of the hill.

The houses were wrecks. After the missionaries had gone, the Japanese Army had camped in them and then left them to fall down. 'The rooms were dirty, and all the plumbing was out of order,' writes Gladys McMullan Murray. The stoves used for heating were broken. And there were only two houses for the hundred people filing in – the hundred who weren't German or Italian, and so on the same side as the Japanese. The hundred who had been foolish, hopeful or desperate enough to stay in Chefoo.

That made fifty prisoners to each family-sized house.

It worked out as anywhere between six and seventeen to a room. Dining room, sitting room, nursery or bedroom. Martha Philips, a missionary teaching at the Chefoo school but moved into a business community house, remembers five of them being put in 'a tiny upstairs room, which was not much bigger than a walk-in closet'. The rooms had bare floorboards, dusty corners, a broken-down broken-up metal stove squatting along one wall and wide windows that had once given a sweeping view of a busy Chefoo – and whose grimy panes now gaped curtainless across a dying town. Men, women, children, all ages, were jumbled up together. I imagine the arriving internees wobbling – nearly all of them, like Lilla, wearing as many layers as they could to take that tiny bit more with them – towards their spaces on the floor. Each dormitory must have looked like some grotesque boarding school or summer camp. Instead of fresh glowing teenage faces, the dried and battered features of a terrified and already malnourished ageing population stared up from the floor.

* * *

The first night there weren't even mattresses to sleep on. Dodging each other's knees and elbows, the prisoners eased open their bags and piled their clothes into bedding on the floor. And then, trying to stick to familiar routines, in a vain attempt to convince themselves that everything was still all right, they tried to change for bed.

It can't have been easy. Especially sitting on the floor in a small room, with no discreet corner in which to hide from several new pairs of eyes. Each time that Lilla's clothes caught on her underwear, baring the folds of skin that she would have struggled so hard to conceal, it must have felt like being forced to reveal a secret that stripped away her dignity.

One elderly lady couldn't bring herself to change in front of everyone else, writes Gladys McMullan Murray. She sat on the floor, not moving, simply unable to do it. When the lights dimmed, she popped out into the corridor to be alone, unaware that the light on the stairs was illuminating her, like a stage spot, to everyone back inside.

By the time I started writing this book, Gladys was no longer around to talk to. But I've often wondered whether that was Lilla.

A couple of days later, the prisoners were allowed home to fetch mattresses and bedding. Those who could brought back curtains to divide their tiny spaces into mini-cubicles. These gave the prisoners a gesture of privacy but made the rooms feel even more jam-packed, leaving little space to move. And they couldn't stop the noises, or the smells.

It was hard to sleep. A single heavy snorer could keep a dozen of them awake all night. One lady 'snored every night, so loudly that the shingles rattled'. And it wasn't just the noise of the irregular, unfamiliar, heaving breathing that would have kept Lilla awake – it was its proximity. I can imagine her lying there, fraying sheets enclosing her and Casey in an area the size of a small double bed, trying to sleep, but surrounded by the stale breath exhaled from a dozen pairs of lungs that belonged to people she knew well – her brother Vivvy, his wife Mabel, Mabel's octogenarian mother – but had never wanted to be quite this close to. The sweating dampness of so many strange feet and armpits in such a small space added to the ageing mist that crept around the room.

But it was fear, rather than physical discomfort, that made the greatest contribution to the prisoners' insomnia. 'We often lay awake,' writes Murray, 'thinking apprehensively of the future.'

Once they had been herded through the barbed wire into the camp compounds and the gates were locked, the prisoners were more or less left to organize themselves as 'the Japanese officials did not want the responsibility'. They were allowed to hire outside workmen to repair the boilers and stoves used for heating and cooking. And then, 'with no more servants around, we all had to pitch in . . . every one of us in camp had our regular chores, from sweeping floors to peeling potatoes'. In Philips's house, 'we selected two teams who worked on alternate days to plan, prepare and serve meals'. And in that of Wiley Glass, a Baptist missionary who was in the business camp with his wife and daughter, 'some chopped kindling and brought in coal . . . The younger men pumped water, two at a time. It was a strenuous job.'

The lack of running water in the camp meant few opportunities to wash. Whether it was for cooking or bathing, every drop was rationed. Once it had been pumped out of the ground it was then carried into the house, where it was systematically heated saucepanful by saucepanful 'with hot water being taken one way and cold water brought from the other direction'. If you wanted the luxury of a bath – in a tin tub filled for the purpose in a barely lit cellar – then the water had to be shared. And even bathing in somebody else's dirt was a treat, says Murray. So much so that one teenage girl, on finding the tub full, leaped in – only to discover the grease and leaves of a cabbage soup clinging to her skin. Nonetheless, 'folks managed to keep fairly decent'.

But it wasn't just their own bodies that the prisoners had to keep clean. Packed like sardines into spaces designed for far fewer, the internees' elbows, knees and ankles must have risked rubbing each other raw, their flaking skins creating a snowstorm of dust to battle with. Added to this was the 'inconvenience', Glass mentions, of the 'lack of a dining room'. This meant that after the prisoners had 'picked up their plates cafeteria style, we took our food to our bedrooms and ate on the small bit of floor space marked out as ours'. Inevitably, as the internees ate squatting on their beds, dropping crumbs, splashing drinks and spilling food, bacteria bred unstoppably. The prisoners did the best they could with the limited water supply but, as the weeks passed, the conditions deteriorated. The outdoor latrines were 'by far the biggest shock of the Temple Hill compound', as they became 'a seething sea of maggots'.

The dirt and ripened stench of such communal living must have been very hard to bear. Especially for Lilla. Lilla who loved to clean, who loved to put things in order, for whom being well dressed and washed was almost a raison d'être. She faced a daily struggle just to make herself feel neat. I can see her, sitting on her mattress in the dormitory, trying to put her hair up in a way that would disguise the fact that she couldn't wash it as often as she'd like. Dabbing a little powder, rouge even, on her cheeks. Checking that her diamond earrings were still in her ears – the safest place for them. Pulling herself up, standing tall, shoulders back, and facing up to the shrunken world around her.

As October passed into November and then December the hours of daylight faded and the internees' spirits dimmed with them. 'A bitterly cold winter descended upon us,' writes Cliff, and 'clothes were wearing out'. Replacements were being stitched together from the curtains and drapes that the prisoners had brought with them. At least the body heat generated by so many souls living cheek by jowl meant that 'it did not take much to keep the rooms warm'. But even then the prisoners sifted all the ashes 'to find any cinders that might burn again'. And, hands and legs chapped by the cold, they often found themselves down to their last bucket of coal, unsure when another delivery might come.

At Christmas there was an attempt to raise the mood in the camp. On Christmas Day, the internees were allowed to visit the other houses in the compounds and each house made a card to mark the occasion. I have a photocopy of the cards from the two houses in the business-community camp. Two long columns of signatures sit beside oriental pen-and-ink drawings on each page. The names of Mabel Eckford and her mother, Josephine Lavers, are written in the same steady hand. This makes me think that Mrs Lavers, a small but once-strong woman heading towards ninety, was already too feeble to write herself. I am relieved to see Casey's signature still scrawled in his own writing on the opposite side of the page.

There are several signatures missing from Lilla's house. Maybe the internees' names have slipped off the edge of my photocopy. Maybe they just couldn't bring themselves to join in the jollity. Or maybe they saw the list for what it appears now – not the mark of a festive occasion, but a sad register of those locked away.

Strangely enough, Vivvy's signature isn't there although he must have been in the same house as Lilla, Mabel and her mother. I wonder if it's because he did the drawings instead? The drawings of a stick-thin temple pagoda perched on top of a hill. Of a lone hunched man on a donkey. Of a tree whose leaves look as though they would pierce your skin, its branches bowed.

Beyond the lack of space and sanitation, there was no orchestrated cruelty to the prisoners' living conditions. The Japanese authorities even encouraged regular visits from the town's German Jewish dentist – unaware that he was passing on in whispered French and German the news he had picked up from the radio. And in early 1943, when Lilla had been a prisoner for about four months, the camp commandant – nicknamed 'Candleblower' for the face he made while listening to the regular morning roll-call – handed over to a Major Kosaka, who was 'immaculately dressed ... with a kindly face and impeccable manners'. Kosaka allowed sand to be brought into the camp for the children to play in, and even gave them a supply of fireworks to let off when crowds of thousands gathered for festivals at the nearby temple.

In general, apart from roll-call, where the prisoners had to call out their number in the line in Japanese – which they had to learn to count in – the guards' interference was limited to insisting that anyone with money helped support his fellow prisoners. 'In polite English, but with a bayonet at his throat, they told a Greek import-export man, "Yes, you put in money, please. Thank you."' For the first few months the internees bought their own food through former Chinese house servants who had been assigned the task of coming to the camp each day to take orders. Even fresh bread was delivered daily from the baker still operating in the town – who also seized the opportunity to pass discreet messages between the three separated camps of the business community and the boys' and girls' mission schools. And a few piglets were smuggled into the children's compounds, where they were hidden under the verandas and fattened up. 'We fed them aspirin to keep them quiet,' remembers the then nine-year-old Mary Taylor Previte.

Before the winter was over, however, the money had run out and the prisoners had to fall back on limited Japanese rations. 'We ran short of meat, butter and sugar,' and 'stocks of flour . . . often ran dangerously low only to be renewed in the nick of time'.

Little more is said about the food here in the Temple Hill camp. The reason for this, I think, is that it was barely any different to the miserable fare of peanuts, beancurd, cabbage and bread that the prisoners had already been scraping by on for almost a year before they had gone into the camp.

But later, there would be hardly any food at all.

In Chefoo, spring had always meant the beginning of summer, glorious summer, visitors and parties, new faces and dancing until dawn. And as the snow melted around them the prisoners must have held their breath in anticipation of something better to come. Surely this war had to end soon?

It didn't. Instead, five months after Lilla had walked into the Temple Hill compound, spring disappeared into a summer that brought a blistering heat to the bursting houses. Whereas sleeping – and living – a dozen to a room had been tolerable in the cooler months, in summer it became unbearable. With temperatures rising to 49 degrees Centigrade inside, some of the younger people moved their mattresses outdoors. But Casey can't have been up to this. And Lilla didn't leave his side. They must have stayed in their dormitory, being cooked alive

like two lobsters in a pan, until the heat drove them to try
to drag their mattresses and belongings out of the oven
that the house had become. And then, bent over the
weight of their bedding, heaved away, tears in their eyes.

It must have been hard for Lilla and Casey to feel
married in the camp. Imprisonment warps relationships,
and everything that people expect marriage to be – a
couple's own living space, moments alone together,
shared dreams – had gone. At least Lilla and Casey could
still share a hope to go on, to return to their old lives
together. But the war ate into even this. Casey grew
feebler. Both his determination to survive and his
physical strength began to ebb. Lilla nursed him as well
as she could. And as she helped him move around, she
had to persuade him that everything would, she was
sure, be all right.

But she couldn't have been sure. The very worst part of
being imprisoned was that as each empty day stretched
into the next, with the prisoners struggling to fill their
time, nobody had any idea how long they would be there.
The internees may have called their prison a camp, but
camp is a deceptively temporary word. Maybe deliberately so. Everything it suggests – packing up and moving
on, starlit nights and open air, fresh game roasted over a
wood fire – is everything a prison is not.

And as the weeks passed into months, the expectation
that the war would end soon must have begun to recede
– replaced by a growing, stomach-emptying fear that it
might never end.

It must have made every gut rumble, stench, pile of dirt
and breath of someone else's exhaled air all the more
painful.

In the middle of all this hunger, this discomfort, this
uncertainty, whenever the daily grind of cooking,
washing, cleaning receded, Lilla was writing her
recipe book. Her recipe book of cosy homes and full bellies.

Of newly-wed lives and grand hopes for the future.

It can't have been easy to think about all that there. But, like her fellow prisoners, Lilla must have been desperate to find activities to fill her days. On arriving in the camp, Cliff and his friends had 'walked round and round the house, six times to a mile, to pass the time'. But after this initial enthusiasm, 'the months at Temple Hill dragged on monotonously'. As the weeks and months passed, the monotony worsened. And, sheltered behind her makeshift cubicle curtains, as if hiding from the oppressive tedium of the camp, Lilla must have perched the typewriter on her knees as she squatted at the end of her mattress and slowly and deliberately punched each letter in turn. 'M-e-l-t t-h-e b-u-t-t-e-r . . .'

As I read through Lilla's book now, my mind stuck in the crowded, smelly house on Temple Hill, it seems hard to believe that the world of her recipes had existed so recently, so close by. A world of freshly pressed clothes, the scent of clean laundry tinged with a hint of hot-ironed starch. Of silver gleaming on long white tablecloths, the sunlight reflecting off it into little spots of light dancing on the wood-panelled walls. Of jazz playing on a gramophone in a room nearby. Of bottles of wine being poured into decanters. Of kitchens full of cooks and steaming pots. Of piles of thinly sliced beef and vegetables waiting on thick wooden chopping boards. Of great white meringues cooling under gauze. Of buckets full of raspberries and mixing bowls stiff with peaks of freshly whipped cream. Of the feeling that guests are about to arrive.

The recipes seem to cast a kind of magic as I read them. Somehow they bring this other, old world to life, take me right there and make me want to reach for a cocktail, hum along with the music. Sneeze because the smell of spice is tickling the back of my nose. And as she typed, Lilla must have escaped there too. Escaped back home for the moments her fingers were knocking the keys and her mind was absorbed in what to write next. Perhaps when Vivvy sat with her, whisking his strokes of pen and ink on to the pages she had finished, all this was easier to believe. Perhaps she read the recipes out to Casey – I can almost hear her doing so, her stutter tripping her at every line, yet still trying to persuade him to believe in it too.

Four decades later, when she pulled out the manuscript from the bottom of the suitcase it had been hiding in for so long, Lilla said that she had written the book 'for my fellow prisoners'. Perhaps, once she was in a prison camp, it was their desire to go on reading page after page that helped her find the strength to keep churning them out.

But each time Lilla stopped typing or reading, the aroma of rich gravy giving way to the damp smell of cabbage leaves, the jazz notes and dinner-party chatter being drowned out by the indeterminate groans and clatter of fifty people and a house bulging to over-capacity, the starched tablecloth dissolving into the crumpled sheets on her bed, the dining room disappearing into the chipped bowl she had to balance on her lap, the searing contrast must have burnt her like the fat from one of her dreamed-of pans.

The order to move came in August, ten months after Lilla had been taken from her home and put into the camp. The initial instructions from the Japanese were almost cryptically brief: 'MAKE IMMEDIATE PREPARATIONS TO BE TRANSFERRED TO THE WEIHSIEN CIVIL ASSEMBLY CENTRE' was barked at the internees by a 'top-ranking' Japanese officer who had appeared from headquarters. The Weihsien Civil Assembly Centre, the prisoners soon learned, was a much larger camp and already contained all the enemy nationals from Peking, Tientsin and Tsingtao, who had been there since March. The Temple Hill commandant,

Kosaka, went to look at it. Take everything you have, he warned the Chefoo internees ominously on his return, the conditions there will be far worse.

By the time they left the camp it was September 1943. Lilla and Casey had already been in a prison camp for almost a year. They packed up their belongings, their mattresses, whatever tins, if any, Lilla had managed to keep, and walked back down the hill to the port.

Even the Chefoo outside the camp was a different town to the one of Lilla's recipe book. The old picnic panorama of town and bay, junks and steamers jostling in the harbour, Consulate Hill just beyond, that she had so often climbed Temple Hill to feast on had long since vanished. The streets were emptier. The harbour was subdued. The mass of Japanese gunmetal hulks that had come right into the shore – the US and British navies had always moored a little way out – had suffocated the usual bustle of tiny boats. If Lilla had been able to see far enough, she might have spotted the strangers who had taken over her home – most of the vacated buildings in Chefoo were occupied by Japanese soldiers – bumping into the furniture, moving it around. If any had been left by the looters. Or even her little houses where, by now, the blue silk curtains she had designed would have been torn, if not ripped away completely by their temporary inhabitants. The furniture gone, every strip of woodwork smeared with black boot polish.

I hope she never saw that far.

The same crowd of Chinese faces that had watched the prisoners walk into the camp swarmed out to watch them pass again in their now dishevelled clothes and worn shoes. Lilla and Casey, the rest of the business community and the couple of hundred Chefoo school-children were, remembers Gladys McMullan Murray, 'literally packed into a small steamer'. Although the old walled city of Weihsien was only about one hundred miles inland from Chefoo, there was no railway between the two towns and the prisoners first had to make the sea journey around the Shantung peninsula to Tsingtao and take a train from there.

The steamer pulled out of the harbour, past the row of red-brick houses Lilla had been born in, rounded Consulate Hill and headed out to the open sea, leaving behind the club, the beach, the hotels, the school and the Casey & Co. building that stood on the waterfront. I wonder whether Lilla was one of those on deck watching the only real home they knew disappear from sight.

The journey was tough. 'It was a miserable voyage,' writes Murray, 'the hold and every available space packed with people . . . our youngest slept in my arms . . . it was unbearably stuffy in the hold . . . and the smells on the ship were nauseating as the plumbing had gone wrong.' The 'floor was hard, the ship was rocking, our stomachs were hungry and rats were running over us', remembers the usually upbeat Cliff.

And it was dangerous. The portholes were 'covered by thick sacking lest American submarines should spot us' and 'there was also the danger of the mines left by the American navy'. Equally chilling was the fact that 'it was the season of the annual breaking-up storm for which Chefoo is famous' – a season marked in Chefoo's long consular records as an annual September toll of shipwreck deaths.

After two days and nights of merciful calm, the ship docked at Tsingtao early in the morning of the third day. Lilla must have wanted to leap for joy. The town's gingerbread churches and wooden chalet houses were untouched. Just as they had been on so many trips to see her brother Reggie, for those picnic lunches, those

Empire Day Sports that he'd organized on the beach each year. But this time Reggie wasn't waiting to meet them. Of course he wasn't. Lilla didn't know whether he had escaped, died, or would be waiting for her at the next camp.

The first they saw of the camp was the watchtowers. The photographs show squat medieval stone turrets with pointed wooden hats, the tips of machine guns pointing out like black teeth. Then they saw that the high walls 'were electrified', writes Murray, and 'our hearts sank . . . we didn't know what was in store for us'. But it was when they drew through the gates that the real shock came. The streets were lined with hundreds of prisoners staring at the new arrivals. The men were barefoot and bare-chested, wearing only shorts, their skinny backs tanned to leather from working in the sun, 'like creatures from another world'.

Lilla must have seen Reggie there. Standing in the crowd. Waving at her, calling out to her and Vivvy furiously. Reggie half his usual size, missing that crisply pressed open-necked shirt and the whistle round his neck with which he always seemed to be starting some race or umpiring some match. Reggie standing alone because his wife had made it back to England and his children had all gone off to nurse or fight in the war. Reggie smiling to see her, his eyes shining with relief that she was still alive.

14
THE BIG CAMP

*Weihsien internment camp, North China,
September 1943, eleven months into Lilla's
imprisonment*

THE NEW CAMP spread out in front of Lilla in row
after row of long, thin, grey huts as far as she could
see. Here and there, the single-storey skyline of this
former missionary compound was punctuated by a taller
building hovering over the tips of the low trees dotted
along the alleyways and open spaces between the buildings. The pictures drawn by inmates show that each
block was peppered with a row of door- and window-
shaped holes, like a long line of animal stalls. A series of
beams protruded out of the front of each row like the side
of a cage that had been temporarily lifted to let the
creatures out. Clothes flapped from the wooden poles. A
few greying sheets and towels seemed to skip just clear of
the quagmire that must have been oozing like a lava flow
through every gap the buildings allowed. 'The monsoon
rains were late that year,' writes Pamela Masters, a
teenager who had gone straight into Weihsien from
Tientsin, with her parents and two elder sisters. The
rains usually came in August, but when Lilla arrived in

September the camp pathways were still inundated, the compound a sticky sea of mud.

The mud stank. The stench must have hit the back of Lilla's nostrils and the top of her throat as her bus rolled in through the camp gates. It was a reek of 'rotting human excrement', writes Masters. Of refuse and sewage. Of the discarded items that life leaves behind – which, in a way, was what the two-thousand-odd inmates of Weihsien, the remnants of the northern treaty-porters, were. The elderly and schoolchildren. Taipans and civil servants. Prostitutes and thieves. An entire jazz band from Tientsin. British, Americans, Canadians, South Africans, Dutch, Belgians, Norwegians, Greeks, Cubans, Filipinos, Jewish Palestinians, Iranians, Uruguayans, Panamanians, a lone Indian and even one German – a wife who had decided to follow her American husband and daughter into the camp. The people whose national governments had simply abandoned them to their fate. They had all been swept up in the great river of mud that was this war. Bundled together, rained on and left to rot at the far end of the world, now distinguished only by the identification badges that they 'had to wear at all times', writes Murray, who, in an attempt to render this vast new camp less frightening to her youngest daughter, stitched a badge on her doll too.

Lilla and Casey were in either block twenty or block eight. The only record of who was where in Weihsien is a column of numbers jotted alongside a camp census typed up at the end of June 1944. The smudged room numbers were inserted after this, but nobody now knows when, or whether the internees were in those rooms for a night, a week or a year. And what those numbers tell me is that, at some stage during their imprisonment, Lilla and Casey spent at least one night apart. Lilla in block twenty, room three, and Casey in block eight, room five.

*Weihsien internment camp: the perimeter fence, walls
and watchtower by the hospital block.*

The camp from the air.

As a couple of pages of prisoners' names are missing, I don't know whether they were alone in these rooms, or temporarily sharing with the husband and wife of another couple. The elderly men in block eight perhaps because it was near the men's showers and latrines, and the women in block twenty. Or, I have been told, Casey may have been ill enough to need nursing care for a while. As there was only one ward in the hospital and many nurses – nursing being one of the few professions open to women back then – an interned nurse would move in with a patient, the rest of the patient's family moving out to make room for her for as long as necessary. I don't think it can have been that long. Casey may have been weakened by interrogation and imprisonment, but he would still make several journeys across the world in the years to come. In any case, although at first sight the number of buildings in the camp made it appear large – there were sixty-odd buildings in total – at just a couple of hundred yards square, it was all too compact a space for two thousand people to eat, wash, work and sleep in. And blocks eight and twenty were both off a black cinder pathway in the north-western corner of the camp known as Tin-Pan Alley or Rocky Road, only a few yards away from each other.

The compound had a few large buildings containing old classrooms that were now being used as dormitories for the single men and women in the camp. The former missionaries' houses – the most comfortable places there – had been taken over by the Japanese. The remainder, and the majority, of the camp's accommodation consisted of those long, thin, grey huts that had been built as rows of single cells to house individual Chinese missionary students. Even before they had been abandoned, looted and occupied first by Chinese soldiers and then by the Japanese, they had been spartan. Now they were miserable, and each had to house at best just a married couple

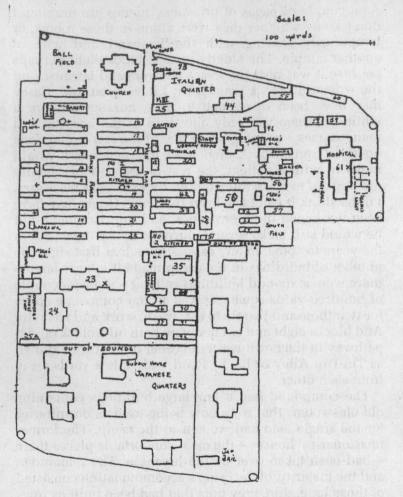

*Plan of Weihsien camp, drawn by Langdon Gilkey,
an internee.*

but often a family of four. The cells measured just nine by twelve feet — barely enough room to cram three mattresses on to the floor. The door and one window stood at the east-facing front, and there was a tiny opening for ventilation at the back. 'The rooms had all been badly neglected,' writes Masters, 'the white plastered walls were peeling and in need of repair, and the only electrical fixture was a ceiling lamp, hanging from a frayed cord.' And 'there was no furniture', points out Murray, 'just a shelf on the wall'.

It was Lilla's greatest domestic challenge yet. Less hospitable — and potentially hotter — than the Indian postings in which she had sweltered. Damper than the 'rat-palace' in Kashmir. Less personal than Mrs Bridges' lodgings in Calcutta — and certainly smaller. And most galling of all, a stay that each day she must have hoped to see the end of. She had already been locked up for a year. Who was to say that she wouldn't be locked up for another, or more — two, three, four or ten years, twenty even? If she survived that long. Perhaps like murderers or other penitentiary lifers, she and Casey would die in prison.

Nonetheless, I can imagine Lilla doing her best to make their cell a home. She starts with the beds. Even the height of a mattress would at least keep them a few inches away from the cockroaches that hopped around the floor at night, occasionally landing on their faces. And from the rats that left their greasy slithers along the bottom of the walls, 'of which there were a number of varieties' — 'providing the noisiest night-time entertainment by far'. She pulls some slightly crumpled embroidered linen out of their cases. After a year in camp, it isn't as fresh as it had been when she left home. Still, it is something with which to make their beds. Next she slides out the photographs and prints that she had taken from her home. Using pins, she tries to stick them on the walls. Some fall back down immediately, bringing slabs of plaster with them and exposing the grey brick. With a great deal of huffing and puffing, she and Casey manage to shunt their cases into the empty corner of their room and arrange them to make a table and chairs, of sorts. Lilla sets out a couple of tiny painted china pots at one end, spreads a small embroidered tablecloth over the middle of the trunk. Finally, she pins up a couple of tea towels over the front window. Something to close them off from the camp outside and its two thousand pairs of eyes.

That's one of the few things Lilla used to mention when she talked about the camp. That she had remembered to pack tea towels. And used them for curtains.

The one aspect of the room that would have defeated her was the light bulb dangling from the ceiling. It hung there, ugly, bare, in the centre of the tiny room, no doubt irritating her every time it caught her eye. Making her think that she ought to have brought a lampshade too.

Still, at last she and Casey had somewhere to themselves. And a precious door with which to shut out the world outside. And here in Weihsien, the world outside their little space needed much more shutting out than it had in Chefoo. Instead of looking out on the familiar, still eerily beautiful ghost town of Chefoo that might any day spring back to life, Lilla now found herself looking out at a painfully brave new world.

Every aspect of the inmates' lives in Weihsien was ordered by layer upon layer of ruthlessly efficient committees – 'everything was so much more sophisticated than at little Temple Hill', comments Cliff. These had been set up by the first prisoners to arrive at Weihsien, on the instructions of the Japanese, and by the time Lilla and the rest of the Chefoo contingent arrived, they were a well-established hierarchy committed to the principles of 'mucking in' and 'pulling your weight' to an almost authoritarian extent. There was a supplies committee that rationed out food. There was an education committee in charge of an almost terrifyingly high standard of prisoners' learning programmes that ranged from biochemistry for children to Russian for adults and athletics taught by the Olympic 400-metre champion Eric Liddell, who had been a missionary in Tientsin. A quarters committee distributed the prisoners among the cells and dormitory places as it saw fit. A discipline committee both decided upon and enforced the laws of the camp. And a labour committee allocated the camp's mainly manual jobs according to each prisoner's fitness and experience. Taipans and thieves alike were sent to clean the latrines, pump water for cooking and showers, eke meals for hundreds out of limited rations in the three camp kitchens and keep the roofs on the decaying buildings.

The committees ran an extraordinary range of camp facilities. These included camp shops offering shoe-mending, watch repairs, clothes-mending, book-binding, a barber and a general exchange known as the White Elephant. There was even a financial service provided by the Tsingtao Swiss consul, a Mr Eggar. Whenever he managed to visit Weihsien, he would distribute Red Cross 'comfort money' to prisoners in exchange for IOUs that would have to be redeemed at the end of the war. There was a fully functioning camp hospital, although with limited equipment and supplies. Urgent cases obviously took priority but prisoners with other medical needs found that these could be satisfied, too. Some female prisoners even chose to have hysterectomies there.

And there was an impressive list of camp entertainments. Baseball and softball matches, cricket matches, soccer matches, rugby, touch football, band practices, plays and musical revues were all put together to take up as much of the prisoners' time as possible. The whole committee system seems to have been designed to hypnotize the prisoners with such an array of activities and duties that their minds had no time to wander to what might be happening outside.

It worked. Weihsien was its own little metropolis. A utopia of prison camps. 'With such centralized organization, our community began to show the first signs of a dawning civilization,' wrote Langdon Gilkey, who was in his early twenties and had been teaching at Yenching University. The committees admirably kept the prisoners alive and more or less healthy and sane. They did the best job they could possibly do. The only thing they could possibly do.

But in doing so they set up a structure that would enable the Japanese to keep them there for a very long time indeed. And, despite the committees' sophisticated arrangements for education and entertainment, the basic facilities the Japanese provided for the prisoners at Weihsien were appalling. Each day began with a long wait at the latrines. As there were only about a couple of dozen lavatories for a camp population of over fifteen hundred, 'the queues for this unavoidable aspect of life were endless'. And so many were continually out of order that there was, on average, only one lavatory for every hundred prisoners. To flush them, each prisoner had to take in their own tin can of slop water from the earthenware jars that stood outside the door. Nor was there any paper. 'The stench that assailed our Western nostrils almost drove us back.' And every able-bodied woman in the camp – Lilla doubtless included – took her turn at cleaning the ladies' latrines for a week at a time.

Showering was even more open than dormitory life in the Chefoo camp. 'There were no cubicles, just open stalls,' writes Masters, who 'couldn't get used to the complete lack of privacy'. Water was pumped through the showerheads by a male prisoner sweating and grunting away on the other side of the wall.

Joan Ward explained to me that, early on, it became clear there were two sorts of people in the camp. Those who let themselves go and 'certain people who made an effort to continue to look nice'. Lilla she remembers as being one of the latter. Just as she would have battled through the loss of dignity as she cleaned the latrines, Lilla must have closed her eyes, taken a deep breath to prepare herself for the freezing water, and shut her ears to the grunts.

For the first few months at Weihsien, Lilla didn't go too hungry. The cartloads of supplies that rolled into the camp still contained green vegetables, potatoes and meat. But the meat was so packed with sinew and gristle that only a small proportion could be eaten.

Like the committees, the three camp kitchens were fanatically well run by the camp oligarchy. Any meat that arrived was pulled off the carts and sent to the two camp butchers, who brushed off any larvae – it had travelled unrefrigerated from a slaughterhouse thirty miles away – and in summer boiled it overnight as the only way of stopping it deteriorating further. The vegetables were sent directly to each kitchen, where a team of fifteen to twenty women spent the day peeling and chopping. At five o'clock each morning two cooks and five kitchen helpers turned up to start breakfast. After they had prepared the cereal and tea, they set to work on lunch. The great challenge was to try to serve a meal other than stew or 'dry – that is put on a plate rather than in a bowl'.

When the mealtime arrived, there was a team of women servers to ladle out the food to the queues of prisoners. A couple of elderly gentlemen monitored the rate at which food was distributed, making sure that there would be some for everyone. And they checked that no one came in twice. Finally, a team of washer-uppers cleaned up after each meal. Throughout the entire cooking process, a pair of storekeepers kept vigil over the quantities delivered and the quantities used – to try to make sure that as little as possible slipped into inmates' pockets instead of the communal pot.

Kitchen jobs were sought after – 'jobs kept you sane'. I have seen some drawings showing groups of women standing elbow to elbow around tubs and chopping boards, scrubbing and peeling vegetables. The drawings are simple, almost sketches, but you can still sense the camaraderie leaping out from the paper. Almost hear the banter. Stories of horse races and hunting around the treaty ports. Of dinner parties. Of sizzling meals of spicy Chinese food followed by English puddings. Of how they would cook the carrots if they were back there. Carrots coated in melted butter, thickened with flour and drowned in parsley. Or carrots so fresh that they could be shredded into thread-thin curls and doused in mustard, oil and vinaigrette.

Lilla would have undoubtedly wangled her way on to a kitchen shift. I imagine her picking up a mouldy carrot, turning it round in her fingers, taking up the challenge of turning it into something edible while saving as much of it as she could. Slicing it into whichever shape the carrots were being sliced that day – a constant rotation of sticks, circles and cubes to give an impression of variety. At the end of the day, after hours standing, arms constantly moving as if she were swimming a marathon, keeping up her end of the conversation, Lilla must have felt exhausted. Looking forward to the next day's rest yet longing to return to the hubbub. Wishing her shift came round more often than the standard one day in three. And dreading the gaps in between.

* * *

On the days they weren't working, the prisoners stretched out the daily chores of living for as long as they could. After queuing at the showers and latrines, the internees took their water buckets to the communal pump, heaving the full ones back to their rooms. Then they'd head off to wait in line for a breakfast at which tea, while it was still available, was such a precious commodity that one person's sole job was to dry out used teabags and bang them back into shape. After breakfast, Lilla set about cleaning their tiny room, sending Casey out – for a walk, a chat, or simply out – and trying to scrub the black dirt and traces of insects out of every crevice she could find. As though, if she scrubbed hard enough, the walls of her cell might dissolve back into the wood panelling of her home in Chefoo.

Mid-morning, the bell rang for roll-call. For the first few months that Lilla was at Weihsien, roll-call was a relaxed affair. The prisoners chatted, the guards made a show of counting. The arrival of Lilla and the other internees from Chefoo had pushed the numbers in the already packed camp to over two thousand. But within a couple of weeks, around four hundred Catholic clergy had been moved to an institution in Peking, and a couple of hundred Americans – including Martha Philips and Dr Glass's family – were repatriated in a prisoner exchange, taking the camp numbers back down to around fifteen hundred. Cliff 'noted that the figures chalked up on the blackboard in the guardroom had one day totalled 1,492 and the next day 1,518, and so on, with little effort to account for the discrepancies' – after all, no Western face could travel far in the Chinese countryside and, in any case, where would they go to? And after everyone had been more or less counted – occasionally a child's doll was mistaken for a baby and counted too – the camp transformed itself into a giant marketplace.

Private supplies of food, or home rations as they were

called, were the be-all and end-all of camp life. There were a few prisoners – mainly missionaries whose Chinese-manned stations in China were still operating well enough to send them food, and knew where to send it to – who were receiving a steady supply. Steady enough for them to throw out tins that the mice or the rats or the cockroaches had found their way into. Cliff remembers finding one such tin with a rat in – 'the rat was duly removed, the syrup was boiled for several hours over the stove, and then three of us spread it sumptuously on our bread for some weeks afterwards'.

And steady enough for them to have more than they wanted for themselves. Or things that they didn't want. Like cigarettes instead of jam or jam instead of cigarettes. And they were prepared to barter. Bartering 'for life's daily needs' was a serious business inside the camp. Gladys McMullan Murray remembers exchanging her 'best dress' for 'a tin of sweet condensed milk'.

At the beginning, cash was still worth something too. People clung on to some savings in the belief that they might need them again soon when they went home. Or they'd sell things for money knowing that they could turn it back into something they wanted and needed more – soap, mosquito nets, things that were still coming into the camp. Or they used it to buy goods on the black market. 'We sold all our belongings, bit by bit,' Gladys's son Jimmy told me.

The camp's black-market operation was run with the same precision as the kitchens and committees. Three Chinese, their bodies 'blackened and greased', would slide through the outer electrified fence and pass boxes of eggs and crates of wine through the inner wire into the camp. Another black marketeer, a Mrs Kang, organized her small sons to help her 'funnel a steady flow of eggs into a drainage tunnel that came in underneath the wall'.

Once the goods were in the camp, a group of former

Black marketeers at the perimeter fence.

businessmen would quickly hide them behind a pile of loose bricks. Lookouts were posted in several directions. If one saw a Japanese guard approaching he would blow his nose ostentatiously and the black marketeers would hide. At one stage, Gilkey reckons, thirteen hundred eggs were coming through the walls each day – 'an equivalent amount of jam, sugar and butter was there for the buying if one knew whom to see'.

For the first few weeks of their stay in the Weihsien camp, black-market eggs were Lilla and Casey's main source of home rations. A whole section of Lilla's recipe book is dedicated to eggs. Boiled eggs. Boiled eggs with mayonnaise. Boiled eggs with fried bacon and tomatoes. Baked eggs with cheese sauce. Poached eggs. Scrambled eggs with ham, with smoked fish, with mushrooms, with asparagus. Egg dishes, she wrote, are useful when unexpected visitors arrive.

Something turns in my stomach as I read this. Its poignancy, its hope, stops my breath. Unexpected visitors. Lilla was locked up in a prison camp. Nobody unexpected would be turning up that day, or the next, or the next. But just maybe, she was writing, maybe one day it won't be like this any more.

And piece by piece, Lilla must have sold almost everything she had to buy eggs. Her clothes, her lace, her embroidery, any tiny china pieces she had with her – if anyone wanted them. And her jewellery. Piece by piece, it went. Except for two items. Those diamond earrings. And the brooch that Ernie had given her. The one she'd torn the emeralds out of when she heard he had died.

And when she had finished washing and queuing and cleaning and bartering, Lilla would have pulled her typewriter out of its trunk and balanced it on the packing-case table in the corner of her damp cell. Wound a fresh ricepaper receipt, blank paper, American Red Cross paper, any paper she could find, into the machine and plunged her fingers on to the keys and into the world that the prisoners tried to remember as they worked in the kitchens. The world of seven-course meals and servants to run steaming baths. The world of food so fresh that you could hear the vegetables crunch as you broke them in two. The world where you had more than you could possibly want to eat. The world in which, long ago, somewhere between the London smog and the fresh Himalayan air, Lilla had learned she could reign supreme.

Perhaps, when she lent her pages out to other prisoners to read, she felt she was reigning supreme again. And that's what kept her head held high in the months to come.

Change came to the camp. Came soon. But not in the way that anyone had hoped. First the rains stopped. The mud dried out. And a couple of months after Lilla had arrived in Weihsien, the black market was brought to a shuddering close. Two Chinese black marketeers were caught and set before a Japanese firing squad. Another was electrocuted trying to slither through the fence. 'His body was left to hang on the wires as a gruesome warning to others.'

Then the cold arrived. A bitter, biting cold that swept down from the north and froze the ground. Froze the water in its pails. Froze the inside of their cell. Froze the very marrow of the prisoners' bones. According to the UN War Crimes Commission, 'only those who have experienced the winter cold of North China can appreciate its bitterness'. The prisoners piled on their clothes. Huddled under their blankets. Paced around the camp to keep the circulation going.

When Lilla sat at her typewriter, her fingers must have jarred stiff as ice blocks against the keys.

15

HUNGER

Weihsien internment camp, North China,
November 1943. Thirteen months into Lilla's
imprisonment.

THE PRISONERS had been freezing for several weeks
by the time the stoves arrived. One stove for each
cell, a leaden square box with an opening for fuel and an
exit for smoke. Something that, even if it couldn't make
them properly warm, should at least keep Lilla and Casey
alive.

Only there wasn't any fuel.

It was another month before that came. A month of the
stove sitting there in their room like an empty promise. A
month of Casey fiddling hopefully with a column of
empty tins spliced together to form a chimney. Another
cold month.

When the fuel came, it was dust. Just dust. Loose dust
that suffocated any match you put to it. Lilla, like everyone else, had to learn how to scratch her nails into the
frozen soil for dirt to mix with the coal dust and water,
turning it into coal bricks.

The dust must have spread over Lilla's hands, up her
arms, into every hollow of her clothing, every crevice of

her barely exposed skin that it could find. And even when she had mixed that first heap of coal and earth with water, pulled the mixture apart into tiny lumps, rolled them into balls and pounded them into bricks, she would still have had no fire – 'we still couldn't burn them, as they were wet through'. It took another week for the coal balls to dry out.

Eventually, Lilla, like everyone else, learned the science of coal balls. How much dust you needed for coal balls that could light a fire. How much soil you should use for coal to burn slowly through the night. Masters and her sisters worked out that 'there were different types of soil in different parts of the camp that bound better, and burned longer'. The biggest question, however, was when to use the coal dust. There was all too little of it and Lilla would never have known when, or if, the next delivery would come.

In December 1943, the Italians arrived. On the other side of the world, in Europe, Italy had surrendered to the Allies. The Japanese had then rounded up all the Italians still living in the treaty ports and herded them into the internment camps. As their country had surrendered, the Japanese regarded the Italians as dishonourable prisoners. And when they arrived at Weihsien they were locked away in the quarantine compound – so as not to contaminate the other, honourable Allied nationals. After a few weeks, the rules were relaxed and they were allowed to wander around the camp. But by then the cold had reached them too.

The winter in North China is arctic. In the treaty ports, on the coast, at least there is a chance of a sea breeze drifting up from warmer climes to take the edge off the cold. But inland, at Weihsien, the winds sweep down from the north, from the Arctic Circle itself. As they cross the great plains, the freezing Mongolian desert, they harden with the toughness of the terrain they are travelling over. The nights are already growing cold by the end of September. By November they are freezing. At New Year you think it is so cold that it cannot grow any colder. And then, in January, the real winter comes.

As Lilla scratched deeper and deeper into the earth to make coal balls, sharing the black dust out among them as thinly as she could, the winter would have dug into her like a ghoul finding a fresh vein and sucking her energy away. It must have been harder and harder to type out those recipes. Even if she kept her gloves on, taking her hands out of her pockets would have exposed her fingers to such cold that they no longer felt attached to the rest of her.

Instead of bending each finger from key to key, Lilla would have had to raise her hand each time and position it above the letter she wanted, then let it fall painfully on to the keypad, waiting for the thin silver arm to slice through the air and hoping that it was swinging fast enough to leave a mark on the paper. But for the moments she had a rhythm going she could leave her cell, the camp, the cold behind for a world of hot soups, steaming buckets of rice and crispy pastry – 'to make it brown nicely, brush it over with milk just before putting it in the oven' – stewed fruit disintegrating into its warm juices – 'do not put hot cooked fruit into a tart, the steam given off will sodden the pastry' – and the baking heat of an oven whose temperature she could just turn up and down. Sitting there in her cell on those bitter, dark, winter afternoons, did she close her eyes and imagine turning it up up up and opening the door, letting the heat blast out over her?

The moments when Lilla's stove was on, when she could warm her fingers enough to move them against the typewriter keys without wincing in pain, she would have had to use her hands for other, more pressing tasks.

314

Stitching up their clothes that were falling apart. Sewing layer upon layer of clothing together to make a coat thick enough to keep warm. How she must have wished she'd brought that fur. At least the kitchen was warm. At least on the one day in three that she must have been there she wouldn't have frozen. But what about Casey? Lilla must have wanted to bundle up the warmth of the kitchen and take it back for him, rushing back to their cell before the cold could reach her. And burrowing deep under the blankets with her husband, glowing like their stove that seemed so rarely lit.

At low points, Lilla's mind must have drifted to what ifs. What if she hadn't come back to China that autumn of '39? Well, she couldn't have left Casey, but what if he'd come with her on the trip to England? What if they'd sold up when times were still good and gone to Europe? What if they'd just left everything and fled for their lives when the Americans had gone home? Or taken those passages on the diplomats' boats? Would they have been caught in the Blitz – or be living in some English seaside town waiting for a German invasion? What if they had managed to take just a little more money out of China before this war? What if they didn't have to start all over again, start saving to retire, when Casey was seventy-something and Lilla had a grandson of almost eighteen?

She must have wondered what was happening to everyone else. Everyone except Reggie, Vivvy, Mabel and Mabel's mother, who were all still with her. Freezing but alive. It was hard to receive news in the camp. The only letters to arrive had nearly always been posted in China. The steadily shrinking English-language pro-Japanese newspaper, the *Peking Chronicle*, edited by the Germans and notoriously inaccurate – over the years, Masters says, it claimed that 'the total US fleet had been sunk at least three times!' – could be deciphered to reveal just how fast the Americans were moving across the Pacific.

Even if it was claimed they were Japanese victories, the names of the islands being fought over, the Tarawa and Makin atolls in Gilbert Islands, Kwajalein, Maloelap and Wotje in the Marshalls, gave away the Americans' progress. The only other source of news, the only hint as to just how long they might have to wait, came from the 'bamboo' or 'cesspit' wireless – tiny linen pellets spat out by the Chinese coolies who came to clear the latrines and that unfolded into treasured newssheets.

But none of these would have given Lilla any idea of what was happening to her family in Europe. Had England been invaded? Were her children, their children, well? Alive, even?

And there was Ada. Lilla had never been so long – almost three years – without exchanging words with her sister.

I find it hard to believe she simply accepted the silence between them. Didn't manage to conjure up some twinly telepathy just to know that Ada was still alive.

The cold ate away at everyone and everything. It 'dampened our mood and stunted conversation'. Fewer people scurried along the camp paths. And when they did, instead of finding themselves stuck in the mud, they slipped and skidded on the ice. Even the Red Cross visits slowed. Home rations, comfort money, contact with the outside world, all dwindled. Sporting matches were unplayable. Musical and theatrical performances were abandoned. 'Every effort was spent acquiring fuel, food and clothing.'

And then, after six months in Weihsien, eighteen months in captivity, just as winter eased, when Lilla must have thought that they'd made it, they were alive and now the cold was abating they would have a chance to build themselves up a little – the rations began to be cut.

Years of war and occupation, followed by a hard winter, had left food in China thin on the ground, the Japanese told the prison committees. What they didn't mention was that, as US forces made their way steadily across the Pacific, Japanese resources were being diverted to try to hold their positions rather than run their new empire. The prisoners' days of filling up on noodles and dough, of longing for home supplies of sweet spreads to smear on abundant bread, were over. Even at the start, the Japanese authorities had calculated food supplies on the basis of 'quantities for two meals per day', which the kitchens had stretched to three. Now this would be almost impossible.

Cereal was the first to go. That glutinous mass of stodgy millet porridge had sat heavy in the prisoners' stomachs from breakfast onwards, choking their insides into believing that they were full. Then it was tea. No tea. In China. The last beaten and rebeaten teabags had disinte-grated, the leaves washed pale. Hot water that you had to wish the flavour into. By the end of the morning, Lilla and Casey must have been struggling to find the energy to stand in the long queue for lunch.

Spring didn't come to the camp in 1944. There was no warm Chinese sunshine and blossom. No gentle awaken-ing and flowering of a new year. Instead 'the climate in the camp switched from arctic cold to tropic heat with clock-like precision'. With the heat came a sun that dried out every inch of the ground. Left the alleyways punctured with ankle-twisting crevasses. Sent clouds of dust swirling through the air, into the cells, under the sheets, into the prisoners' lungs. The prisoners must have felt their skin, still cracked by the winter, begin to shrivel further as the heat stole the last drops of moisture from them. 'The heat was unbearable. Although we wore only khaki shorts (without shoes [which wore out easily and so were saved for the winter months] or shirts), the perspiration just poured off us,' says Cliff, who was so desperate for water that he often drank straight from the camp pumps – in direct contravention of the health committee's orders to drink only boiled water. Obviously others had too, as 'throughout the night there was the pitter-patter of feet down the corridor to the toilet of those suffering from dysentery'.

And, as the heat rose, the camp's other inhabitants flourished, especially at night. 'Mosquitoes buzzed around us persistently . . . Rats ran over us and became such a menace that the Japanese authorities organised a competition to stamp them out.' Bedbugs swarmed up through any gaps they could find in the floors and walls, and surfaced from the depths of the mattresses. The prisoners tried to slow them down by pouring boiling water into the cracks, but still 'by the light of our two- and four-wick candles we could see clusters of little black-red bodies scurrying across the sheets'.

The heat besieged the prisoners in a different way to the cold. Cold chills you from the inside. Heat punches you in the face and chest as you step in it, awake in it. You feel as if a great fist will knock you over, evaporate you the moment you step into its glare. I can imagine Lilla trying to keep to the shade of the trees as she made her way round the camp, each step producing a trickle of sweat that defied gravity as it worked its way into every fold of her skin. Sticking her together with a persistent dampness that inevitably turned into the itchy red rash of prickly heat.

One afternoon in June 1944, a rumour ran round the camp that two prisoners had escaped to join a band of Chinese rebels. Avoiding the electrical fence, they had climbed through a watchtower during the guard's evening cigarette break. The inmates' initial reaction was elation. For a few precious hours, excitement buzzed from cell to cell. The knowledge that somebody, anybody, had made it into the outside world gave even the oldest and weakest prisoner a glimmer of hope. 'The effect was electrifying.'

But by nightfall elation had been replaced by fear. How would the Japanese react?

Until this point, as in the Chefoo camp, the rule of the Japanese Consular Guard had been relaxed. The soldiers had been on reasonably friendly terms with many of the prisoners, giving some of the boys ju-jitsu lessons, helping others to dig their toy gardens in the dirt and even fielding a baseball team. And, perhaps because they were preoccupied with the bands of Chinese guerrillas fighting in the region around the camp, the Japanese had stated that their only responsibilities in respect of the internees 'were to see that none escaped and to supply coal and wood for cooking and heating and "adequate" food'.

This escape therefore meant a great loss of face for the Japanese guards. Yet worse was the fact that the Japanese had not picked up on the escapees' absence in the morning's roll-call – and had had to be informed of the escapes by the prisoners themselves. The captain in charge was 'livid with rage'. He ranted and raved at the camp's committee leaders. He doubled the daily roll-calls to morning and evening and made the prisoners stand outside in the burning sun for hours on end as soldiers counted and recounted, barking at any internee who fell out of line. He imprisoned every other man in the escapees' dormitory for several days, questioning them again and again as to what they knew.

And then he cut the rations. For two weeks there was no meat. Not even horsemeat or the 'tablespoonful of donkey' that the prisoners were becoming used to. Yet, however hungry they felt, every single one was grateful that his anger had stopped at that.

After a couple of weeks of punishment the meat ration was restored. Shortly afterwards, the summer rains came. Water poured out of the heavens and seemed to turn to steam as it hit the baking ground. The hot, damp air hovered above the ground, as if trapped by the thick cloud above. With every inch of water, the earth softened and gave way, dissolving back into the rivers of stinking mud that had greeted Lilla a year beforehand. When the rains moved on, they took all the warmth with them. As quickly as winter had turned into a baking summer, so the summer flipped back into winter.

It was then, in September 1944, at the beginning of Lilla's third year in a prison camp – as, unknown to the prisoners, the US military was pushing its way into the Japanese-held Philippines – that the more systematic cuts in rations began. I don't know whether this was a calculated cruelty or whether the camp authorities were running out of the money or men needed to obtain the food. They admitted to neither, and simply told the prisoners over and over again that there was no more food to give them. The clearly ragged state of the Japanese soldiers that winter must have made these assertions all the more believable – 'we looked at our bedraggled clothes and barely-shod feet and saw our reflections in the young, forgotten guards. They had put newsprint in their boots to keep their feet warm, and wrapped their legs in whatever rags they could find, as they, like us, had no socks to wear. Their uniforms were in shreds, and their bare hands, as they checked off the roll, were cracked and bleeding from the cold,' writes Masters.

First to go was meat again. Not cut entirely, just halved. But halved from very little to almost nothing. I can imagine Lilla studying the stew that was ladled into her bowl at lunchtime. Sweeping her spoon through it, catching each lump and bringing it to the surface to see whether it was meat, or just another piece of aubergine. SOS, the prisoners called it, Same Old Stew, as each day's ingredients were indistinguishable from any other's. Flour went next. Just as the autumn weather was growing colder again. At the next monthly meeting between the supplies committee and the commandant's men, the Japanese imparted the news with deadpan faces. The flour ration would be cut by half. From now on, Lilla would be lucky to see two slices of bread at each meal to go with her stew, thinned down to a cup of soup at supper.

The following month it was oil. Peanut oil. The prisoners used it for frying, baking and, most importantly of all, to supplement their diet. Peanuts are full of goodness, Lilla had written in her recipe book. Peanuts can be used as a substitute for meat when it is scarce. In a few weeks their fingernails would crack more readily than usual, a little more of their hair would fall out on their brush each night, their skin would feel even drier and, as the increasing cold bore down on them, would split into crevasses at every joint.

They came to dread these monthly meetings, wondering what would be taken away from them next. Whether they would be left with anything at all.

Not a hungry soul could open his mouth without talking about food. 'Our stomachs, like implacable slave masters, completely supervised our powers of thought. A conversation might begin with religion, politics, or sex, but it was sure to end with culinary fantasies.' Adults talked about meals they'd had, evenings out, New Year's feasts, in 'intricate detail and tasting in our excited imaginations long forgotten dishes in restaurants visited in some dim past'. I can almost hear Lilla's voice joining in, chatting away about h-h-how to bake this, h-h-how to cook that, as she scribbled down notes of new recipes before rushing back to her cell to type them up.

In conversation the images were there for a few tantalizing seconds – and then they were gone. Vanished. Not waiting to be turned over and rediscovered as they were in Lilla's recipe book. She could flick back through the pages, though carefully, as most of the ricepaper was too fragile to stand heavy handling, and gaze at food words she'd typed days earlier. Eggs. Mix. Stir. Sift. Until steam rises. Chop the pork finely. Add garlic. Add cream. Add wine.

It was as though, by writing down the recipes, or even just the words – chocolate, sugar, tomatoes, lamb – Lilla gave them a life of their own inside the camp. And, as the book progressed through category after category, from meat to game to Chinese dishes to savouries to ice creams, Lilla recreated in her tiny grey cell an entire universe of the good old days. The good old days back in her grand apartment in Chefoo. The smell of course after course being carried into the dining room. The tastes changing from dish to dish so that you could eat more than you really had room for. That slightly bloated feeling of having overeaten. Or the good old days in a crisp-white-tablecloth restaurant in Shanghai, the long low-ceilinged room sending the noise and clatter of plates and the latest news echoing back around her ears. Waiters charging past, steaming platters held high. Even the good old days in Kashmir. Roasting the goose that Ernie had stormed in with so triumphantly, still wearing her nightdress over his coat. The good old days that would now always exist on the paper pages of her recipe book, ready to be picked up again the moment she was free.

As the chasm grew between the food that Lilla was

eating and the food that she craved, or knew that she needed in order to survive, even bringing herself to type out these recipes must have begun to feel like self-torture. Chop the onions. Onions. Just onions. Raw, cooked, even sprouting with age. As she typed out the word 'o-n-i-o-n', Lilla must have yearned to feel its weight in her hand, brush off the dirt, peel away its papery skin. Wanted to bite into it. Even a raw onion. Crunch through the layers with her teeth. Feel its juices squirt into her eyes, making them sting.

By the end of 1944, food supplies were so low that children's teeth were growing in without enamel. Girls were not reaching puberty – some would never be able to have children. The queues for what little food there was brought out the very worst in the internees. Everyone was desperate to see his or her own bowl filled. As they neared the serving hatch, starving prisoners would literally pounce on the servers, accusing them of handing out too much to those ahead of them. Gordon Martin, a teacher at the Chefoo school, remembers feeling 'filled with black poison' when he saw the food run out before his family's bowls were filled, leaving his young children to go hungry.

I don't think that I could even have rasped out the words 'roast beef' at this stage. Let alone written a recipe. I would have cracked at the mere prospect of doing so. I think most people would.

Lilla, however, didn't.

Maybe it was because she was so used to picking her-self up off the floor that she knew how to take a deep breath and make the great mental leap required. Maybe it was because she had learned she had to fight to survive. And then, surviving this far might have weakened the prisoners' bodies, but it had given them a lean inner strength. Enough to keep almost all of them alive.

It is still dumbfounding to read what Lilla was writing then.

By this stage she must have reached her recipes for pastries and puddings, desserts and cakes. Lilla had a sweet tooth and wrote chapter after chapter full of sugary, gooey treats. They take up a good part of her book. Recipe after recipe of indulgent dishes. List after list of cakes. Large cakes, tea cakes, scones, 'i-c-i-n-g', she typed. Dripping raisin cake. Chocolate layer cake. Honey gingerbread. Raspberry sandwich cake. Swiss roll. Cream puffs. Treacle scones. Waffles. A warm, sweet orgy of cakes and puddings. Steamed sponge puddings, hot enough to burn your tongue, coated in a thick, sugary syrup that stuck to your spoon until you had licked every last sticky drop away. Trays of freshly baked apples just out of the oven that you could slide your spoon into as smoothly as butter, their cooked insides melting into a white sugary soup. Or bread and butter pudding. Thick, yeasty bread layered with eggs and milk and butter and sugar and raisins and baked until the crusts were still crisp but the centre had melted into a single hot sweet soggy mass.

This was Lilla's feast.

∽ 16 ∾
SURVIVAL

Weihsien internment camp, January 1945. Lilla has been in a prison camp for two years and three months.

HOPE COMES in many guises. It can float in on the wind as a familiar scent or a changing season, just a rumour or even a definite piece of news. Or it can take a concrete form. A gift, a home, an item of clothing. Or food.

Hope came to Weihsien camp in the form of American Red Cross parcels. They appeared out of the thick white snow one morning, rolling into the camp on the back of donkey-carts. Donkey-cart after donkey-cart. Piled high, overflowing, almost tipping with huge parcels three feet long and half as wide again and full to bursting, the prisoners knew, with food. The entire camp downed tools, dreams, or whatever was keeping them busy, and stumbled through the snow to watch this epiphanical caravan arrive.

The Americans were the first to weep. These parcels usually came to them. The rest of the camp had to use their cash to bargain for a share. But nothing had arrived for over six months. Food had become priceless. 'In utter amazement, tears streaming down our faces,' remembers Gilkey, who was American himself, 'we counted fourteen of those carts, each one carrying well over a hundred parcels!' As more and more parcels came in through the gate, quick calculations were made and a rumour ran through the British and the Belgians, the Canadians, the Dutch, the Norwegians, the Greeks, everyone else — there's enough for us, too.

Tears ran down the prisoners' cheeks, cutting paths through the frost that was settling on their skin the moment they stood still. Each of them was imagining opening their own parcel. Imagining sinking their teeth through the firm flesh of tinned meat, the kick of caffeine in their veins, the fizz of sugar on their tongues. Tastes that had haunted their dreams. Tastes that — if supplies ground to a halt, and they well might — could keep all of them alive. A Red Cross parcel each!

But that wasn't how everyone saw it. Just as the prisoners' dreams seemed to be turning into reality, they were snatched away. The camp commandant was 'mobbed by a contingent of angry Americans' arguing that the parcels should go to Americans only. And, 'afraid of an uprising', he took the parcels and locked up every single one in the camp's assembly hall until he could work out what to do. A 'heavy guard', adds Gilkey, 'was posted to watch over them'.

The prisoners waited two days for a decision from the Japanese. For two long cold days the assembly hall seemed to bulge with promise. Finally a notice was posted on the hall door. Every internee would receive one parcel. The two hundred Americans would receive one and a half. The parcels would be distributed at ten o'clock the following morning.

The line for the parcels began at dawn.

* * *

The queue was a jolly affair. The prisoners' lips were buzzing with pleasure as they looked forward to what was to come. A late Christmas present for their children. A late Christmas present for themselves. Something to ease the pain in their bellies. Something to go on keeping the cold at bay, the cold that – even though it was January and so bitter that they had stopped counting the degrees below zero – none of them felt as they waited for their packages. 'What blessed security was promised to every father and mother with three, possibly four, parcels for their family, enough surely to last through to the spring, whatever might happen to our camp supplies,' explains Gilkey. As they stood in line, every British, Canadian, French, Russian, Dutch, Belgian and Italian prisoner loved the Americans for their generosity.

A few minutes later, the Americans were more reviled than the Japanese.

Shortly before ten, as the queue began to shuffle forward to the doors that at any moment would open, letting them into an Aladdin's cave of food, a new notice was posted. Seven American prisoners had again protested against the handing out of parcels to any non-Americans. The commandant had referred the matter to Tokyo. There would be no parcels today.

It was as though the internees had jumped off a cliff only for the sea beneath them to vanish. Gilkey overheard an Englishman explain to his crestfallen children that the Americans had taken away Santa. 'For the first time,' he says, 'I felt fundamentally humiliated at being an American.'

If, at any point, Lilla found herself simply unable to think about a recipe or type it out – the sight of what she had already written bringing her not comfort but pain – then now must have been one of those moments. The entire camp was on edge. However hard the non-Americans tried not to point their fingers, however well everybody knew that it was just seven out of the two hundred who had made a fuss, an ugly tribal instinct reared its head, threatening to cleave the camp in two. Lean and mean on their empty stomachs, the prisoners began to remember where each of them had once come from. Fist fights broke out over the parcels. Over old grievances. Over new grievances. Over nothing at all – if you can call a year of near-starvation and the worry of whether you would have enough food to keep your family alive nothing at all. For ten long days, every prisoner's stomach ached for the treasures that were just out of their reach. And then the decision arrived from Tokyo. One parcel each for everybody, including the Americans. The remainder would be sent to other camps.

Lilla and Casey must have staggered back to their cell with their parcels – each weighed about fifty pounds – and unwrapped their new-found wealth on their beds. An endless picnic of powdered milk and tinned butter, spam and cheese, salmon and raisins, concentrated chocolate and sugar, jam and several packs of cigarettes spread before them.

Nobody had to taste the food to feel its effect. Simply having it, possessing it, knowing it was there was enough to keep them going. It was as though 'our small community had been whisked overnight from the living standard of a thirteenth-century village to that of a modern affluent industrial society. Now we had food to keep us all from hunger,' says Gilkey. And whereas, before the war, the food-loving Lilla would have turned up her nose in disgust at all these powders and tins, now she must have been close to tears at the sight of it. I can see her, in her freezing cell, prising open the pages of her recipe book again and rereading the recipes that she had already typed. The scent of fresh basil and garlic, the rustle of brown-paper bags squelching with fruit, the feeling of dough between her fingertips, the warmth of the oven all flooding back. She pulls the leaden typewriter out of its trunk with ease. Winds a new piece of paper – a new piece of American Red Cross paper that had arrived in the package – into it, throws a couple of extra coal balls on the fire and starts to type. Drifting back as she does so into the comforts of that old, familiar world without feeling her stomach, her guts, her entire body, trying to claw her back to a bitter reality.

Lilla, like everyone else, would have strung out her and Casey's food through the rest of winter, each little nibble of sugar and protein becoming a great feast. Rolling it around inside your mouth, pushing it to every corner, could turn it into an entire ham, a whole cheese, a side of salmon, keeping you going for hours. By the time most of the parcels were finished, the corners of the tins licked clean, the snow had gone. It was spring 1945 and after over two years in camp, just as the trees were blossoming, a new hope – halfway between rumour and certainty – was arriving.

The cesspit-wireless coolies had spat into the camp the news that, over in Europe, France had been invaded and the Nazis were on the retreat. And then, one night in May, the nocturnal calm was shattered by the clanging of the bell that hung in the tower over the single men's dormitory block. The noise stopped and the Japanese guards – convinced this was marking another escape – pounded through the camp, turfing the internees out of their beds for a roll-call. And as the prisoners fumbled their way through the darkness, they saw to their horror that the guards surrounding them were carrying not clipboards but machine guns.

They waited, shivering in the still bitingly cold night air. The dark silence was punctuated by infants' cries, children's whimpers, guard dogs barking and soldiers shouting at any of the older internees who tried to sit down in the dirt. And a single machine-gun volley that had one lady screaming: 'We're all going to be killed! We're going to die! We're going to die!'

Lilla, unusually half-dressed, her hair still down, must have been clinging on to Casey's arm to keep him up off the ground.

After they had waited for 'what seemed like hours' with little idea of what was about to happen to them, the camp commandant appeared and ordered the prisoners back to their cells. There would, he said, be no more food for them until the bell-ringer confessed. But as the dazed prisoners dispersed, the rumour began to buzz from mouth to mouth that the bell had been marking the end of the war in Europe. And, with this, the prisoners' spirits soared. For the next few days the adults thrived off the rumour, 'cinching our belts in tighter', and any remaining food supplies and home rations were handed out to the children.

A week later the perpetrator owned up and was put into solitary confinement by the Japanese in the hope that he would reveal the whereabouts of the shortwave radio set from which he had learned the news, and the rumour was confirmed. The prisoners' attention now rapidly shifted to events in the Pacific. The pro-Japanese *Peking Chronicle* was now recounting 'victories' in Japan itself, where American bombers were allegedly being shot out of the sky. As the crow flies, the Allies were now close. But how long would it take to beat Japan? One year, two more years? What would it take to make the Japanese give up China?

By now, Lilla must have been running out of recipes to

type. She'd composed a chapter on almost every topic she could think of – starters, soups, fish courses, meat dishes, game, puddings, ice creams, cakes and dishes from almost every country, many of which the average British person wouldn't have dreamed of cooking back then. Before the war, and for several years afterwards, only those British who could afford to hire chefs from Paris ate French food, and pasta could be bought only from specialist shops in London's Soho.

But Lilla wasn't an average British person. She had been born in China, surrounded by French, German, Italian, Russian and even Japanese friends. And her recipe book is packed full of French fare and pasta recipes, Russian concoctions and Chinese chow. Recipes that, over in England, would make news when they were eventually published years later, turning their authors into household names. Even a Japanese recipe is included. 'Sukiyaki', she typed as Japanese guards manned the gates and watchtowers around her.

After Lilla's cakes come her sauces. Sauces to go with everything she could think of. 'Let your sauces display an important factor in your menu.' Melted butter sauce, she typed. Brandy sauce. Mayonnaise. Hollandaise. Take this, add that, melt another, stir in . . . It's as though Lilla was trying to weaken the Japanese with sauces. Coat them in sauce, simmer them in sauce, drown them in sauce. Anything that might soften them up. Lilla typed and typed. Broken eggs were tossed from shell to shell. Ingredients were chopped into the tiniest of pieces. Still liquids were whisked with a fork until they spun in a whirlpool of their own.

And if she was trying to cast a spell, it worked.

It was in June that the mood among the Japanese began to waver. Cliff, who had built up enough Japanese for a conversation, found the usually rigorously disciplined soldiers 'now critical of their senior officers'. Some started behaving more aggressively towards the prisoners. Others seemed overly keen to make friends, 'perhaps subconsciously wanting to save their necks'. Guards off duty staggered back to their quarters drunk. One night there was a rumpus when a guard escaping an infuriated colleague slipped into a family cell and hid under a bed. Lilla wrote a chapter on cocktails as if to encourage them on their way. A Gin Fizz with sugar and lemon. A Manhattan, a jumble of whisky and Italian vermouth. A Flash of Lightning. The brandy to knock them out. The Tabasco to burn the roofs of their mouths. Then a Monkey Gland. The gin and absinthe to finish them off. Make them drunk enough to surrender.

Soon, the Japanese guards appeared eager to earn what cash they could by buying what valuables the prisoners had left and reselling them to the Chinese outside at a profit. The internees were keen to comply. They desperately needed money to buy lavatory paper and soap at the White Elephant. And the scarcer these items grew, the more their prices rocketed.

And then, fired by a potent combination of alcohol and fear, the Japanese soldiers began to boast to their prisoners, in a combination of 'Chinese, Japanese and sign language', that if the war ended, rather than surrender they would shoot every single one of them, before falling on their own swords.

Change bore as many threats as promises for the prisoners. Would the Japanese really shoot them all? Or would they simply abandon them? If they did, who would bring them food? Would they be able to leave the camp? Where would they go? The countryside that they could see around them was hot, dry and empty, save for the sound of gunfire from the Chinese guerrillas fighting off anyone who came too close. Would they, too, shoot the fleeing prisoners without stopping to ask who they were? If they knew, would they care? Would the Chinese welcome them back – or want to humiliate them? What if the Russians reached them before the Americans? Soon, what might happen when the war ended was all anyone in the camp could talk about.

Towards the end of Lilla's recipe book is a section on sandwiches. Picnic food. Food that she could eat while travelling. Cheese sandwiches, she typed as if preparing for the journey she was about to make. Egg sandwiches. With beetroot, the juice finding its way through the yolks and whites, staining even the bread a dark purplish-red. Sweet sandwiches. Crushed currants mixed with sugar. Melted cocoa oozing out of the sides of the bread in warm, sugary globules asking to be licked off.

17
FREEDOM

Weihsien internment camp, August 1945. Lilla has been a prisoner for just under three years.

WHEN THE NEWS CAME it was like a bolt out of the blue. Spat into the camp by the bamboo wireless. The committees tried to keep it a secret, not let anyone know until it was confirmed. But this was a rumour that was fast on its feet. Within a few hours, everyone was murmuring its name – armistice. Peace. Nobody quite dared believe that it was true.

Still, just some hope of an end was enough. 'The whole camp looked, felt and even smelled different,' Gilkey writes. The odour of the ubiquitous mud from the seasonal rains stopped grating against the back of the prisoners' nostrils. Tired, shambling gaits quickened into lively steps. Eyes glazed over by years of malnutrition were glinting again. Smiles began to hover at the edge of long-cracked lips.

Two days later, on Wednesday 15 August, the news came again. 'The rumour factory in camp was never busier,' says Michell. There had been an offer of peace, the war was over. Again, no-one could quite believe that it was true. Everyone was waiting for some convincing sign, some proof, some messianic apparition.

There was no call to gather that evening. No message was spun around the camp telling people to come. Like hungry bees, every adult prisoner who could walk simply joined the swarm around the commandant's office. They literally buzzed with excitement as they waited for the official bulletin that the war was over. When a door opened, the commandant didn't appear. Another 'well-hated but secondary official, small, arrogant and mean', stepped out, writes Gilkey, barely looking where he was going until, suddenly, he saw the crowd around him. His face turned white with fear. And he ran for the cover of the Japanese quarters. 'The sight of this hated tormentor transformed before our eyes into a fleeing rabbit caused a howl of delight and laughter to rise . . . as the most promising clue to the real state of things that we could have had.'

For the next day and a half, the camp held its breath.

Then, on Friday morning, they came. The plane passed overhead once, twice, its wheels skimming the tops of the trees. All the prisoners threw down what they were doing. They splashed their way along the muddy paths to the assembly field, the games pitch, whatever you called it, and stood mesmerized, their heads thrown back, chins in the air, mouths and eyes wide open as though they were witnessing the Second Coming. The engines stopped. For a moment there was a deathly silence, the silence you expect before a bomb. Then they appeared. Seven billowing parachutes floating to the ground, with arms and legs dangling below them. And the bold American flag painted on the side of the aircraft glinting in the sunlight.

The prisoners charged. Charged in a single pounding mass, squealing and hugging and weeping on the way.

Out of the gates. Past the guards who half raised their rifles before lowering them again in astonishment. On across the fields to where the parachutes were landing. The crowd surrounded the men. Stared at them. Danced around them. Then, with a whoop of joy, picked them up, carried them on their shoulders, and marched back to the camp gates. As the prisoners strode back in triumphantly, the camp's Salvation Army band struck up a victory march – and the national anthems of every prisoner echoed, one by one, around the camp. The notes reverberated around the cellblock walls. Swept into each room. Blasted the hopelessness away.

When the prisoners and the American paratroopers at last stood face to face they looked like dwarves meeting giants. Even the healthiest internee was wizened compared to the soldiers. Two and a half years of wartime rations followed by three years of imprisonment had ravaged the internees' bodies. Their skin hung off their cheekbones in flaps, the whites of their eyes had reddened, the hair they had left was dry and brittle and their clothes were now a size, maybe two sizes, too big.

Then the chief giant, an American major, asked where the Japanese commandant's offices were. Once directed, he cocked the two pistols on his hips and, with a hand on each, strode in to meet him. The two men stared at each other across the room. Neither moved a muscle. Then the Japanese soldier reached into the drawer in front of him and drew out his samurai sword and his gun – and handed them over to the American. The American handed them back. From now on, he said, you are under my command. We need you to protect the camp from outsiders.

And once their enemy had become their friend, nothing else was quite as the prisoners had expected.

There was no swift departure. No rush to pack and catch

a train back to Tsingtao and then a boat on to Chefoo, Peking or Tientsin. There wasn't any train back to Tsingtao – Chinese guerrillas had broken the tracks. And, the Americans told the prisoners, they needed time to be reorientated, re-educated even.

And they had a lot to learn.

First, the internees had to learn how to eat again. The standard of food that they had become used to in the camp was so low that even when one kitchen prepared the best meal they possibly could for two of their liberators, drawing out 'specialities from our store . . . what to us seemed quite a treat', writes Cliff, 'quietly and politely, the food was left uneaten . . . to them [it] was unpalatable'. And the food that they had dreamed about, that Lilla had written about, that they all believed would save them, had now become their poison. Cartloads of vegetables, grain and meat – food that the Japanese had told them they were unable to obtain – were rolling in through the camp's open gates. But after years of malnutrition and at least a couple of years of near-starvation, their bodies couldn't cope with it. 'During that first week, we could not eat a full meal without vomiting,' Gilkey remembers.

Then there was everything else. The world of empires and great social divides, of grand houses staffed by dozens of servants – already rocked by the First World War – was fast being sunk by the Second. 'Magazines [were] distributed and a library set up, all for the purpose of paving the way for our much-anticipated departure,' recalls Michell. And the prisoners had to learn history. 'Realising how little of the events of the previous four years we knew,' writes Cliff, the Americans organized classes to bring them up to date. 'An officer sketched the initial retreat of the American forces following Pearl Harbor,' and then spelt out how the war had turned around in mid-1942, as they had begun to advance across the Pacific.

How deeply ironic this must have been for the internees. The Allies had already been winning the war by the time they were imprisoned. But then maybe it was because the Japanese had found themselves on the defensive that they had decided to round up all their enemy nationals in the first place.

And then, finally, the lessons came to the two atomic bombs that had fallen on Hiroshima and Nagasaki. The grim reasons why the Americans were at the camp now, and not in a year or two's time. There was a long list of vocabulary to learn, too. Words that had been rolling off the tongues of people in almost every corner of the world, but which the inmates of Weihsien had never heard – GI, jeep, kamikaze.

Lilla must have wondered whether she'd ever use them back home in Chefoo. The Chefoo that she longed to return to. She would only have had to close her eyes and remember the sweeping bay, the smell of the salty air, the sound of the gulls, to feel a great rush of energy through her body. In a week or two now, she and Casey must have whispered to each other at night, we'll be home. We'll be home.

The hardest lesson was to come.

On a cold, grey day a month after the Americans had arrived, a British colonel turned up at the camp. He had come to speak to the British subjects, he said. Lilla, Casey, Vivvy, Mabel, Mabel's mother, Reggie and the eight-hundred-odd other British in Weihsien gathered in front of him. The moment Lilla and her siblings recognized him their spirits must have soared. The colonel was the younger brother of Bob McMullan from Chefoo. Bob who had died at the hands of the Japanese and Bob who had rescued Lilla's family from bankruptcy a decade earlier. This was another McMullan, he had to be rescuing them again. I can see their chests puffed up with excitement, their eyes gleaming – ready to catch every gesture, every word.

Then the colonel began. He began by warning them that they would not like what he had to say. But the situation was this. Their businesses had been destroyed. The Chinese had now occupied their homes and buildings. The British Army would not be turning the Chinese out. Nor would there be any money to help them start again. While they had all been locked up in the camp, it had been agreed with Chiang Kai-shek's Chungking government that the days of the treaty ports, and the foreigners' immunity to Chinese law that came with them, were over. They should all leave China. Those who had relatives in England should go there. Those who had no other roots apart from China, who had no connection with England at all, should try Australia, New Zealand, Canada. And start again.

The crowd was silent, every face around Lilla as white as a sheet. Some were shaking their heads. Some had tears running down their cheeks. 'Others merely clung together mute, emptied of life,' writes Gilkey. Many were murmuring that they didn't know anyone anywhere else apart from China. That they'd never been anywhere else but China. 'When that is taken from us,' one internee told him, 'we have no place on earth that is ours.' For many of them, every single thing they had taken for certain had been swept away.

Eventually the railway was repaired and Lilla and Casey were taken by train to Tsingtao. Tsingtao was one of four key ports in China that the American forces had agreed with Chiang Kai-shek, whose Nationalist government they were now backing, they should occupy as soon as possible after the Japanese surrender – taking them out of

Chinese Communist hands if necessary. Now it had British and American ships moored in the harbour. And its hotels, and a few other recently deserted buildings, were put at the disposal of the Weihsien internees.

The Chinese and Allied troops set up a great welcome for the prisoners. As their train pulled into the port, 'every roof was covered with Chinese waving British and American flags', Joan Ward told me. 'It was a very emotional moment.' And as the internees came out of the station into that Bavarian town square so strangely untouched by the war, the band of HMS *Bermuda* began to play. A vast crowd of Chinese schoolchildren cheered, waving a sea of victory banners, remembers Cliff, 'with slogans in Chinese and English, such as "Victory of the Allied Nations is the base of World Peace"'.

Some of the prisoners cheered and waved back. Some of them cried. But I don't think Lilla did either. It couldn't have felt like much of a victory to her. She and Casey, her brothers too, were beginning to realize that they had probably lost almost everything they owned. Many of the treaty-porters were ignoring the advice they had been given in the camp and going back to their old homes in China to see what was left and what sort of life they could pick up again. But Lilla couldn't even do that. Unlike Tsingtao, Chefoo had fallen into the hands of the Communists, who, in their search for a new China, were deeply opposed to all elements of the treaty ports and imperialist rule – their viewpoint no doubt hardened by America's decision to lend its support to their enemy, Chiang Kai-shek. They made it clear that they would not welcome any of the internees back to Chefoo. It wasn't even safe enough for Lilla to go back and look.

Lilla stayed in Tsingtao, waiting to see if the situation in Chefoo improved. For the first time in three years she and Casey were living not just in comfort but in luxury, as they had been given a room in the former German consulate – one of the grandest houses in Tsingtao – where they were being waited on hand and foot by Japanese prisoners.

But I think all Lilla wanted was to go back to her home in Chefoo.

A few days after they arrived in Tsingtao, as the family legend goes, Lilla's old houseboy turned up on a bicycle. He had cycled the whole way across the Shantung peninsula from Chefoo with Lilla's fur coat tied to the back. It was the only thing he had managed to save, he said. Everything else had been stolen and vandalized. Not a single one of her possessions remained.

Lilla was devastated. She had worked hard, so very hard, to build her life in Chefoo. At long last she'd had everything she wanted – a beautiful home, a business of her own and money to give to her children. And now the Japanese had taken everything she had worked for. And although Casey was still there with her, the weeks of interrogation, those years in the camp, had taken most of him away too.

She must have wondered what she had done to deserve this.

But she wasn't giving up yet.

If she was going back to England, she was taking something for her children with her.

The German consulate in which she was staying was still full of pictures and furniture and silver and china and every type of possession under the sun. The Japanese had taken everything from her, she reasoned, and the Germans were the allies of the Japanese. Lilla reckoned she was entitled to something for her family. There were a couple of pretty china pots standing on the side. A pair of graceful, slender blue-and-white vases with lids, about a foot high, I think.

There are two vases just like this sitting quietly on a

bedroom windowsill in my parents' house in Hampshire, thousands of miles and several decades away from war-torn China.

Lilla's son Arthur left them to my mother in his will.

Back in Tsingtao, Lilla stuffed the china in her suitcase and headed south to Shanghai. There the city itself appeared relatively untouched. 'Shanghai bore few physical marks of war . . . apart from the street fortifications and air-raid shelters,' writes Bernard Wasserstein, in a rare account of treaty-port Shanghai that goes on to describe life there after the war. As in Weihsien, the 100,000 Japanese troops in the city remained on duty, under Allied orders, and then disappeared into the Japanese civilian popu-lation, which, in an eye-for-an-eye gesture, was compelled to wear armbands.

Despite this, 'the Shanghai party hardly missed a beat', continues Wasserstein. American sailors thronged through the shopping streets and 'like manna from heaven, goods of every description suddenly descended on the Shanghai markets; electric kettles and toasters, typewriters, cameras, radios . . .' The bars and brothels found themselves taking off, notwithstanding the 'spectacularly unenforceable orders given to the victorious soldiery' to avoid them. On a tamer front, in November 1945 Shanghai's Amateur Dramatics Society revived its production of *Richard III*, banned by the Japanese three and a half years earlier.

But this wasn't a party that everyone could join in. Like Lilla, many of the internees found their homes and possessions gone. Another 'bitter pill for the former internees to swallow', as Wasserstein quotes from a US intelligence report, was the sight of 'scores of former collaborators' flashing their money around the town, in sharp contrast to 'the gaunt looks and threadbare clothes of the camp residents'.

Either it was poverty in a bustling Shanghai none-theless short of food and fuel, or a need to see her children and Ada, or both drove Lilla back to England. Anne Eckford, who was married to Reggie's son Donald, remembers Lilla and Casey still living in Shanghai in January 1946. But, shortly afterwards, clutching a suit-case containing Lilla's recipe book and fur coat, the few pieces of clothing that hadn't disintegrated in the camp and their stolen china, they sailed back to England.

At least Lilla had someone to go to there. Although Reggie had gone straight to see his wife and children in Britain, Vivvy was still in Tsingtao, trying in vain to start a business in a post-war economic environment that still didn't know what was going to happen when the Allied troops left. His son Erroll had disappeared in Burma, but Rae had survived the war in a camp near Shanghai and was staying in China. I don't think Vivvy – a huge, hand-some and desperately kind man but somewhat hopeless when it came to finance and trade – had it in him to move to a new country and start all over again. After all, he was now sixty-eight, and had lost everything not once but twice, the first time being when Cornabé Eckford had gone bankrupt. He, his wife Mabel and her mother must have stayed in Tsingtao with little to look forward to and a great deal of apprehension as to what might happen next.

Lilla was met at Southampton by her son Arthur. She must have known by now, and I wish I could have seen her when she heard, that he had more or less fulfilled her ambition for him. He had been promoted to brigadier, the first and lowliest rank of general but a general all the same, and had even held the post of acting major-general for a while. He wasn't Sir Arthur, and as he had rejoined the army just for the war he could only call him-self Colonel now. But I imagine Lilla's smile, when she at last saw her son, almost cleaving her shrunken frame in two.

Maybe it was a good thing that Arthur couldn't tell her then, had to keep from her for years, what else he had been up to. For, while Lilla had been freezing and starving in the camp, he had been in the eye of the storm, working in the tiny team in the Cabinet War Rooms hidden beneath the London streets. His job had been to collate all the information coming in from the forces on land around the world. (A naval officer and an air force officer covered the sea and air.) He then briefed first Churchill and later, after the British public had voted their wartime leader out of office in July 1945, Ernest Bevin. Bevin was Foreign Secretary in the Attlee government that followed Churchill's, and Attlee delegated the War Rooms to him.

Bevin – a Churchill-shaped man (short but heavily built), whose thick round spectacles made him look like a frog – needed some guiding through the system when he came on board. Hidden at the back of a former broom cupboard in the War Rooms was a highly secret transatlantic telephone booth that had provided a direct link between Churchill and Presidents Roosevelt and Truman. Arthur found himself repeatedly being called down the corridor to help his new chief make the telephone work during his calls to Truman and Byrnes, the US Secretary of State, during the last days of the war. Bevin, a self-educated man who had taken control of the entire trade union movement in Britain, was an immensely powerful figure. This transatlantic telephone was probably the first thing in his life to defeat him. 'He used to shout at it [in his thick cockney accent] as though shouting at it would make it work,' Arthur told my father years later, in 1970, when he became a very junior minister in the Civil Service Department in the same building. After hearing this story, my father took the lift down two floors below the usual ground-floor entrance and emerged into the underground labyrinth of the War Rooms. They had been sealed up when the war had ended twenty-five years beforehand and barely touched since. 'It was very dusty,' he tells me. 'There were hand-written lists still pinned to walls, and sugar cubes, which everyone had hoarded in the war, still in the desk drawers.' And, at the back of the broom cupboard, the transatlantic telephone booth was still there.

If Lilla had heard about all that then, she would have burst with pride.

And then she went to see Ada. Even though they had been apart, unable to write for almost five years, the twins' lives had been so similar that whilst Lilla had been resurrecting mouldy vegetables in the camp kitchens, Ada had been filling her days serving in the Australian Troops' Canteen in London. Just about the time when Lilla had first been herded into a prison camp, Toby had died. While Lilla had been locked up in China, Ada had been in an internal prison of her own. For months and months after Toby's death, she had sat down every afternoon, all afternoon, and cried her heart out on the shoulder of her postcard-collecting cousin Lulu. Lulu, whose womanizing husband had left her to pursue his interests in Paris, and died too.

When Lilla and Ada met, they didn't look like twins at all. Not even sisters. Ada was healthier, taller, fleshy, full. Compared to Lilla, she even looked fat. Lilla could hardly fill her own clothes. However far she pushed her shoulders back, they no longer met the seams where the sleeves began. She didn't just appear thinner, older, ill-fed. As one of her grandsons, my cousin, tells me, 'She seemed half the size of Ada.'

⪢ PART IV ⪡
Refuge

BEEF ROAST

Fillet, ribs, sirloin or topside.

Put the joint in a baking tin large
enough to take it comfortably. If it is
not a very fat piece of meat, lay one
or two pieces of dripping on top of the
joint. Put in a very hot oven for the
first 10 minutes, then reduce to a mod-
erate oven. Allow ½ hour to each pound
of meat and 20 minutes extra. Baste
frequently and serve with horseradish,
gravy and Yorkshire pudding.

18

STEALING CHINA

England, 1947

IT TOOK almost two years for Lilla to fill out to look like her twin again. Her cheeks gradually fattened. The thin layer of muscle that had been stretched over her frame thickened. Her shoulders expanded to fit her clothes. Her eyes lost that rheumy look of hunger. Her hair, now completely grey, began to shine and the clumps that, for years, she had found in her hairbrush each night faded away. Slowly, either from relief at being out of the camp or sheer determination to catch up with Ada, her old energy returned.

It can't have been just the food. Food in England was still tightly rationed. There was even less to go round than there had been during the war. The only way to obtain a decent amount of meat each week was to have been friendly with the local butcher throughout. Lilla and Casey, as good as foreigners pitching up from China at the end of things, wouldn't have made it into this category. In the summer of 1946 even bread had started to be rationed – something that had never happened before. Nine ounces a week each, of a loaf made from flour so fully extracted from wheat husks that it was a

349

dark grey, and barely digestible. Nor was there enough fuel. In the cold of early 1947, an already shivering British population was working in their offices by candlelight and forbidden to cook on an electric stove between nine in the morning and noon, and two and four in the afternoon. Traffic lights and lifts stopped working altogether. Even the national newspapers were cut to just four pages each. All this took an inevitable toll on the business environment – over two million people lost their jobs. In 1947, England was a far from comfortable place to be.

As Lilla and Casey sat in their room in a small hotel in Richmond, on the outskirts of London, the news that they were receiving back from China made it sound a golden land again. In January 1947, America had withdrawn its support from Chiang Kai-shek in the face of his continuing use of violence against the Communists attacking him. But Chiang's Nationalists were nonetheless advancing, and his pre-war government had appeared well-disposed to foreign residents. Vivvy's son Rae was living in Shanghai, and half of Lilla's family was already back in Tsingtao. Mabel and Vivvy had never even left the town. Reggie had been sent straight back out in 1946 to act as British consul in Shantung. His children had followed. Jean, his youngest, sailed out with her mother and started working as a decoder in the consulate. Gerry, his eldest daughter, and her husband, Murray Zimmerman, returned from Washington, where Murray had been in charge of foreign funds control during the war. Rugs and Audrey, whom he had just married, moved back too.

Lilla and Casey heard from them all how the tennis and golf clubs had reopened. Lilla would have remembered, even from her short stay in Tsingtao after the camp, that there had been no shortage of food. The news from Reggie confirmed this. Fresh fruit and vegetables were being delivered daily to everyone's door. And some sort of business life seemed to be starting up again.

Back in grey-as-ever London, Lilla must have felt that she and Casey really were the flotsam and jetsam that – even before the war – she had feared they might become. They were refugees, drifting along on the far from welcoming waters of British life, with no apparent purpose or use. Not even to Lilla's own family. Her daughter-in-law Beryl, my father tells me, regarded Lilla as 'irrelevant'. And Lilla would have felt that she and Casey were only a burden on her daughter Alice and her husband, Havilland. Even Ada had apparently recovered from Toby's death and was sailing along. She might not have had a husband any more, but she did have something else that Lilla didn't. Money.

Lilla and Casey had a little money in England and stocks and shares worth about two thousand pounds before the war (sixty thousand pounds today). It was not nearly enough for a long, comfortable retirement in Britain. Even a Britain which Attlee, having wound up the war, was reforming to provide a free health service and welfare state for all. Nor was it enough to leave Lilla with anything much to pass on to her children and growing grandchildren. In China, she and Casey had had twenty thousand pounds (half a million pounds today) of property, possessions and Casey & Co. embroidered linens. The possessions were no longer there but, as far as she knew, the houses were. And back with them in China was the possibility of starting up the business again. Lilla's family in England 'thought she was mad to go back'. But to Lilla it clearly made perfect sense. In September 1947, obviously aware of some danger in what they were about to do, she and Casey handed power of attorney in all their affairs to Lilla's son Arthur 'should anything happen to us' and, at the ages of sixty-five and seventy-six, set sail for a still war-torn China.

* * *

Lilla must have hidden her recipe book at the bottom of a suitcase she left with Ada. She'd had a pair of loose bindings made from black leather embossed in gold leaf with Vivvy's sketches and tied her manuscript up between these covers before hiding it away. Ada didn't even know it was there. Didn't even know it existed. Never would.

I've often wondered whether this was because Lilla didn't want implicitly to challenge Ada to write a recipe book too. Or whether back then in 1947, surrounded by the particularly horrific stories that unfolded in the aftermath of the Second World War, her recipe book didn't feel like much of an achievement.

The ship was packed. Just as disillusioned as Lilla and Casey by the state of affairs in England, many 'old China hands', as the treaty-porters called themselves, were flooding back. For the six-week journey east, men and women were segregated into cabins stacked with bunk beds. They must have reached Shanghai in the late autumn, Rae bounding up to meet them as they came off the ship. He found them an apartment to rent and Lilla and Casey decided to spend the winter there, looking up friends and trying to pull the threads of their life back together. Trying to make it just as it had been before. Trying to ignore, I'm sure, what the British colonel, the McMullan boy, had told them back in the camp. That life in China would never be the same again. Shutting their eyes and ears to the chaos of the continuing civil war between Chiang Kai-shek's Nationalists and the Communists. Perhaps forgetting that foreigners were no longer immune to Chinese law, so they would be at the mercy of whatever happened next.

That first winter, Lilla and Casey's hope of restarting their old China life didn't seem too far-fetched. There were fuel shortages and an erratic power supply. But that was nothing new. Many of their old contacts had vanished and inflation was out of control. Between December 1946 and July 1947, the amount of money that the Westerners paid their house-servants had rocketed from a bundle of banknotes two inches thick to one almost a foot long. By the time Lilla and Casey arrived in Shanghai even a daily trip to the shops meant carrying a suitcase in order to have enough cash to buy food with. But an expatriate life was struggling on. The old hotels had reopened. The bands were playing again. There was an air of hope around, an aspiration to return to the old life that had been missing in Britain – where the horror of the war in Europe had made most people feel that life could never be the same again. And for a great many so-called British who had spent their entire lives in China, it was the only home they knew.

However, although expatriate life in Shanghai seemed superficially to be working, by the time Lilla had boarded that packed ship to return to China, Chiang Kai-shek's government had already begun to look fragile. The country was still in ruins. The transport infrastructure – especially the railways – had been ripped up and destroyed at random. Most of the buildings in China's towns had been severely damaged. Those still standing were likely to have had the plumbing torn out by the Japanese army, who had intended to turn the metal into guns. In many places, piles of old radiators and lead piping were found sitting on the edge of towns. Even though agricultural areas like Shantung, around Tsingtao, were providing ample fruit and vegetables for the local inhabitants, elsewhere in China there was a growing risk of famine. And while Chiang Kai-shek struggled with this wreckage, the Communists were waiting to step into any breach that appeared.

*   *   *

In May 1948, about six months after Lilla arrived in Shanghai and as the summer heat began to rise in the city, she took Casey to join the rest of her family in Tsingtao. They arrived, as Audrey wrote in her diary, 'ostensibly to visit Chefoo'. They must have hoped, fingers tightly crossed, that they might be able to return. But, as soon as Lilla and Casey left Shanghai, they would have begun to realize just how much China had already changed. The railway between Shanghai and Tsingtao was in shreds. Flights were hazardous and involved abandoning your baggage to its fate by sea. Neither Lilla nor Casey wanted to be parted from their possessions again. They chose to stick with their luggage and sail up the coast, arriving by boat. Tsingtao's harbour, however, was now closed to any non-Chinese vessel. So, instead of spending a couple of days on a Western liner that could offer its passengers some luxury – even if they still had to be locked below decks some of the way for fear of pirate attacks – Lilla and Casey travelled on a Chinese steamer.

Conditions on board were grim. The passengers were crowded into bunk beds in mixed-sex cabins, wrote Audrey. Every inch of space on the ships was packed. At mealtimes, squatting passengers were cleared from on top of and underneath the dining-room tables so that those entitled to could eat. The distinctly unappetizing – and unidentifiable – food on board was hardly helped by the failure to change the tablecloths even once throughout the journey, allowing them to gather an increasing number of equally unidentifiable stains from both the meals served upon them and the passengers camping around them. By the time they reached Tsingtao, the smells on board these ships were 'well-nigh unbearable'. No doubt reminding Lilla of the latrines back in the camp.

But after two days at sea, Lilla and Casey stepped off

into a balmy late spring in Tsingtao. The acacia trees that still lined the town's rolling hills were in full blossom, their waxy white flowers giving off a sweet scent that the sea air would have swept into their lungs. There were ballboys at the tennis club and 'caddies by the dozen' on the golf course. Lilla and Casey rented a seaside cottage near Mabel and Vivvy – Mabel's mother had died in Tsingtao at Christmas 1946, ninety-one years old but still in China – just along the coast from the main port in Tsingtao's resort area, a place known as Iltis Huk. And a couple of weeks after Lilla arrived, her brother Reggie threw a party to celebrate his daughter Jean's wedding to Jack Polkinghorn, the son of a treaty-port war hero.

Jack's father had been a boat pilot on the strip of river that ran from the coast at Taku to the treaty port of Tientsin and an unofficial 'eyes and ears' for the British government. In 1941, he had been the first person to fire on the Japanese in China. Swiftly realizing that he was outnumbered, he had then sunk his vessel rather than allow the code books with which he telegraphed London to fall into the hands of the Japanese. He remained on board. The admiring Japanese had fished him, minus a finger, out of the water and swept him off to Japan. There they had treated their prisoner as well as one of their own heroes as, like them, he had been prepared to die for his country.

As Lilla stood on the consulate lawn at the wedding party, surrounded by her family, breathing in that sweet Shantung sea air, she must have felt that she was almost home. Almost back looking over that perfectly curving bay, with those storybook dragon spines arching their way through the water.

The Communists were still in Chefoo. And not just in Chefoo, but in nearly all of Shantung except a narrow strip of land between Tsingtao and the inland city of Tsinan – one of just four strategic corridors in North

Avalon, Vivvy and Mabel's home in Chefoo, before and after the Second World War.

China that the Nationalists were fighting to keep open. And which, within weeks of Lilla's arrival in Tsingtao, the Communists would manage to close. Nonetheless, shortly before Lilla reached Tsingtao, her nephew Rugs had managed to make a brief trip back to Chefoo. He had sailed round the coast on a US Navy transport ship with the US vice-consul and six representatives of other countries. The only foreigners left in the town were the German civilians who had not been imprisoned but were now stranded there – their 'home' country being in no state to pick them up. The American vessel stayed out at sea and the group landed from a launch, carrying signal lights to flash to the ship in case they found themselves in trouble. Once ashore, Rugs took them all to stay 'at the house of a German friend from the old days'.

They stayed just under a week. Each of them visited as many of their nationals' former houses and offices as they could. Rugs went to where Vivvy's house, Avalon, had once stood and took a couple of photographs of the few bricks scattered there. The Casey building still towered over the seafront, but was very much occupied. And its new occupiers, whoever they were, had no intention of letting Rugs in. Once he had given up trying to gain access, he walked to the far end of First Beach and climbed East Hill to the remains of the Woodlands Estate. As in the rest of the town, the furniture and plumbing had been torn out of every house. But Lilla's houses were still standing. Two of them still had glass in some of the windows. Rugs wandered through the buildings and made a few notes.

On his return to Tsingtao, he wrote up a lengthy report for the Consulate-General in Shanghai. Lilla pored over its contents, and I think she took the description of every stone standing as hope that the town she remembered could come alive again. She couldn't go back to Chefoo until Chiang Kai-shek's Nationalists regained control –

but surely they would. After all, a couple of months
earlier, in March, a new Chinese National Assembly had
been set up in Nanking. And Chiang Kai-shek had been
elected president of it.

So Lilla decided to wait. Unaware that she, like the rest
of her family in Tsingtao, was standing right in the
enemy's path.

While they waited, Lilla and Casey kept on trying to
carry out some sort of linen trade from Tsingtao. But
business was far from easy. Lilla's niece Gerry and her
husband Murray were finding it hard to restart his
business of shipping frozen eggs to the US. Vivvy and
Mabel seemed to be having no luck at all and were 'so
pauperish', says Lilla's niece Jean, that they were living
off chilli con carne and little else. Still, they can't have
been completely penniless as – although fruit and
vegetables were abundant – any sort of meat was hard to
come by. It was mainly available on the black market
and, even with cash, it was hard to buy. 'Rugs came back
one lunchtime jubilant,' remembers Audrey, 'to have
found a ham.' The one form of protein that seemed to be
in endless supply was caviar, sent in to the British
consulate from passing Russian ships. At times, Reggie
and his wife, Jessie, resorted to feeding it to their dog.

As the summer passed, Lilla's hope that the
Communists would be defeated began to look increasingly unlikely. Chiang Kai-shek's first term as president of
the new assembly was not proving a success. The country
was still in chaos, and the assembly had decided to issue
a new national currency. This was to be based on the
price of gold and – perhaps ill-advisedly – required
the surrender of all gold, silver and foreign currency held
by individuals. At this proposal, public opinion swung
firmly against Chiang Kai-shek and his Nationalist Party.
And, at almost the same time, the military tide began to

Red Army troops parade through Peking, June 1949.

turn against them too. In the bitter northern province of Manchuria — where the Nationalists had long been fighting off the Communist forces — the Communists were now gaining the upper hand. By the end of 1948, they had taken the town of Mukden and control of Manchuria with it. In January 1949, just as the Japanese had done a dozen years beforehand, the Red Army swooped down out of the windswept province.

It was two more months before the Red Army marched into Tsingtao. But long before the army's arrival, the town was already feeling the effects of its advance. As the Japanese had removed the radiators from every house, the only form of heating was a coal stove in the kitchen. And the coalmines were now in Communist territory, so no coal was reaching the Nationalist-controlled areas such as Tsingtao. Once more, Lilla and Casey found themselves grubbing around in the dirt to make coal balls to keep warm. 'Even the Chinese coolies found squatting in the mud to do this too degrading at any price.' At least there was still some electricity. Kettle by kettle, Lilla would have been able to heat herself a bath. Unless it rained — when the electricity shut down altogether. As the Red Army drew closer in the early months of 1949, even this capricious power supply grew more and more erratic. And a new hazard reared its head as 'Nationalist bullets began to fly around the town indiscriminately.' Not even the supposedly inviolable British consulate was safe. One evening bullets flew through its bathroom walls, narrowly missing Jean, who, heavily pregnant, was manoeuvring herself into the bath. Even the official consular car was fired at — as it was trying to speed Gerry to hospital before her new baby arrived. Already in the throes of labour, Gerry had to fling herself 'to the floor of the car to dodge the bullets'.

When the Communist Army eventually entered Tsingtao in March 1949, the Nationalist soldiers showed little resistance. They had been so poorly paid – if at all – that some took the opportunity of making a fast buck by selling their rifles to the advancing enemy before disappearing. Lilla's hopes for a Nationalist victory in China must have disappeared with them. But as the red flags rolled into the town, I think she found herself nurturing the same optimism that had kept her going under the Japanese. Maybe, just maybe, once the Communists had settled down, sorted the country out, life in China could continue as before. Lilla wasn't going to give up everything now. Not now that she was this close to home.

She'd spent so many years forcing herself to keep on going that she must have forgotten how to stop.

First to go were the books. All books – all evidence of learning, education, the old culture – were destroyed. It didn't matter whether the books were on Chinese Confucian philosophy – which the Communists were particularly keen to eradicate – or were simply the American detective thrillers collected by Lilla's nieces. It didn't matter whether they were written in Mandarin, English or German.

The Communist officials started with the libraries of the British-American Institute, the Tsingtao Club, the Masonic Hall. As if to demonstrate the extent to which Westerners and their culture were now the enemy, 'every single book was carted away in wheelbarrows and burnt', remembers Rugs. Then they moved on to the houses, where 'all Chinese who worked for foreigners were ordered to inform on their employers or face unspeakable consequences'. The party officials turned each home upside down in their manic hunt for now illegal literature. Even newspapers were destroyed. Audrey had packed some china in a combination of spare dressmaking material, underclothes and old Chinese newspapers – every sheet of which was pulled out and destroyed, page by page. In one foreign family's house, the Communists found something even more incriminating than books and papers – a photograph album containing pictures of half-Chinese, half-Western children. A suggestion that China could mix with the West. The political official who found that destroyed it on the spot.

Eventually, the Communists reached Lilla and Casey's house in Iltis Huk. Lilla would have known they were coming. Would have been sitting on a kitchen chair, waiting for a knock on the door. When it came, she had to stand by and watch them sweep through her home, picking up piles of business documents – just as those Japanese soldiers had done in the Casey offices in Chefoo. By now, Lilla must have begun to think that her optimism here in Tsingtao might be just as misplaced as it had been back then. At least this time they hadn't taken her husband away for questioning. Not yet.

Then the Communists seized control of all the businesses in the town. Or rather shut them all down, cutting off any chance of earning a living. It was as though Lilla had been caught up in some infernal historical loop where events were repeating themselves again and again, in slightly different shades of red. What would happen next if she stayed, she must have wondered. Another camp?

This time, Lilla wouldn't have been sure that she could do it all over again, and still survive. Casey wouldn't. He wasn't a complainer but his hands and legs were beginning to tremble. He was starting to mumble about seeing tigers hovering outside their house. And even if they did survive another camp, it was extremely unclear what would happen afterwards. The Communists weren't some foreign invading force like the Japanese. There would be no American Army making its way across the Pacific to rescue them.

It must have been about now that Lilla realized she couldn't stick out this war in China. As much as she longed to return to Chefoo, it wasn't about to happen. She would have to go back to England – she couldn't call it home – and watch her grandchildren grow up while she plotted her return. At least this time the rest of the world wasn't at war and she and Casey could still go back there.

But as soon as she tried to book a passage out of Tsingtao, Lilla discovered that it was already too late. She could no longer go anywhere at all. In order to leave, she was told, she needed an exit permit from the authorities. When she applied for permits, one each for her and Casey – an elderly Western couple who just wanted to be out of the way – she was refused.

There may have been no room for Westerners in Communist China. But Lilla's new rulers were making it clear that they weren't about to let her walk away. After what the Chinese felt the foreigners had done to their country – appropriating land for themselves, dominating its trade and selling opium to millions of its inhabitants – they were going to make an example of their new prisoners first.

As the weeks passed, Lilla and Casey simply ran out of money. They had nothing left with which to buy anything at all. Not even food, which was becoming scarcer and scarcer. Together with Mabel and Vivvy, each day they trekked over to Reggie's house, the British consulate, to eat and wash.

And then the interrogations started, just as Lilla must have feared. The Communists began hauling off all the young Western men for questioning, at eleven at night, at two in the morning. 'I was questioned three times a day for two hours at a time,' says Rugs. Each time they were dragged out of their beds, Jack Polkinghorn and Rugs found themselves sitting in front of the same interrogators in the same cell, being asked the same question, again and again and again. In Rugs' case it was, 'What day did you go to school?' As if the Communists were trying to obtain an admission that he was in possession of some of the education that they were so keen to destroy. Half asleep, confused and scared – because he never knew whether one of his questioners might simply pick up his gun from the table and shoot him, and they had already shot a German this way, while the Chinese British vice-consul had disappeared overnight – he struggled to remember what he had answered before. 'You had to say just one thing, give the same answer again and again.' 'It was very harrowing,' remembers Jack. 'You never knew when they would turn up to take you away.' He was asked about 'opium and religion', both of which the Communists were against. 'I had to reply, "I don't know much about that," and look down as I spoke,' he told me.

Rugs and Jack were interrogated for three months.

This time, Lilla must have thought when she saw her battered and exhausted nephews, at least they have left Casey and Vivvy alone. Casey was now seventy-eight. Vivvy was seventy-two. Reggie was seventy. As British consul he seemed to have some immunity. But who knew how long it might last?

Lilla and Casey spent months trailing between Iltis Huk and the consulate in the centre of town for meals and baths. The journey seeming longer every day. Months of Casey finding it harder and harder to make the trip, and Lilla coaxing him there and back. And then, suddenly, in August 1949, the exit permits came through. Four permits. For Lilla, Casey, Mabel and Vivvy. The old folk. The old folk could go home, the new authorities said. Had to go home, they said.

But my home is here, Lilla must have wanted to scream. But she couldn't. She was lucky to be getting away alive.

19

HEAVENLY TWINS TOGETHER AGAIN

The London suburbs, 1949

BACK IN LONDON, Lilla was an exile. She floated on the surface of the city, one of the thousands of pieces of human debris that the disintegrating British Empire was throwing up on British shores. People whose families had left Britain two, three or even four generations earlier to fly the flag in far-off lands. People who had barely known Britain. Some may have been educated 'at home' for a couple of years, others not even that. Yet, even though they felt they belonged in the tropics, in dusty desert cities or, in Lilla's case, junk-filled harbours, they had still felt that Home would be there for them when they needed it. An often unfamiliar, deific power, waiting to reclaim them in an afterlife. But now that, finally, their Time Had Come, this afterlife was proving a far from celestial affair.

Many of these families had worked tirelessly as civil servants, soldiers or diplomats for the great machinery of the British Empire. Even those who had been running their own businesses, like Lilla and her family, had still been throwing coins into Britain's gleaming coffers. But instead of returning to a glorious fanfare of trumpets, they now found themselves unwelcome and superfluous in a war-battered, rationed and overstretched land. Those still young enough took off straight away for the former British dominions – Australia, New Zealand, Canada – that offered them the chance to start again. Many had no choice but to try to make a resting place in Britain, surrounded by mementoes of their past adventures.

One of the most dignified and heart-rending stories I have heard comes from Gladys McMullan Murray. She ended up in 'a camp for displaced persons in Bridge-of-Weir' near Glasgow. Eventually, after she had spent some time in a factory job 'within walking distance' while her husband remained unemployed – he 'tried everywhere to find a job but was told that he was too old – he was barely fifty' – they both found posts as a warden and cook in an old folks' home. It must have been a crushingly different life to Chefoo, where she was the wife of a successful businessman and the sister of the biggest taipan in town.

Others – the lucky ones, perhaps, who could – chose to return to the former colonies that had become home, and eke out their days chasing the ever-fading shadow of empire life. This was what Lilla had tried to do. But her far-off land, the China she knew, had ceased to exist. Thankfully, all Lilla's family, my family, eventually escaped alive. But few of them went to Britain. Gerry and Murray had left for America just before the Communists marched into Tsingtao. A few anxious months after Lilla and Casey had sailed from Tsingtao, Rugs and Audrey sailed straight out to a new life in Vancouver. Jean and Jack, their car heart-stoppingly halted and searched on the way to their ship out, eventually slipped south to Hong Kong in the summer of 1950 with a 'very important letter' from Reggie to the British Foreign Office sealed at the bottom of their baby's crib. Lilla's brother Reggie was the last to leave, staying on alone for a year after his wife had sailed to England. He manned the consulate until 1951, when it was finally closed. By then he was over seventy and, like Lilla, too old to start again. And Vivvy's son Rae never really left China. He moved to Hong Kong and ended up alone in a home for impoverished and slightly confused former treaty-porters. Somebody sent me a photocopy of an interview with Rae published in the *Hong Kong Standard* in July 1990. He could no longer remember when he'd arrived in Hong Kong but recalled being treated 'as the taipan's son' in Chefoo. 'Perhaps I should go back to England and settle down,' he said – although he can have had neither the money to travel nor anywhere to go. The only living relative he knew of was his elder brother's widow, who lived in South Africa. And when, a couple of years later, Rae died, Vivvy's book on the history of Chefoo vanished with him.

Sitting in the Public Record Office in Kew fifty years after Lilla left China, I leafed through the British consular registers for Chefoo and Tsingtao. There were the births of Lilla and Ada and their siblings. The death of Jennings. The most poignant entries, however, were in Tsingtao. The first entry in the British births register is that of Reggie's daughter Gerry in 1911. The very last is in Reggie's own handwriting. It is for his granddaughter, bearing the same name, Geraldine, born in May 1950 as her parents, Jean and Jack, were desperately trying to escape the country. Lilla's family's roots were plunged so deeply into China's treaty-port earth that when they were finally torn out of the ground, the patch where they had once been concreted over by the Chinese, part of them shrivelled and died. All the family, like Lilla, found themselves floating on the surface of wherever they went next, yearning for the China that had been their home. In Vancouver, I celebrated Chinese New

Year with Rugs and Audrey in a huge, bustling restaurant where ours were the only non-Chinese faces, Rugs automatically ordering in still fluent Mandarin. And when Gerry took me to a Chinese restaurant in Kent – half a century after she had last left China – she bantered a little with the waiter before turning back and whispering to me, 'You know, his Chinese isn't really very good. I am certainly more Chinese than him.'

For China, the treaty ports had been a brief wrinkle in a long history. For Lilla and her family, the treaty ports had been their life.

Back in 1949, almost as soon as her feet touched British soil, Lilla started trying to recreate something of her old life back in China. She and Casey rented a flat in the London suburb of East Sheen and she filled it with the dragon-covered furniture that she found on the Sheen Road. She stood in their kitchen, using Worcester sauce for soy, trying to reproduce the sticky, spicy, sweet foods that reminded them both of Chefoo – shreds of pork and beef coated in sauce, tiny deep-fried parcels of whatever she could scrape together, noodle dishes floating in clear soup made from dried pasta that she hunted out from Italian shops. At home, she ate only with chopsticks. In the evenings she flung on a traditional Chinese coat of woven silk that she had brought back to England before the war. And, snug inside her oriental refuge, she must have felt a little less of a refugee.

Her recipe book, however, stayed hidden at the bottom of a suitcase.

But this tiny China haven wasn't enough for Lilla. After almost seventy years of fighting her way through life, she couldn't just shut up and put up with what she had left. And justified or not, she didn't only feel that she had a birthright to be in China, she felt that she had a blood, sweat and tears right to be there too. And if the Chinese government was going to prevent her from living in the country in which she had been born, then it could at least give her something in return. In return for her business, her property and the life it had taken away. Something to make all those years in the camps worthwhile. And as she watched Casey, exhausted by the to and fro, exhausted by losing everything not once but twice over, die in 1951, Lilla – as if entering into some otherworldly pact – seems to have vowed not to let go of life until China had given her something back.

Whoever she struck a bargain with – and maybe it was just with her own sheer determination – held her to it.

Shortly after Casey's funeral, Lilla started with the Foreign Office. She fired off a series of letters asking whether she was entitled to compensation from Japan or China. The replies were clear: 'The peace treaty with Japan has not yet been ratified'; property in China now needed to be registered with the Chinese authorities either in person or through an agent and 'at present, unfortunately, it is proving most difficult to find persons willing to act as agents in China'. The country was in the middle of a series of purges of anybody who did not adhere to strict Chinese Communist Party lines. There was a Three Antis Campaign against 'corruption, waste and obstructionist bureaucracy' aimed at administrators and managers, even party members themselves; a con-current Five Antis Campaign to dig out any remaining industrialists and businessmen, and a campaign to uncover hidden counter-revolutionaries. Many of those found guilty were sent to labour camps. Nobody dared hold any links with the West.

Lilla moved on to the Chinese Embassy in London. Its first rejection letter pointed out that 'it would be more appropriate' if Lilla were to write in Chinese. She did.

The second, nonetheless written in English, quoted a report from Chefoo that made it clear where the Chinese government believed responsibility lay — with everyone else but itself:

> *After the outbreak of the Second World War, Mrs Casey's property was confiscated by the Japanese authorities occupying the city. Part was destroyed by them. After the end of the Second World War, the property was occupied by Chiang Kai-shek's soldiers, who completely destroyed it. Therefore the Casey property was long out of existence during the liberation of Chefoo.*

However incorrect this was — for Lilla's houses had still been standing when the Communists occupied or, in their view, 'liberated' Chefoo after the Second World War — there was little she could do about it. Like millions of other refugees around the world, Lilla's life in China had been swept up and tossed from pitchfork to pitchfork in the chaos of war. So many different boots had trampled it underfoot that the Chinese government felt no need to shoulder the blame for her loss. By the late 1950s, Lilla had tried every avenue she could think of and had received rejection after rejection in return. Far from staking a claim to her old life, making her feel that she really had belonged somewhere once, she must have felt her life in China slipping further and further away. She took a deep breath, put down her pen and gave up.

Perhaps forgetting the pact she had made.

Living alone after Casey's death, Lilla began to spend more and more time with Ada. They took carefully counted turns to make the long bus ride across the London suburbs to meet each day. Now that they were both in the same city, both without husbands, and with a son and daughter and grandchildren each, their relationship settled into a wobbly equilibrium. It was almost as if keeping up with each other was the motor driving them through their days. If they couldn't meet that day, they'd write instead. And when they argued, an iron curtain fell across south-west London as each sent her children, her nieces, her cousins, to spy on the other while feigning a total lack of interest herself.

And then in 1958, when Lilla and Ada were seventy-six years old and still going strong, something happened to Ada that – just as her falling in love with Toby had done half a century earlier – turned Lilla's world on its head.

Ada was offered a 'grace and favour' apartment in the royal palace of Hampton Court on the outskirts of London. The last British monarch to live at Hampton Court was George II. He moved out in 1727, leaving his courtiers to move in. When Queen Victoria took over a hundred years later, she decided that the widows of high-ranking servants of the state – soldiers, clerics and civil servants – might make more deserving tenants.

Toby had been distinguished enough for Ada to qualify as just such a widow and her move into Hampton Court Palace elevated her on to a grand social plane. Nearly all the other widows there bore household names – many of them prefixed by a title. Ada's new neighbours were Lady This and Lady That. When she talked about them, it must have sounded as though she was reading out a history book.

Lilla was so jealous, I'm told, that she could hardly bring herself to talk about Ada's new home. And, no longer to be outdone if she could possibly help it, she wrote to the Lord Chamberlain's Office – which allocated the apartments – arguing that Ernie's limited successes entitled her to one too. She was turned down. But, perhaps out of loneliness, perhaps out of sympathy, perhaps because as much as she vied with her twin she now couldn't really live without her, Ada invited her to move in.

There was more than enough space for the two of them. Ada's apartment consisted of the nurseries used by Henry VIII's short-lived son, Edward VI. It was a rambling succession of rooms that were reputedly haunted by several ghosts. Lilla's daughter Alice, a firm believer in the supernatural, was convinced that she'd seen a Tudor nursemaid outside her bedroom when staying overnight. After that, few of Lilla and Ada's family were willing to stay.

Ada was completely unperturbed by these stories. She slept in the room in which Henry VIII's third wife, Jane Seymour, had died shortly after giving birth to Edward VI. If Lilla was even the slightest bit scared, she wasn't going to show it. Not even the Four Horsemen of the Apocalypse would have driven her from that apartment once she was in. She did, however, claim to have seen one ghost when walking in the palace grounds after dark. She said she'd spotted a lady looking lost and approached her to help. When the woman turned to her, Lilla said she had recognized her as Henry VIII's faithless and beheaded second wife, Anne Boleyn.

I strongly suspect that she made this up. Not just to tease the more gullible members of her family but to bait Ada. Ada might have been sleeping in a Tudor queen's bedroom but Lilla had met one. Once they were living together, the old twinly rivalry took on a new, even more energetic lease of life. At times they'd bicker like mad, then sit down together for a cup of tea or a stiff drink. Whatever one did, the other had to do too. Now, however, towards the end of their lives, at least it wasn't always Ada who went first.

Within the apartment, each twin had her own sitting room. Lilla moved in her dark dragon-covered furniture

and bought more, again from the Sheen Road, to fill the
room. Walking into her apartment was like stepping into
China. Ada copied her. She bought identical furniture
and created her own Chinese chamber across the hall-
way. And although by then she could only cook curries,
Ada copied Lilla in eating with chopsticks only – even
making her daughter and grandchildren eat turkey with
them on Christmas Day.

It was here, in the kitchen, that Lilla could have really
outstripped Ada if she'd shown her the recipe book. But
for some reason she didn't. She cooked Chinese, Indian,
English, French and Italian food, winding Ada up from
day to day. But she never showed her twin her cookery
book. Maybe she was so successful in chasing away her
memories of the camp that she had forgotten about it. But
I find this hard to believe. Surely every time she went
through a recipe, went into a kitchen, felt the resistance
of fresh food in her hand, she remembered the hunger
she had felt and the effort of typing those pages letter by
letter in the baking heat and searing cold.

I think that Lilla kept her book hidden because from
day to day there was still a chance that Ada could learn
to cook a few more dishes and catch up, moving their
game on. But Ada could never have written a recipe book
like hers. Could never have bridged that crevasse. And
she would have tried, certainly.

Lilla knew all too well what it was like to feel that far
behind. I don't think she wanted Ada to have to feel it
too.

Still, however hard the twins tried to keep up with each
other, there remained one glaring difference between the
two of them. Even though she never appeared to put on
a single pound – and she had done from time to time
when younger – Lilla 'ate like a horse', without a trace of
self-discipline. Whenever she went to a restaurant, she

collected up the leftovers and took them home, as if she was still worried that there might not be any more food the next day. She did this at parties too – as one of her grandchildren burst out, 'Even at my wedding.' And Lilla had a desperate need to eat on time. Lunch had to be by twelve and supper early. Some days, she couldn't even wait until noon. Her daughter Alice would go to meet her for lunch in a department store – the combination of eating and shopping together was Lilla's idea of a perfect day out – only to find that Lilla hadn't been able to stop herself from eating before Alice arrived, gorging herself on cakes and cream buns as though they might vanish at any moment.

But of course, after those years in the camps, she would have still felt they could.

The twins busied themselves through their eighties. Vivvy and Reggie and their wives passed away. Even their younger sisters Edith and Dorothy, who – safely back in England with their families – had avoided the camps, grew old and died. But Lilla and Ada were still going at their lives hammer and tongs. Each was up at six to clean out her fireplaces, tidy her sitting room, make it sparkle just a little more than the other's. Then they dressed. Each twin's hair swept up at the back of her head, each wearing an immaculate suit, diamonds in her ears, the two of them went out shopping. Not that they bought much. They thrived on the process rather than the act of shopping. Occasionally they went together but usually each went off on her own, hunting out some piece of oriental paraphernalia that the other had found. Or something that the other hadn't yet found. Shopkeepers throughout the area must have thought they were seeing double as, a day or so after one twin had bought something from them, the other appeared to buy it again. They made the most of looking identical.

Whenever one bumped into somebody she didn't like, she unhesitatingly pretended to be the other.

Back in the apartment, the Heavenly Twins were as gregarious as they had been all those years ago in Chefoo. They were endlessly throwing parties, inviting family, friends, anyone who had been in China. Anyone they knew. One relative out of a job found herself recruited to the filing department of MI6 – at the height of the Cold War – by someone she met in Lilla's kitchen. And whenever the two of them wanted to retreat into their private twinly world in front of other people, they lapsed into a private language. 'It sounded by then,' says one of Lilla's grandsons, 'like a form of kitchen Hindustani.'

Lilla and Ada stayed together in Hampton Court until 1970. When Ada grew so frail that she had to move into a nursing home, Lilla took her to one in the Chefoo-like seaside town of Hove on the south coast. She rented an apartment nearby and sat at her elder sister's bedside holding her hand until Ada – eighty-nine years old and still vowing to outlive Lilla – eventually let go of life.

After Ada died, Lilla moved in with her daughter Alice. Alice and her husband Havilland lived on the lower ground floor of a rambling house in the commuter town of Tunbridge Wells in Kent. They gave Lilla a bedroom next door to the sitting room. The room that she turned into that through-the-looking-glass museum of furniture and clothes from every corner of the world. The room that I remember being invited into to be shown how to brush my hair. Lilla unpinned her hair and, even in her nineties, it fell to below her waist. She showed me how to comb through my tomboy locks with her silver-backed hairbrush. 'I b-b-brush my hair one h-hundred times a night,' she whispered. I remember my arm aching as I tried to do the same that evening back home.

Six years after Ada died Lilla brought out her recipe book. She showed it to Alice. Alice showed it to her daughter Liz. Liz showed it to her husband, Donald, who took it to the Imperial War Museum in London. The museum asked to keep it. Lilla agreed. The museum wrote to her expressing their 'warmest appreciation ... We are delighted to be able to add this most unusual item to our collections and are certain it will be of great interest to visitors and researchers alike.'

Lilla had the letter framed.

That summer Lilla's son Arthur, my grandfather, led a family expedition to see her recipe book in the museum. I was eight years old and wanted to climb on top of the great gun that still stands in front of the main door, but Grandpa, still a soldier at heart, ordered us on. The recipe book stood in its own glass case, in the centre of an open hall near the entrance. My father lifted me up so that I could peer at the pages that lay open. I remember seeing the yellowed paper, the lists of ingredients and Vivvy's pen-and-ink drawings. At the time I didn't understand why Great-Granny's book was so important when there were far more exciting things like guns and tanks in the museum. Then, while the grown-ups stood around the recipe book talking and talking, Grandpa took my sister and me down into the basement and showed us the guns he'd commanded in the North African desert.

Lilla didn't come to the museum with us. She was as proud as punch that her 'b-b-book' was in the museum and she regarded it as a great honour. 'Both my book & my name are placed there for ever!!' she wrote. But – unlike so many people who used to boast of their experiences in the war – it wasn't a time that Lilla wanted to dwell on.

After all those years of feeling a foreigner, at the age of ninety-five Lilla found herself suddenly welcomed in by the British establishment. And she felt it was parading her at least as high as it had ever paraded Ada. Lilla was made an honorary vice president of her local branch of the National Council of Women of Great Britain. The tiniest of honours, but Lilla boasted of it as though she had been given a medal. It was then that the BBC sent a television crew down to interview her about her time in the Japanese camps. The crew unpacked their bags in Liz's drawing room, set up their cameras, arranged the lights. Lilla sat there in silence, watching them. This would have been her great moment, but by the time the crew were ready to start, Lilla couldn't speak. She just sat there in a black beaded outfit, her elegant legs crossed, her hair up, diamonds in her ears. And unable to utter a word about what she'd been through.

Lilla was now in her late nineties. Yet the years hardly seemed to touch her. Having had a far tougher life than her identical twin, there was something a little uncanny about the way in which she seemed to be sailing on after Ada had gone. She was still as bright as a button and quick on her feet. Still walking a mile each day to do her shopping. She even had her teeth capped at the age of ninety-seven. It was as though Ada really had taken Lilla's share of good luck at birth and, now that Ada had died, Lilla had taken it back. But it was when Lilla had outlived both Arthur and Alice, and an emptiness had begun to creep into the back of her eyes, that her family began to wonder whether it wasn't good luck but something quite different that was keeping her alive.

Arthur was the first to die, of cancer, in 1980. Lilla was ninety-eight. A few months later, Alice had a heart attack on her way into an operating theatre.

It was only then that Lilla told her granddaughter Liz about her other child. The one whom she thought she had bounced out of her in order to keep Ernie. The child whose death I fear she thought she was being made to pay for again and again. It was only then, eighty years later, that there was somebody to tell her that she couldn't possibly have killed that child.

After Arthur and Alice died, something in Lilla weakened and she had to go into a nursing home in Tunbridge Wells. I can remember her deep red room, crammed with her Chinese furniture. And Lilla sitting at a small darkwood table under the window, throwing her arms up, fingers and hands extended as if she were about to throw herself forward on to her knees in prayer as she welcomed us in. 'D-d-d-darlings,' she smiled at us. She still dressed immaculately in those beaded black cardigans and diamonds. Still wore the brooch that Ernie had given her. Her fingers still just nimble enough to fix her hair. She wasn't like other old people, my mother used to say. Not at all. And Lilla could still twist a man round her little finger. When one of her other great-granddaughters popped in to see her on the way to the cinema with her boyfriend, Lilla greeted the strange young man with a 'd-d-darling' and he was spellbound, rooted to the spot. Unable to tear himself away until long after the movie had begun.

In the hours she was alone, Lilla leafed through her scrapbooks of China photographs. Photographs of Chefoo, the bay, her little houses. Photographs of Peking and the Forbidden City. Photographs of the places to which she longed to return – but knew she never would.

And then, out of the blue, came a glimmer of hope. A glimmer of something that Lilla thought she had given up on. Perhaps all those years in the camps might have been worthwhile. Perhaps she might have something to give, if not to her children, to her grandchildren.

In the early 1980s China decided to talk to the West. It decided to open its doors enough to let a sliver of light through. It wanted to borrow money and lure investors back. It had to show that it could honour its debts. It was prepared to settle all outstanding claims.

My father filled out all the forms for Lilla. Attached copies of the lists she had made on the day after Pearl Harbor. Copies of the lists she had made when she returned to China after the war. Copies of her title deeds to the land upon which she had built her houses. He sent them off from his office as Secretary of State for Energy – Lilla was always brimming with pride over her grandson's success – with the British passport that she had been given back in 1939.

The reply from the British government department dealing with the claims was stark. Lilla's passport was no longer enough to make her British. In order to stem the flow of immigrants from its former empire, the British government had introduced new laws making it difficult to claim British nationality unless you could show that you had been born in Britain or were married to a British citizen. And to claim under the arrangements with China, Lilla had to provide birth and marriage certificates to prove her nationality and changes of name.

Pieces of paper like that don't always survive wars. Lilla had clung on tightly to her lists and title deeds. But the documents she needed now – that she could never have imagined she would need – had gone.

My father didn't know what to say to Lilla. She had been so excited, so thrilled to hear that China was about to acknowledge her life there and give her back something for her grandchildren. He couldn't bring himself to tell his dear sweet granny that now, even after the Imperial War Museum had taken her recipe book, she was still regarded as a foreign refugee. That she couldn't give her grandchildren the money she felt should be hers to give.

Lilla was not alone in believing herself British but being classed as a stateless foreigner. The new laws had caught hundreds, if not thousands, of returning empire-builders in its nets, including most of Lilla's family. Nearly everyone I spoke to had had problems with their nationality. Lilla's niece Gerry, returning to Britain from the US with her young children after her husband Murray had died of cancer in 1950, very young, found herself shuffled from windowless room to windowless room deep in the bowels of the Home Office until she let fly, 'Of course I'm bloody British. My father was the British consul in Shantung.' Rugs, who won a Military Cross for single-handedly leading an infantry charge up a hill in the Second World War, hasn't held a British passport since.

And when Ernie's youngest brother, Evelyn – who had been Foreign Secretary to the government of India and received a knighthood – had gone to renew his passport, he had been told he was no longer British. He had been planning his first trip abroad in years, as a lifetime serving his country had left him with a great deal of pride but very little money on which to retire. Now even that pride had been stolen from him.

Luckily, he had made it back to Britain first. There are some people whose families set off for the empire's outposts a couple of generations ago who, turfed out of the former colonies they have been living in, are still trying to return.

The British Empire, and colonial life generally, offered a deal. It encouraged people who were prepared to work hard to take risks abroad in exchange for a better life than was open to them at home. But once imperialism fell out of favour, troops were withdrawn and some of the former colonies became set on expelling all trace of colonialism, the families of those who had first taken up the challenge began to discover that they no longer belonged to the country they regarded as Home.

* * *

My father wrote back to the Foreign Office. He told them about the camps. He told them about the Communists. He pointed out that it was almost a century since his grandmother had been born. And then he waited.

And, ignorant as to why her claim was taking so long, Lilla waited too.

Lilla turned one hundred while she was waiting to hear from the Foreign Office. My father decided to take no chances and wrote in advance to Buckingham Palace to check that Lilla would be receiving the traditional telegram of congratulations from the Queen on reaching a hundred years old. It arrived at her party. A large room in her nursing home was packed with relatives, and plastered with cards that Lilla had received from all over the world. Thirteen years old, gawkily dressed in a drop-waisted tartan mini-dress that I now cringe to think about (it was 1982), I watched Lilla, elegant as ever in diamonds and black, sitting resplendent in the bay window. All she'd lost was her long hair. When her fingers could no longer twist it up at the back of her head, she agreed to have it cut and curled. She still, I thought, looked better than me. But in the moments between conversations, I saw a faraway look in her eyes as she fingered her telegram from the Queen.

I wonder whether she was remembering another telegram from the Queen. Another King, another Queen. One written in a pencil scrawl on yellowing paper pinned into that little black album that she still kept in a drawer. The telegram that she'd received almost seven decades earlier, confirming that Ernie was dead. Ernie, whose reddish hair was still floating around the room in front of her on the top of several heads. Including mine.

* * *

Two months later, the news came through that Lilla's claim to her property in China had been accepted. And suddenly, whatever had been pinning her to this life began to loosen its claws. Old age came pounding down upon her. 'It's so m-m-maddening, d-d-d-darling,' she whispered to my mother. 'First your legs go, then your hearing goes, then your eyes go.' But at last she was free. 'Now I can go to Heaven,' she wrote to my father, her writing so shaky that I still want to applaud each word. She longed, she said, to join her children and Ada. And, though far from devout, she claimed to hear heavenly music and choirs in her head. It was as though she was listening to what she thought Ada could already hear. As though she was slipping back to be one with her twin again. And the following January, on the 6th, Epiphany, the day after Twelfth Night, the last day of Christmas – the day the decorations are taken down and the revellers go home to rest – Lilla died.

Lilla's funeral was the first funeral that I had been to. The church was packed. The overflowing pews were buzzing with excitement. As I found my way to my seat I saw the same faces I had seen swarming around the room at her birthday party a few months earlier. The only person missing was Lilla.

Her grandson John, a clergyman, led the proceedings. Lilla had lived so long that even her daughter's son had grey hair. Each time John referred to Lilla, instead of saying 'the deceased' or giving her name, he called her 'dear Granny'. That was what made me want to cry.

I sat staring at the coffin throughout the service. The stretched wooden hexagon in front of the altar didn't seem to bear any relation to Lilla, to all that life, at all. And if she was there, hiding inside, I was amazed that she was keeping so still. I kept my eyes on the box, waiting for the flowers to tremble, the lid to slide away and Lilla to pop out stuttering, 'D-d-d-darlings, how w-w-wonderful you could all come.'

But she didn't. She had at last gone.

EPILOGUE

London, November 2003

LILLA NEVER made it back to Chefoo, but I did. In May 2000, I went to China with my younger sister, Kate. We landed in Beijing – the city Lilla called Pékin – marvelled at the Forbidden City as she had done, and then flew south to Chefoo. Only the town isn't called Chefoo any more. Now it's known only by its Chinese name of Yantai. For the Chinese, Chefoo had never really been the town's name. Chefoo, or Zhifu, was the name of a fishing village just along the coast, and the foreigners had misappropriated it for their port next to the city of Yantai.

I didn't expect to find many traces of our family's life in Yantai. For the past half-century, China had been such an isolationist country that it felt like another planet. It seemed, frankly, weird to think that, just over fifty years ago, its coastline and rivers had been scattered with American and European enclaves. Places full of Western buildings, Western businesses, Western people, Western lives. Places that had been – and were still – home towns for the Americans and Europeans born there, including Lilla and the host of other relations I had dug out of Vancouver, New Zealand and a variety of British seaside resorts. All of whom still felt displaced in the non-Chinese countries in which they had ended up. But of course the treaty ports, with their foreign domination of Chinese trade and their importation of opium, are one of the unspoken reasons why China decided to cut itself off from the rest of the world.

As Kate and I were driven in from the Chefoo airport by a friend of Norman Cliff's called Liu Xingbang, we were hoping at best to grasp the geography of the place. The perfectly curving bay, the dragon spines in the water, Consulate Hill dividing the port from the harbour, the hills rising up behind.

We were surprised.

In the gaps between the modern towers that now make up the Yantai waterfront stood the remains of the treaty port that the town had once been. European buildings poked up between the concrete blocks like the lost ruins of an ancient civilization. Germanic alpine chalets gathered in groups of three or four along First Beach. There was the mission boarding school, now a heavily guarded military training ground. The Casey building still loomed up on the seafront just as in the photographs I had seen, though now a wide road had been tarmacked between it and the beach. The church had gone but I squealed as I saw the Chefoo Club straight ahead of me, instantly recognizable from the photocopies of the family albums that I was clutching. There were even Westerners sipping cocktails at the front. They were, we were told, the new wave of foreign investors in China, lured over from Canada's West Coast. The owners of the club – by then known as the Hundred Years Golden Club – showed Kate and me around. They took us downstairs to the nineteenth-century wooden bowling alley – whose far end was decorated with a vista of what looks like London's Houses of Parliament and Big Ben. Then they took us into the new basement bar. Western style, they proudly said. Next door to the club the old white-gabled hotel that used to stand there had been replaced by an unpainted concrete block containing a hotel and sushi restaurant, designed to appeal to the Japanese who still frequented the Shantung – now written as Shandong – coast.

Behind this lay the path up to Consulate Hill.

Consulate Hill had become a park. The gardens of its old mansions had overflowed, opening out into public lawns. The long-empty consulates and grand dwellings served as a form of entertainment for the passers-by to gawp at, as they were being steadily knocked down to make way for new property developments.

Kate and I meandered through and over the top of the hill to the customs officers' red-brick houses. The row was still there, but boarded up and ready to go next. We tried to peer over the high wall in front of them, hoping to catch a proper look at the place where Lilla, our great-grandmother, had been born. Where her real father, our great-great-grandfather Charles Jennings, had blown his brains out in the garden shed.

It felt very strange to walk around this town perched on the Chinese coast and think that, in a way, this is where I am from. As we followed the steps on down to the port, I glanced inside the terraced houses on our left and saw eerily familiar tiled Victorian hallways, wooden banisters rising up beside the stairs, as in a hundred London houses I have seen. The same view that a toddling Lilla must have glimpsed as she trotted by.

The next day we walked along the beachfront and up East Hill, clutching Lilla's photographs of her houses. Not a brick remained. The rich brown earth had been recently ploughed and then flattened to make way for the new China rising up around us. I looked at the photos and then back at the bare hill and thought that this was what it must have looked like when Lilla had started to build her houses almost seventy years earlier. She'd loved those houses, spent hours leafing through the photographs I was holding in my hand. To Lilla those five houses had meant independence and a guarantee that no child, grandchild or great-grandchild of hers would ever be abandoned because they weren't rich enough. They were, she believed, worth a fortune. A fortune that made all those years in the camps, her whole life, as she put it, 'worthwhile'.

When Lilla put in her claim she was hoping to receive this 'fortune', somewhere between a quarter and half a million pounds in today's money. As I stood on East Hill, looking along First Beach to Consulate Hill and the dragon spines curving through the water beyond, I wondered what would have upset her more – the destruction of her houses or living long enough to learn how small this fortune turned out to be. A few months after Lilla's funeral, the cheque arrived that Lilla had died believing would make her six beloved grand-children rich – and which left her free to join her own children and Ada. But the cheque was for just fourteen hundred pounds (three thousand pounds today). She was paid just one fifth of the 1935 value of her houses – the only property she was deemed to have lost in the Communist takeover in 1949 and not during the war with Japan beforehand. If Lilla had been alive to discover that, I think she would have been so angry that she would still be alive now, battling with the latest Chinese regime.

Before we went home, Kate and I took the train across the Shandong peninsula to Tsingtao, now Qingdao. As we stepped out of the railway station into that untouched Bavarian town square that looks like a Second World War film set with an extensive Chinese crew, our jaws dropped. Qingdao still has mile after mile of avenues lined with European stone mansions. It was mind-boggling to see such a perfectly preserved European town standing in China. Clutching an old photograph, Kate and I found Reggie's old house at 5 Liang Road – the mansion he had to sell when Cornabé Eckford went bust. We broke in through the garbage bins at the back and sneaked round the front. The stone balustrades and trees outside were intact. But instead of the clutch of English children peering over the balcony in my photograph, we saw lines of washing and signs that at least one family if not two lived on each floor.

Our final stop was Shanghai. Here block after block of mock-Tudor suburbia fanned out from the grand waterfront buildings. The palaces knocked up in the Twenties and Thirties by the port's magnates sprawled alongside new motorways. Kate and I roamed the streets, shopping for silk, popping into restaurants, meeting up with friends of friends as Lilla and Ada must have done on their visits. Just as in Chefoo, although on a far grander scale, Shanghai is welcoming foreigners again. And a new generation of Westerners is flocking back. They are opening jazz bars, printing English-language newspapers and talking in reverent tones about 'old China hands'. The city buzzes with an explosive energy that can make Manhattan feel provincial. Its former treaty-port mansions are once more changing hands for millions of pounds. Its old five-star hotels have become new five-star hotels. The bellboys have returned, as have the dancing girls. 'Shanghai,' the neon signs seem to flicker, 'is starting all over again.'

ACKNOWLEDGEMENTS

THIS BOOK HAS BEEN a long journey, and there are a great number of people who deserve my thanks for helping me to complete it. Very sadly, not all of them are still alive to see this book's publication but I have included their names as they are certainly far from forgotten.

Much of the research in the latter half of the book I owe to Lilla's fellow internee Norman Cliff, without whose generosity in both thought and time this book would not have been written. Others who have been equally unstinting in their help include Ron Bridge, Peggy Caldwell, Martin Cornish, Joan Croft, Colonel Patric Emerson, Alison Holmes, Rosie Llewellyn Jones, Bob McMullan, George McWatters, Colonel Patrick Mercer MP, Lord Montagu of Beaulieu, Jimmy Murray, Patricia and Brian Ogden, Algernon Percy, Mary Taylor Previte and James H. Taylor III; Dan Waters and Sarah Parnell of the Royal Asiatic Society in Hong Kong, Christopher Hunt of the Imperial War Museum, Sarah Parker of Historic Royal Palaces, Sarah Dodgson of the Athenaeum, Frances Wood and the staff of the Oriental and India Office reading room at the British Library. And, of course, Elizabeth Filby, my researcher, who managed to unearth long-forgotten documents and details from the recesses of London's archives with a flourish.

My research in China could not have been completed without the help also of Susan Liu, Liu Xingbang, Mark O'Neill, Sun Liping and Zhang Tao, who all extended me generous hospitality during my visit. The other great set of people who threw open their doors to me are my many rediscovered relations, whom it was a joy to meet. Rugs and Audrey Eckford in particular showed me the sights of Vancouver while producing a treasure trove of memories, photographs and diaries that form the backbone for several chapters in this book. Carol Bartlett, Anne and Shelagh Eckford, John and Nan Elderton, Nicholas Gibbs, George Howell, Phyllis Morley, Liz Murton, Dilys Philps, Jean and Jack Polkinghorn, Gerry Simmons, and John, Maureen, Nicky, Tom, Mike and Belinda de Sausmarez each gave me several pieces of the jigsaw puzzle of Lilla's life, and have discussed and rediscussed their reminiscences with me at length.

Several of my friends, too, have provided me with both their advice and encouragement at crucial points along the way. Chief among these is Amanda Foreman, who has nudged me in the right direction both professionally and as a friend. I can safely say that, were it not for her enthusiasm at several critical stages, *Lilla's Feast* would still be one of those many books that were never quite written. And Corisande Albert, Matthew d'Ancona, Catherine Fall, Simone Finn, Henrietta Green, Edward Heathcoat-Amory, Santa Montefiore, Catherine Ostler, Kate Pope, Albert Read, Andrew Roberts, Sarah Schaefer, Simon Sebag Montefiore, Victor Sebastian and Alice Thomson have each passed me a few pieces of information worth their weight in gold.

And I can boast a handful of new friends that I have made along the road, namely, Claire Paterson, my agent, and Jane Lawson and Elisabeth Dyssegaard, my editors.

They are the ones who ultimately teased *Lilla's Feast* out of my mind and on to its many pages, guiding me up the vertiginous slope of writing my first book, cajoling me back to work after the arrival of Liberty midway with their eagerness to read it. And, with the exceptional skill of haute couturiers, Jane and Elisabeth used their great expertise in all things editorial to help me tuck and pin this book into its final shape. Thank you.

And thank you, too, to everyone at Transworld. Especially Sheila Lee, who seemed to enjoy looking at my family photographs and has done a fantastic job in finding more. And Deborah Adams, who went through my text with a toothcomb.

My most long-suffering companions on this voyage, however, have been my family. My sister, Kate Bain, for coming with me to China. My brother, Toby Howell, and my parents, David and Davina Howell, for being pestered for facts morning, noon and night. My grandmother, Prue de Winton, and my aunt, Jane Townsend, for helping them to provide them. My mother-in-law Felicity Osborne for her expertise in all things foodie. My children, Luke and Liberty, for letting me work, their nanny, Suzie, for keeping them so blissfully happy while I did so. And last but far from least, my husband George, for his reading and fact-finding, for his opinion so gently offered, and for putting up with my erratic hours and moods as *Lilla's Feast* neared its end.

London, January 2004

Picture Credits

THE LINE DRAWINGS used on the inside covers, the part openings and the chapter headings come from Lilla's cookery book, which is now kept in the Imperial War Museum.

All other photos and illustrations in the book have been supplied by the author and her family, except for the following: 48: Hulton Archive; 123: from *Living London: its work and its play, its humour and its pathos, its sights and its scenes*, edited by G. R. Sims, 1906; 218: courtesy Patricia Ogden; 229: hairnet girls sketch by Claire Malcolm Lintilhac from her privately published memoirs; 243: both images © Bettman/Corbis: view of Weihsien hospital [top]: from the collection of Ida Jones Talbot, courtesy of her daughter Christine (Talbot) Sancton; general view of the camp: courtesy Ron Bridge; 300: plan of the camp courtesy Langdon Gilkey; 309: drawing by Father Louis Schmid by courtesy of Leopold Pander and Father Wiel Bellemakers; 359: © Baldwin H. Ward & Kathryn C. Ward/CORBIS.

Illustrations section: 1: Ada and Lilla as children: MS 201813 Box 20, Bowra Collection, School of Oriental & African Studies, University of London; 2/3: marines taking a ride in a rickshaw: © Lake County Museum/CORBIS; 6/7: drawing of emblem by N. Piculevitch; woman cultivating the ground outside the kitchen hut and the liberation of Weihsien: courtesy Ron Bridge; Father Frans Verhoeven's view of Kitchen no. 1 by courtesy of Leopold Pander and Father Wiel Bellemakers.

BIBLIOGRAPHY

Martin Booth, *Opium*, Pocket Books, 1997

Eloise Glass Cauthan, *Higher Ground* (first-person biography of her father, Dr Wiley B. Glass, constructed from his manuscripts), Boardman Press, Nashville, Tennessee, 1978

Norman Cliff, *Courtyard of the Happy Way*, Courtyard Publishers, 1977

N.B. Dennys, Trubner & Co., *Vade Mecum: A Guide to China's Treaty Ports*, London 1867

Langdon Gilkey, *Shantung Compound*, Harper & Row, 1966

Peter Hennessy, *Never Again: Britain 1945–51*, Sidgwick and Jackson, 1971

Michael Holroyd, *Works on Paper*, Little, Brown, 2002

Peter Hopkirk, *The Great Game*, Oxford University Press, 1990

Claire Malcolm Lintilhac, *China – A Personal World*, privately published, 1977

Gordon Martin, *Chefoo School 1881–1951*, Merlin Books, 1990

Pamela Masters, *The Mushroom Years*, Henderson House Publishing, 1998

David Michell, *A Boy's War*, Overseas Missionary Fellowship, 1988

Jan Morris, *Pax Britannica*, Faber and Faber, 1968

Gladys McMullan Murray, *China Born*, privately published

Martha Philips and Mary Haddon, *Behind Stone Walls and Barbed Wire*, Bible Memory Association, 1991

Mary Taylor Previte, 'A Song of Salvation', published in the *Philadelphia Inquirer* Magazine, 25 August 1985

J. A. G. Roberts, *The Complete History of China*, Sutton Publishing, 2003

C. W. Schmidt, 'Glimpses of the History of Chefoo', lecture given at the Unity Club, Chefoo, October 1932

Jonathan D. Spence, *The Search for Modern China*, Norton, 1999

Mary Taylor, *The Women's Century*, The National Archives, 2003

Paul Tritton, *John Montagu of Beaulieu: Motoring Pioneer and Prophet*, Golden Eagle/George Hart, 1985

Bernard Wasserstein, *The Secret War in Shanghai*, Profile Books, 1999

Clive Wood and Beryl Suitters, *The Fight for Acceptance: A History of Contraception*, Medical and Technical Publishing, Aylesbury, 1970

Frances Wood, *No Dogs and Not Many Chinese*, John Murray, 1998

AN INTERVIEW WITH
THE AUTHOR

Lilla's Feast is curious in that it is a book about the writing of another book: Lilla's recipe and housekeeping guide which is now in the Imperial War Museum in London. For Lilla that recipe book embodied her life's struggles. She was writing it in order to survive mentally when she was starving in a concentration camp. And its content consisted of her means of survival in her earlier great struggle – the one to stop her husband abandoning her and their small son. Despite the generations and miles that separated us, I did find parallels between my own book-writing story and Lilla's. Incidentally, I was writing about Lilla and my grandfather, a chatterbox of a toddler charging around whilst she was pregnant with her second child, a girl – and I was in an identical situation at the time. More broadly, I had always longed to be a writer and was at a stage in my life where I felt acutely aware that I had only one life to do what I wanted with and it was now or never. As I wrote *Lilla's Feast*, I felt I was writing for my own survival too.

1. Is *Lilla's Feast* your first stab at writing non-fiction?

Lilla's Feast is my first stab at writing any book! I had intended to use Lilla's story as the basis for a novel but the true story that I uncovered was so compelling that I wrote it as non-fiction.

2. You are a natural story-teller. Did you have to resist the temptation to alter or invent facts to satisfy your imagination?

I wasn't tempted to alter any facts but, time and time again, I found myself imagining vividly the story just beyond the point to which my research had taken me. I could hear and see the characters continuing beyond the 'script'. I decided to include some of this, but making it absolutely clear to readers when I was doing so.

3. Your book has been described as 'Wonderfully evocative, vivid, distilled'. From the wealth of original family material, how did you know what to include and what to leave out?

I ruthlessly stuck to the essential story of Lilla's life: her growth from spoilt teenager to strong woman. However curious the detail was, if it didn't fit in, it didn't go in. Paradoxically, I think doing so enables the reader to 'feel' the rest of the characters' lives hovering around the book – and makes it richer.

4 How easy was it to empathise with Lilla? Would you have been equally content to write the life story of Lilla's twin sister, Ada, instead?

Although Lilla and Ada were identical twins, their lives were very different. Apart from one or two, particular, aspects of her life, Ada suffered far less hardship than Lilla and there are fewer places to be willing her on. So, no, I would not have been equally content to write Ada's life. In any case, I felt an instinctive empathy for Lilla. Partly because I knew her, fragile and strong, partly because I am her descendant, but also because she was, for much of her life, the underdog and a real trier.

5. There is a clear sense of place in your book. What were some of your research methods?

The hard part to researching some of the places in *Lilla's Feast* was that they are no longer there – at least not as the characters knew them. In order to gain a sense of atmosphere I had to reconstruct the places in Lilla's life by combining reading contemporaneous eye-witness accounts, working out what was going on from official documents, interviewing people who had lived there – and visiting the remains myself. Often, even though the buildings have changed, the landscapes are unaltered. For example, Chefoo, Lilla's birthplace in China is unrecognizable as a town (even the name has changed) but the mesmerisingly beautiful bay and its strings of pointy islands are still there – and with them some of the atmosphere that Lilla knew.

6. When did you know you wanted to become a writer?

I have wanted to write books since the age of five, when I wrote a gory story about monsters and it was pinned up on the wall at school in the full glory of its orange and purple felt-tip border. However it took me until my thirties to find the courage to follow that ambition.

7. How did your legal training affect the process of writing?

My legal training both helped and hindered the writing process. On the research front it helped as I knew how to dig out documents, read between the lines and reconstruct what had happened. When it came to writing it was arguably a hindrance as I found myself unable to pass off my imagination as fact.

8. What objections do you think Lilla would have made to the book? And what would she have especially liked?

What a bundle of mixed reactions Lilla would have had to this book about her: first a flurry of modesty whilst being unable to disguise her pleasure with it; then even greater pleasure when she realized that her identical twin Ada didn't have a book written about her, followed by anguish that Ada didn't have a book written about her, too; and then she would have objected strongly to being portrayed as the underdog to Ada and claimed that her mourning for Ernie was totally genuine, t-t-t-totally genuine, not put on at all.

9. Which chapters were particularly difficult to write? Why?

The writing of *Lilla's Feast* posed two very different types of challenges. The first was a technical challenge of recreating life in a concentration camp which was a totally alien experience. I ended up immersing myself in both conversation and reading with former inmates to the extent that I felt I had been there myself! The other challenge was an emotional challenge. The sharpest point to this was writing how my beloved Grandpa had let his mother be sidelined at his wedding. And then the chapters covering Lilla's early, painful, marriage quite literally reduced me to tears in the process. By the time I reached the last two chapters revealing Lilla's expulsion from China and non-welcome back to Britain, I had run out of tears and simply ached as, for me, they are the most poignant.

10. Do you have any interesting anecdotes behind the writing of *Lilla's Feast* that you would like to share?

Lilla's Feast is partly a book about dispossession and the unravelling of the migrations of nineteenth-century empire. It is about people losing their homes and finding new places for themselves in the world. This was made very real to me when I interviewed some of the people involved: from Lilla's niece who said that she was rootless to the extent that the town in China where she had been born had fallen into the sea following an earthquake; to another of Lilla's nieces who took me to a Chinese restaurant in Kent and tested the waiter on his mandarin before turning to me and whispering that she was certainly more Chinese than him. Perhaps the most amusing anecdotes about the writing of *Lilla's Feast*, however, come from my research trip to China with my sister and these show the great chasm in understanding between East and West which Lilla and her family, for a while, managed to breach. One Chinese woman in her forties told me that when she was at school they had read Dickens – and been told that it was an accurate representation of contemporaneous life in London, right down to the smog. When she arrived in Britain for the first time in the nineteen-eighties, she couldn't believe what she saw! A more basic misunderstanding occurred when my sister and I visited Tsingtao, which is still a spa town. We decided to make the most of it by trying to book what we thought was a foot massage in the health centre downstairs in the hotel. Five minutes later two young Chinese men turned up at our room. There had clearly been some confusion as to what we were after!